OWNERS OF ALTHORP AND THEIR FAMILIES

John (d. 1497) of Hodnell & Wormleighton   Thomas

Thomas   William of Badby

THOMAS SPENCER of Everdon

Dorothy, Lady Catesby   Isabel, Lady Strelly

Mary Boles   Jane, Lady Brydges   Anne, Lady Goodwin

Anne { Lady Monteagle / Lady Compton / Countess of Dorset Alice, Countess of Derby Margaret Allington Elizabeth, Lady Hunsdon Katherine, Lady Leigh

Mary, Lady Anderson   Margaret Spencer   Elizabeth, Lady Fane

Elizabeth, Lady Craven Anne, Lady Townshend Alice, Countess of Drogheda Margaret, Countess of Shaftesbury

Dorothy, Viscountess Halifax   Lady Penelope Spencer

Anne, Countess of Arran   Elizabeth, Countess of Clancarty

CHARLES, 5th EARL OF SUNDERLAND, (1706-1758) 3rd Duke of Marlborough, K.G., Quitted Althorpe 1734. HON JOHN SPENCER (1708-1746) *m.* 1734, Lady Georgina Carteret (1716-1780) Anne, Viscountess Bateman Diana, Duchess of Bedford

JOHN SPENCER (1734-1783) created Earl Spencer (1765) *m.* 1755, Georgiana Poyntz (1737-1814) Diana Spencer

Georgiana, Duchess of Devonshire   Henrietta, Countess of Bessborough

Robert Richard Sarah, Lady Lyttelton Lady Georgiana Quin Hon. & Rev. George Spencer

m. (2) 1854, Adelaide Horatia Elizabeth Seymour (1825-1877)

CHARLES ROBERT, 6th EARL SPENCER, K.G. (1857-1922) *m.* 1887, Hon. Margaret Baring, (1868-1906) Victoria, Lady Sandhurst

2 sons. Lady Delia Peel Lady Margaret Douglas-Home Lavinia, Lady Annaly

Lady Sarah Spencer *m.* Neil McCorquodale Lady Jane Spencer *m.* Robert Fellowes Lady Diana Spencer *m.* H.R.H. THE PRINCE OF WALES

William

Christmas 1984. From Michael.

Georgina Battiscombe

THE SPENCERS
OF ALTHORP

Constable · London

First published in Great Britain 1984
by Constable and Company Ltd
10 Orange Street London WC2H 7EG
Copyright © 1984 by Georgina Battiscombe
ISBN 0 09 465700 9
Set in Monophoto Ehrhardt 11pt by
Servis Filmsetting Ltd Manchester
Printed in Great Britain by
BAS Printers Ltd Over Wallop

CONTENTS

Illustrations   6

Acknowledgements   10

Prologue   11

1 Sacharissa   23

2 The Sunderlands   49

3 The Devonshire House Set   74

4 Althorp of the Reform Bill   113

5 George Spencer, Father Ignatius of Saint Paul   148

6 Sarah Lady Lyttelton   173

7 The Red Earl   198

   Epilogue   240

   Select Bibliography   262

   Sources of Illustrations   264

   Index   266

ILLUSTRATIONS

South-west view of Althorp. Engraving by Woolnooth after a drawing by Blore, 1823   *page* 1

George John, second Earl Spencer, with his sisters, Georgiana and Henrietta. Painting by Angelica Kauffmann, 1774   *Frontispiece*

Sir John Spencer. Engraving by Worthington   13

Robert Spencer, First Baron Spencer   14

The hawking tower, or 'staninge', in the park at Althorp, built in 1612–13   15

Henry Wriothesley, third Earl of Southampton. Painting after Daniel Mytens   18

Elizabeth Vernon, Countess of Southampton. Artist unknown   19

Monument to the first Baron Spencer and his wife in St Mary's church, Great Brington   20

A line of Spencer memorial tombs in St Mary's church, Great Brington   22

'Sacharissa' – Dorothy Sidney, wife of the first Earl of Sunderland, after the Petworth version of the painting by Sir Anthony Van Dyck   25

Henry Spencer, first Earl of Sunderland   27

'Sacharissa': the Chatsworth version of the painting by Sir Anthony van Dyck, c.1642   *Facing page* 32

Three of the children of Charles I. Painting by Sir Peter Lely, c.1646   *Facing page* 33

Penshurst Place. Engraving by Tomlinson after a drawing by J.P. Neale   34

The staircase built at Althorp between 1653 and 1662   37

Dorothy Osborne, later Lady Temple. Painting by Caspar Netscher, 1671   38

Sir William Temple. Painting by Sir Peter Lely   40

Sir George Savile, later Marquess of Halifax. Painting attributed to Mary Beale   41

Charles II. Painting by Sir Peter Lely, c.1675   43

Louise de Kéroualle, Duchess of Portsmouth. Painting by Sir Peter Lely, c.1671   47

Edmund Waller. Painting after John Riley, c.1685   48

'The Little Girl in Green'. Painting by Sir Peter Lely, c.1650   *Facing page* 48

Robert Spencer, second Earl of Sunderland. Painting by Carlo Maratta   *Facing page* 49

Althorp. Engraving after Knyff, c.1702   53

James, Duke of York. Unfinished painting by Sir Peter Lely   54

Algernon Sidney. Painting after Justus van Egmont, 1663   57

Lambeth Delft charger portraying King William III, c.1690   *Facing page* 64

Anne Churchill, wife of the third Earl of Sunderland, with her son, Robert Spencer. Painting by Sir Godfrey Kneller, 1709–10   *Facing page* 65

Sarah Jennings, Duchess of Marlborough. Painting by Sir Godfrey Kneller, 1705   69

John Spencer and his son John. Painting by George Knapton, 1745   70

'The Shooting Party'. Painting by John Wootton, 1740   71

The Stable Block, Althorp, built for Charles Spencer, c.1730   73

A gaming-table at Devonshire House. Drawing by Thomas Rowlandson, 1791   74

Spencer House, London. Aquatint by Thomas Malton, 1800   76

George John, second Earl Spencer. Engraving after the painting by Hoppner, 1809   77

Georgiana Poyntz, wife of the first Earl Spencer. Painting by Thomas Gainsborough, 1781   78

Georgiana, Countess Spencer, with her daughter Georgiana, who became Duchess of Devonshire. Painting by Sir Joshua Reynolds, 1759–61   *Facing page* 80

Saint Christopher, coloured block print dated 1423, formerly in the Althorp library   *Facing page* 81

Georgiana Spencer, Duchess of Devonshire, watercolour drawing by John Downman, 1787   82

William Cavendish, fifth Duke of Devonshire. Painting by Pompeo Batoni   85

Charles James Fox. Painting by Sir Joshua Reynolds, 1784   86

Richard Brinsley Sheridan. Painting by John Russell, 1788   88

George, Prince of Wales. Painting by Thomas Gainsborough, c.1795   89

Lady Elizabeth Foster, later Duchess of Devonshire. Painting by Sir Joshua Reynolds, 1788   90

Georgiana, Duchess of Devonshire. Unfinished sketch by Sir Joshua Reynolds, c.1780   91

Georgiana, Duchess of Devonshire, with her daughter Georgiana. Painting by Sir Joshua Reynolds, 1786   92

'The Two Patriotic Duchess's on their Canvass'. Caricature by Thomas Rowlandson, 1784   95

Mrs Fitzherbert. Painting by Sir Joshua Reynolds, c.1788   97

Charles Grey, Viscount Howick. Painting by George Romney, 1784   99

Henrietta Frances, Viscountess Duncannon, with her children. Painting by John Hoppner, c.1787   101

Lady Caroline Lamb. Painting by Miss E.H. Trotter   106

Georgiana, Duchess of Devonshire, and her sister, Viscountess Duncannon. Watercolour drawing by Thomas Rowlandson, 1790   Facing page 112

Lavinia, Countess Spencer, with her son, John Charles. Painting by Sir Joshua Reynolds, 1783–4   Facing page 113

John Charles, Viscount Althorp, aged four. Painting by Sir Joshua Reynolds, 1786   115

Lavinia, Viscountess Althorp. Painting by Sir Joshua Reynolds, 1782   119

Charles King, Huntsman of the Pytchley Hunt. Painting by Ben Marshall   120

Wiseton Hall, Nottinghamshire. Early nineteenth-century engraving   124

John Charles, third Earl Spencer. Painting by Sir George Hayter, 1816   Facing page 128

The Peterloo Massacre. Coloured engraving by George Cruikshank, 1819   Facing page 129

The Trial of Queen Caroline in the House of Lords, 1820   131

Charles Grey, second Earl Grey. Painting by Sir Thomas Lawrence   135

The House of Commons, after passing the Reform Bill. Painting by Sir George Hayter, 1833   136

The Bradwell Ox. Aquatint after the painting by H.B. Chalon, 1830   140

A Durham Ox. Engraving by Walker after a drawing by W.H. Davies   143

Father Ignatius of St Paul   148

The School Room at Eton   151

The Quadrangle of Trinity College Cambridge   154

St Mary's church, Great Brington. Drawing by George Clarke, c.1832   156

Augustus Welby Pugin   164

Oscott College, Sutton Coldfield. Engraving c.1840   165

Sarah, Lady Lyttelton. Miniature   173

William, third Lord Lyttelton. Miniature by Bone   174

Hagley. Engraving after a drawing by J.P. Neale, 1818   176

Queen Victoria at Windsor. Lithograph after Chalon, 1838   179

Albert, Prince Consort. Drawing by G.B. Champion, 1839   180

Victoria, Princess Royal, 1856	187
Reception to King Louis Phillippe. Painting by Winterhalter	188
Claremont. Aquatint by Havell after a drawing by J. Hassall	191
'Bertie', the Prince of Wales, aged seven. Painting by Winterhalter	195
'The Red Earl'. Caricature by Harry Furniss	198
Charlotte Seymour, wife of 'the Red Earl'. Painting by G.F. Watts	206
Shooting at Wimbledon. Painting by H.T. Wells, 1864	209
The Prince of Wales in shooting dress	211
The arrival of Princess Alexandra for her marriage to the Prince of Wales	213
Lord John Russell. Painting by G.F. Watts	214
William Ewart Gladstone. Painting by Sir John Millais	216
Music title for *The Christmas Waltz*, 1865	218
The courtyard of Dublin Castle. Nineteenth-century engraving	219
The Viceregal Lodge, Phoenix Park, Dublin. Nineteenth-century engraving	220
'The Red Earl' on 'Misrule'. Painting by John Charlton, 1878	222
Will Goodall breaking up fox. Painting by John Charlton, 1878	223
'Death of the Fox'. Watercolour drawing by John Charlton	*Facing page* 224
The Empress of Austria at Althorp. *Vanity Fair* cartoon	*Facing page* 225
Cover of *The Illustrated Police News*, May 20, 1882	228
Earl Spencer's arrival in Dublin after the assassination	230
The eighth Earl Spencer. Painting by Rodrigo Moynihan, 1945	*Facing page* 240
The marriage of Lady Diana Spencer to the Prince of Wales	*Facing page* 241
The sixth Earl Spencer. Painting by Sir William Orpen, 1916	242
The sixth Earl at a meet of the Pytchley Hunt, 1914	243
The sixth Earl as Lord Chamberlain at the Coronation of George V	244
Bobby with 'Jock'	245
Spy cartoon of the sixth Earl from *Vanity Fair*	246
Family Group at Althorp, 1911	247
Bobby's private army of Brownies, 1917	247
Viscount Althorp, 'Jack', hunting at Althorp	248
Jack's coming of age	249
The entrance hall at Althorp, 1921	251
The seventh Earl. Painting by Augustus John, 1930	252
Cynthia, Countess Spencer. Painting by Sir William Nicholson	253
Viscount Althorp and Frances Roche	256
The porch at Althorp	257
On the balcony at Buckingham Palace	261

ACKNOWLEDGEMENTS

I would like to thank the many people, some of whom wish to remain anonymous, who have allowed me to use their personal reminiscences, given me access to letters and papers, or helped me in any other way. Among them I am particularly grateful to Sir Alexander and Lady Reid, Mrs Daphne Pollen, Lady Jane Fellowes, Lady (Henriette) Abel-Smith, Mrs Margaret Pawley, Miss Rachel Trickett, the Rev. Henry Thorold, Mr David Hopkinson, Miss Jane Langton, Sir Trenchard Cox, Mr P. I. King and the staff of the Northamptonshire County Record Office, and the Keeper of Manuscripts, the John Rylands Memorial Library.

Mr Ellis Archer Wasson, of Weston, Massachusetts, most generously sent me over the typescript of his as yet unpublished book on the third Earl Spencer and allowed me to make unrestricted use of it. Finally, I owe a special debt of gratude to Henry and Mary Augusta Markham; without their unstinted help and hospitality this book would not have been written.

Acknowledgements to those who generously provided the illustrations will be found on pages 264–265. Picture research by John Hadfield.

PROLOGUE

'Sheep may safely graze.'
J.S. Bach.

In the House of Lords one day in May 1621 Robert Lord Spencer was discoursing at length about times past. Lord Arundel interrupted sharply—'When these things were doing the noble Lord's ancestors were keeping sheep.' Quick as lightning came the riposte—'When my ancestors were keeping sheep the noble Lord's ancestors were plotting treason.' The House burst into excited uproar; both Arundel's father and his grandfather had been beheaded as traitors.

Lord Arundel was right; the first known ancestors of our Princess of Wales were sheep-farmers. Tudor heralds made out an imaginary descent from the Despencer Earls of Gloucester and Winchester, and while giving the Spencers their own coat of arms, allowed them also to use the Despencer arms. In fact no real link existed between the two families. In 1330 one William Spencer held land in Worcestershire of the Abbey of Evesham. His great-great-grandson, Henry who died in 1476, was the first Spencer to hold land in Northamptonshire. His son John is described as of Hodnell, Warwickshire, thus establishing the family's connection with that county. His son, another John, was feoffee of Wormleighton in Warwickshire and tenant of Althorp in Northamptonshire, the two properties which were to be most closely connected with the Spencer name. This John's nephew, yet another John, bought both Wormleighton and Althorp outright and so became the true founder of the family fortunes.

Almost alone among the great families who rose to affluence in the sixteenth century the Spencers owed their wealth not to the favour of a monarch or to the acquisition of monastery lands but to their own skill as farmers and business men. Sir John Spencer, as he had now become, can best be described by the Scottish adjective 'canny'. He bought much land and he bought it wisely, choosing pastures of first-class quality so situated that they could be grouped into two vast sheep-walks, the one centring on Wormleighton, the other on Althorp. Here he and his descendants grazed large flocks though according to local tradition the number of animals never reached 20,000 since disease or some other catastrophe always struck whenever the total approached that fatal figure. Sir John also invented a new and very successful marketing technique. Bypassing local markets, he sold

[11]

direct to London butchers and wool-merchants and disposed of his surplus breeding stock to neighbouring farmers anxious to improve their own flocks by the introduction of the famous Spencer strain.

Although he lived at Wormleighton rather than at Althorp Sir John was a person of considerable importance in Northamptonshire. A document dated 1511 and headed 'A Plea of John Fermor, Richard Knightley, John Spencer, Edward Olney, Thomas Spencer' shows that by that date the Spencers were of sufficient standing to sign alongside some of the best-known names in the county. They also married into the families of these local worthies; John Spencer's son William was married to Sir Richard Knightley's daughter Susan, his daughter to Sir Richard's son. This Knightley connection was to involve the Spencers in a long and bitter series of lawsuits. On the death of William Spencer the Crown claimed custody of his heir, a claim hotly disputed by the Knightley family who maintained that custody should go to the widow and her relations. Much was at stake for the Spencer property was worth the huge sum of £3,000 per annum and the pickings during a long minority would be considerable. Both sides cheated shamelessly, but the Crown finally won by the trick of invoking the intervention of the Lord Keeper.

The young Sir John Spencer who had been the cause of all this litigation built the Tudor house at Althorp which forms the core of the present mansion. The Spencers had a happy knack of marrying well. This Sir John married Katharine Kitson, daughter of a wealthy merchant-prince; his son John married Mary Catlin, an immensely rich heiress who brought the Spencers valuable property in Bedfordshire, Leicestershire, and Dorset. Three of his daughters married into the peerage, one of them successively marrying three peers, another two. Of Anne's three husbands the most notable was Thomas Sackville, Earl of Dorset. Lord Treasurer and later Lord High Steward; he presided over the trial of the Earl of Essex and also had the unpleasant task of informing Mary Queen of Scots that sentence of death had been passed upon her. He was a diplomat of some note and an author, his best-known works being *A Mirror for Magistrates* and *Gorboduc*, the first English tragedy to be written in blank verse. Anne's sister Alice first married Fernando, Earl of Derby, and secondly Thomas, Lord Ellesmere. A third sister Elizabeth who married George Carey, Lord Hunsdon, was herself a patron of poets, the most famous among them being Edmund Spenser, who claimed kinship with the Spencer family. He dedicated to her a poem with the curious title, *Muiopotmos*, and mentioned her in the introductory sonnet to *The Faerie Queen*. 'Divers well-deserving poets have consecrated their endeavours to your praise',

Sir John Spencer (1533–99), father of the first Baron Spencer.
Engraving by Worthington after an English School painting at Althorp, inscribed with the date 1590.

wrote Thomas Nash, another poet whom she befriended; 'Fame's eldest favourite, Master Spenser, in all his writings he praiseth you.' Either Elizabeth herself or her daughter, another Elizabeth Carey, wrote and published a remarkably dull poetic drama entitled *The Tragedy of Marian, the Fair Queen of Jewry*.

Robert, son to the Sir John who married Mary Catlin, is the first Spencer to emerge from the mists of history as a recognizable person, and in many respects a typical Spencer. A sportsman and farmer who combined a liking for country pursuits with an interest in things intellectual and antiquarian—'his skill in antiquities, arms, and alliances was singular'—like some of his best-known descendants Robert Spencer found himself, almost against his will, caught up in affairs of state and like those descendants he played a considerable part in the history of his time. But, for all his involvement with kings and parliaments Robert Spencer was first and foremost a very successful sheep-farmer. His annual receipts from the sales of wool, meat and breeding-stock over-topped £4,000 and his total income was in the neighbourhood of £8,000, an enormous sum in his day. Add to

Robert, first Baron Spencer (1570–1627). Engraving, half-length, by W. Skelton, after the full-length painting by Marcus Gheeraerts which is at Althorp.

this the large reserves of ready money accumulated by his thrifty Spencer forebears, and it will be seen that public opinion was not far wrong in believing him to be the richest man in the kingdom.

Thriftiness had been a marked characteristic of the early Spencers and an important factor in their rise to riches and influence. Nobody called them mean; they did not stint themselves but they eschewed the extravagant building schemes and the heavy expenditure on ostentatious luxury which ruined many of their contemporaries and above all, they saw to it that their income was always in excess of their expenditure.

With the family wealth Robert Spencer also inherited the family distaste for overspending. It was typical of his prudent, down-to-earth attitude that although he accepted a barony in 1603, thus becoming the first Lord Spencer, fifteen years later he refused an earldom offered him at the price of £10,000. He entertained on a large scale but not extravagantly; as the preacher of a sermon at the time of his death declared. 'It was his great wisdom to make a careful frugality the fire of his continual hospitality.' He undertook no major additions or alterations at Althorp,

[14]

The hawking tower or 'staninge', in the park at Althorp, built by Robert, Lord Spencer, in 1612–13. Engraving by Barenger after a drawing by E. Blore, in *Aedes Althorpianae*, by T.F. Dibdin, 1822.

but being a keen sportsman, and having a great liking for falconry, then the most fashionable of sports, he built the hawking tower in the park which bears the inscription, 'This Staninge was made by Robert Lord Spencer, 1612 et 1613.'

Like many of the Spencers Robert made an advantageous marriage which was also a very happy one, judging by an oddly worded note scribbled in one of his account books—'Margaret, my most loving wife, having borne me all those children. She was one of the daughters and co-heirs of Sir Francis Willoughby, of honourable parentage, but her virtue surpassed all.' Born in 1570, he was only twenty-seven when Margaret died in 1597, but he remained a widower for the rest of his life. If a reference to him in a poem by his friend Ben Jonson is to be taken at its face value he avoided all contact with women:

Who, since Thamyra did die
Has not brook'd a woman's eye,
Nor allowed about his place
Any of the female race.

[15]

In April 1603 Robert Spencer was one of the notables who rode out to welcome James I on his arrival in England and to accompany him on his journey to London. 'It shall never be blotted out of my mind how at my first entry into this kingdom the people of all sorts rin and ran, nay, rather, flew to greet me,' James told his first parliament. Some of these people rin and ran not out of disinterested loyalty but with a wish to gain lands or honours—James was showering manors and knighthoods on all around him—or to obtain the redress of an old grievance. When the Huntingdonshire commoners waited on the new King they put forward a complaint about the enclosure of land by Sir John Spencer. James listened and granted them what they described as 'their hearts' desire', regardless of the fact that Sir John's son was among the loyal subjects attending on the royal progress.

James's Queen, Anne of Denmark, later made a more leisurely journey south with her children. They stayed for some days at Althorp where a masque specially written for the occasion by Ben Jonson was performed out of doors in the park. Robert Spencer was not present, maybe because his dislike of women's company extended as far as the Queen, maybe because he was detained in London by business to do with the accession of the new King. In July he was created Baron Spencer and shortly afterwards he was chosen as ambassador to head a mission to invest the Duke of Wurtemburg with the Order of the Garter. Garter King-at-Arms was to accompany him and perform the actual investiture.

Spencer made careful preparations for this important journey. He commissioned two cabinets to be specially made for him, the smaller to be used for letters, and he ordered a new sumpter or pack-saddle, and a splendid saddle-cloth for his own horse embroidered with armorial bearings. He carried bills of exchange as the most convenient way of taking money abroad, and he added an interpreter to his already large retinue because he himself spoke no 'Dutch' as German was then called. When estimating the expenses of the journey he allowed each person the curiously large sum of four pounds a day 'for diet', though that term may perhaps include living-expenses other than food.

On 18 September 1603 Spencer took leave of the King at Woodstock and on 8 October set sail for France. What he saw of the French people did not predispose him in their favour: 'The nobility of France are poor; the gentry of France are courteous and crafty; the vulgar are rude and unconscionable.' He made a further comment which comes oddly from a misogynist who presumably did not concern himself with female looks: 'There is not one handsome woman in all these parts.' He had a farmer's eye for the local breeds of sheep, cattle and horses, and he was distressed to see the desolation on every side: 'All the villages and all the churches with the most part of the gentlemen's houses were spoiled by civil wars and the Spaniards, and not re-edified, a pitiful spectacle.'

The party travelled by way of Abbeville to Amiens, where they were kept waiting three hours outside the city gate before it was unbarred to allow them to enter. Crossing the Moselle, they set out for Nancy but were forced to spend the night in 'a paltry village', a league short of their destination. At Nancy they were lodged 'very royally' and sumptuously entertained by the Duke of Lorraine. They found that the Lorrainers were 'not unlike the English and affect them well, not affecting the French'. Leaving the hospitable Court of Nancy they crossed the Rhine and on 1 November met the envoys of the Duke of Wurtemburg, who greeted them politely and escorted them to Stuttgart. On 3 November Spencer presented his credentials to the Duke; and next day the party were taken hunting, Spencer noting that the Duke's son was 'the best marksman with his piece that ever I did see.'

The investiture took place on Sunday, 6 November. The Duke, magnificently dressed and bejewelled, met Spencer and Garter King-at-Arms in the great hall of the castle, where he was arrayed in his Garter robes. From there they accompanied him to the church, 'walking on red cloth spread for the purpose' (it seems it was already obligatory to roll out the red carpet on grand occasions) where the ceremony of investiture took place to the accompaniment of much fine music. A great feast followed, ending with the serving of some remarkable pieces of confectionery: 'After exceeding plenty, state and variety of dishes there were served all manner of curiosities in paste, as the figures and shapes of several kinds of beasts and birds, also the statues of Hercules, Minerva, Mercury, and other famous persons.'

The investiture over, the Duke continued to entertain the company with a series of balls and hunting expeditions and a visit to a school for the sons of noblemen and 'gentlemen of the greater sort'. These aristocratic pupils led a very pleasant life for as well as studying 'learning and all languages', they were taught such enjoyable subjects as riding, fencing, dancing, singing, and 'all other laudable exercises'. When the time came to take farewell Spencer was presented with a splendid piece of plate. He also discovered that the Duke had paid all the expenses of their visit, a piece of generosity which probably pleased him more than the grand gift, since ambassadors usually found themselves out of pocket at the end of such a mission and on returning to England had the greatest difficulty in extracting payment from the Crown authorities.

For the next few years little or nothing is heard of Lord Spencer. His eldest son

Henry Wriothesley, third Earl of Southampton (1573–1624), father of Penelope, Lady Spencer, and patron of Shakespeare. Painting after Daniel Mytens.

John died at Blois leaving no issue. The second son, William, who now became heir, was married to Penelope Wriothesley, daughter of Henry Wriothesley, Earl of Southampton, thus forming a tenuous link between the Spencer family and Shakespeare. Southampton was Shakespeare's friend and patron. Blue-eyed, golden-haired, and famous for his good looks, he may possibly have been the handsome young man of the Sonnets. Shakespeare dedicated both *Venus and Adonis* and *The Rape of Lucrece* to him, writing in the latter dedication, 'the love I bear you is without end', and again, 'what I have done is yours; what I have to do is yours; being part in all I have, devoted yours.'

Of all the handsome and able young men who flocked to Queen Elizabeth's Court, Southampton was reckoned the most accomplished and the most charming. Prudence, however, was not one of his characteristics. Risking the Queen's displeasure, he made love to one of her ladies, Elizabeth Vernon, who became his mistress. In 1599 they were secretly married. News of the marriage leaked out; the Queen was predictably furious and banished Southampton from

Elizabeth Vernon, lady-in-waiting to Queen Elizabeth; mistress and later wife of the Earl of Southampton.

Court. Wisely, he withdrew to Ireland with the Earl of Essex; less wisely, he entangled himself in Essex's plot against the Queen. Plans went astray; Essex and Southampton were arrested, tried for treason, and condemned to death. Essex was beheaded, but Southampton's luck held. He was reprieved and committed to the Tower where he languished for four years until released on the accession of James I. Now once again he found himself high in favour at Court. The new King took a great liking to him, appointed him Governor of the Isle of Wight, and created him a Knight of the Garter.

By 1621 the situation had completely changed. Buckingham was now first favourite, and Southampton was prominent among the King's opponents in the House of Lords, where he closely co-operated with his relative by marriage, Lord Spencer, in attacking such scandals as monopolies and corruption in high places. The third Parliament of James I, summoned in January 1621, was roughly divided into the Court party and the popular party although of course no party system existed in the modern sense of that term. Robert Spencer was one of the most

Monument to Robert, first Baron Spencer (1570–1627), and his wife, by Jasper Hollemans of Burton-on-Trent, in St Mary's parish church, Great Brington.

active and outspoken members of the popular party, but nevertheless he was considered essentially a moderate man. Today he would be regarded as standing a little to the left of centre, a position occupied by many generations of Whig and Liberal Spencers.

In March 1621 Spencer proposed a motion stating that 'no lords of this house are to be regarded as great lords, for they are all peers', he himself being merely a baron. Much more important business, however, was soon to hand. The Lord Chancellor, Francis Bacon, famous as essayist and philosopher, was believed to have taken bribes. Parliament could not attack the King but they seized on this opportunity to attack his minister. 'Those who strike at your Chancellor it is much to be feared will strike at your crown,' Bacon warned James who, however, was powerless to withstand the anger of Parliament. In the House of Lords Spencer and Southampton were among those who attacked Bacon most bitterly, demanding that he should be stripped of his peerage and severely punished. The case against him was clear; he himself admitted to taking presents though he maintained that he had never allowed these bribes to influence his judgements. He was impeached, found guilty, deprived of his peerage, fined £40,000 and committed to the Tower. The King remitted most of these penalties; but Bacon was driven from public life, never to return.

James took some slight, ineffectual revenge against the most prominent of Bacon's enemies. Southampton was confined to his house for a few months; but Spencer was left unmolested, perhaps because he was so generally liked and respected. In 1622 he was appointed a member of a committee to investigate 'the unemployment of land'. He died two years later and was buried at St Mary's, Great Brington, the parish church of Althorp where, nearly thirty years previously, he had erected a magnificent monument commemorating both himself and Margaret, the loved and loving wife of his youth.

Unlike his father, William second Baron Spencer played no part either in Parliament or at Court beyond entertaining Charles I and Henrietta Maria at Althorp. He may perhaps have made some improvements and alterations to the house there; but his claim to an important place in the family history is connected not with building but with sport. In 1635 Mr Anthony Samwell wrote asking him for 'two couple of unentered hounds, well bred, three of them bitches, in order that they might be sent to France for the use of our Ambassador'. Though this is the first known reference to the existence of any hounds at Althorp clearly the breed there already had a good name among sportsmen. The term 'unentered' suggests that the Spencers kept a regular pack, but not necessarily of foxhounds.

William Spencer seems to have been a kindly man with a care for his own relations to judge from a letter written by his nephew Henry Anderson and dated 18 April 1633. 'That fatherly interest which your Lordship was pleased to bestow on me shall be religiously observed,' Anderson writes. 'It hath been a credit and a comfort to me that I have been advised by my friends, among whom your Lordship has chief place in dignity and affection.' The formal sentences have about them a ring of sincerity in spite of the hyperbole which was a commonplace of seventeenth-century letter writing.

William Spencer died in 1636 at the comparatively early age of forty-five, and his sixteen-year-old son Henry reigned in his stead. There were of course to be deviations, but the pattern which, for the most part, future generations of

A line of memorial Spencer tombs in Great Brington church.

Spencers were to follow was now becoming clear. Masters of great estates and considerable wealth they were to be little kings in their own neighbourhood and persons of repute and high standing in the country at large. Duty rather than ambition was to compel them to take part in politics and public life where they were to win considerable success without ever reaching the heights. The friends of kings and princes and perfectly at ease among the complication of life at Court they were always to be homesick for Althorp and the pleasures of the countryside. Some of them were to develop scholarly and artistic tastes, and, having the collector's instinct, to enrich Althorp with magnificent pictures, porcelain, and, above all, books. But even in the most sophisticated of the Spencers something of the old sheep-master still lingered. Many of them were to turn with relief from politics and statecraft to the more pleasurable business of farming and in particular of stock-breeding. Wise in the ways of sheep and cattle they were never so happy as when among their flocks and herds except perhaps when galloping over Northamptonshire pastures behind a first-class pack of hounds.

[22]

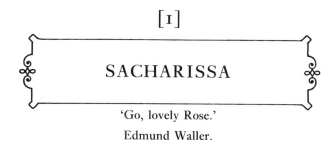

[1]

SACHARISSA

'Go, lovely Rose.'
Edmund Waller.

From early times down to our present day Lady Diana the women of the Spencer family have been as important and as interesting characters as the men; and of all the notable women who were Spencers either by birth or by marriage the first of whom we have any clear picture is Dorothy Sidney. Coming from one of the most famous and gifted of English families she had Philip Sidney for great-uncle and for great-aunt the Countess of Pembroke:

> Sidney's sister, Pembroke's mother,
> Death, ere thou hast slain another
> Fair and learn'd and good as she,
> Time shall throw a dart at thee.

Like her great-aunt Dorothy was fair and learned and good. The eldest of the thirteen children of Lord and Lady Leicester, she was born in 1617 and brought up at Penshurst in Kent. She had inherited the bookish tastes of the Sidneys, a characteristic which particularly endeared her to her scholarly father, but although by nature quiet and studious, she was gifted with a pretty wit and quite exceptional beauty, and she grew up to become one of the most sought-after young women of her day. Lord Devonshire, Lord Lovelace and Sir William Temple were among her many admirers, but the best-known and most persistent of them all was the poet Edmund Waller.

The Wallers were a family of Buckinghamshire squires living near Amersham. An older branch came from Kent; and it may have been through this connection that Edmund Waller first met Dorothy. A remarkably clever and amusing young man, educated at Eton and King's College, Cambridge, he soon made his way in Court circles, 'caressed by all the people of quality who had a relish for learning and wit'. He married Ann Banks, a rich heiress who died after two years of marriage; and it was as a wealthy young widower of twenty-four that he first met and fell in love with Dorothy. He named her Sacharissa and wrote poem after poem to her, professing his profound devotion and lamenting her hard-hearted refusal of his suit.

[23]

It is difficult to make out the truth about this love-affair, if indeed it merits so definite a description. Dorothy certainly did not return Waller's love; from the little that we know about her response she does not appear to have treated his protests at all seriously. But what precisely was he looking for? Marriage was out of the question; a country squire, however rich and gifted, was not a suitable husband for Lord Leicester's eldest daughter. Born and brought up as she had been, an aristocratic girl of unimpeachable virtue, it was unthinkable that he should make her his mistress. He himself was well aware of the obstacles in his way:

Such cheerful modesty, such humble state
Move certain love, but with a doubtful fate,
As when beyond our greedy reach we see
Inviting fruit on too sublime a tree.

Yet Dorothy clearly meant very much more to Waller than the many other ladies who served as inspiration for his tuneful and well-turned verses. Even the worst of the poems to Sacharissa have a truth and a poignancy which is lacking from the poems to Phillis, to Chloris, to Mira, or to Amoret. 'Go, lovely Rose' and 'That which her slender waist confined' have rightly found a place in all good anthologies; but it is a less well-known poem of smaller merit which best describes the real nature of Waller's love for Dorothy. The verses entitled 'To Amoret'— sadly, we do not known who Amoret may have been—suggest that he had fallen far more deeply in love with Sacharissa than ever he had intended. He is infatuated with her; Amoret is the woman 'Who already has of me All that's not idolatry', but he adores Sacharissa with a passion beyond his own control:

Sacharissa's beauty's wine
Which to madness doth incline;
Such a liquor as no brain
That is mortal can sustain.
Scarce can I to Heaven excuse
The devotion which I use
Unto that adored dame;
For 'tis not unlike the same
Which I thither ought to send;
So that if it would take end
T'would to Heaven itself be due
To succeed her, and not you.

[24]

'Sacharissa': Dorothy Sidney, Countess of Sunderland (1617–84), engraving by J. Thomson, after the painting by Sir Anthony van Dyck at Petworth House.

How can his affection for Amoret compete against this 'strong flame'? It is Amoret whom he wishes to love but Sacharissa who compels his devotion:

All that of myself is mine,
Lovely Amoret, is thine.
Sacharissa's captive fain
Would untie his iron chain,
And those scorching beams to shun
To thy gentle shadow run.

When Dorothy at last chose one out of her many suitors Waller's reaction is enlightening. His anonymous biographer has it that 'he was not of a disposition to make any other use of the willow when she married than to hang his harp upon it'; but his letter to her sister Lucy, though light-hearted enough on the surface, has bitter undertones:

May my Lady Dorothy suffer as much and have the like passion for this young lord whom she has preferred to the rest of mankind as others have had for her, and may his love, before the year go about, make her taste the first curse imposed on womanhood—the pains of becoming a mother . . . May she, who always affected silence and retiredness, have the house filled with the noise and number of her children . . . And then may she arrive at that great curse, so much declined by fair ladies—old age!

The young lord whom Dorothy had preferred to the rest of mankind was Henry Spencer the third baron. Being only eighteen he was three years younger than Dorothy herself but, according to Clarendon, 'a man of tender years and an early judgement'. Loving books and country life, he occupied himself with study and with the management of his great estates. As handsome as she was beautiful he seemed the ideal husband for Dorothy, and so indeed he proved during the brief time that they were to have together.

The marriage took place at Penshurst on 20 July 1639. Oddly enough, the married couple did not set up house at Althorp but joined Dorothy's parents in Paris where Lord Leicester was acting as Ambassador Extraordinary. There they remained for two years; and during that period two children were born to them, a daughter christened Dorothy, nicknamed Poppet, and Robert, who was almost twin to his own uncle Henry Sidney, last-born of Lady Leicester's children.

Henry Spencer (1620–1643), first
Earl of Sunderland, husband of
Dorothy Sidney ('Sacharissa'),
killed at the battle of Newbury. At
Althorp.

Following Strafford's execution in May 1641 Lord Leicester was recalled to England and told to hold himself in readiness to take over the post of Lord-Lieutenant of Ireland. His family returned with him; but even now Henry Spencer could spend very little of his time at home at Althorp. He was deeply involved in the political struggles of the day and constant in his attendance at the House of Lords where he was among the moderate men in company with Dorothy's uncle, Algernon Percy, Earl of Northumberland, and Lucius Cary, Lord Falkland, a man 'of a wit so sharp and a nature so sincere that nothing could be more lovely'. Henry Spencer is believed to have been one of those 'men of eminent parts and faculties' who came out from Oxford to Falkland's home at Great Tew to enjoy a spell of country life and to debate topics of literary, philosophical and religious interest. If so, he must have been very young at the time since 'this college situated in a purer air' virtually came to an end in 1638: but it is not impossible that he should have been there since in the seventeenth century boys often went up to the university at the age of fourteen. Now, in 1641, he was

[27]

certainly one of those favoured persons 'who first became known to the world as a friend of Lord Falkland's, and that was enough in itself to raise a man's character.' For the present he followed Falkland in supporting Pym and the Parliament party. Both men urged peace and reconciliation on the extremists of either side, and when the moment for decision came with the passing of the Grand Remonstrance and the attack on the bishops, both men decided, though with grief and reluctance, that their ultimate loyalty must be to Church and King.

One of the saddest features of any civil war is the division within families, and nowhere was this more marked than among Dorothy's relations. Her husband and her father held by the King, though with some hesitation; her uncle, the Earl of Northumberland, and her cousin the Earl of Essex equally reluctantly took the Parliamentarian side. All these were essentially men of moderation; but her brother Algernon Sidney was a convinced republican, and both he and his elder brother Philip Lord Lisle were hot in support of the Parliament.

In March 1642 the King moved North to York where Falkland and Spencer joined him. We do not know if Spencer was present when Charles raised his standard at Nottingham but he was certainly with the royal army a few weeks later at Shrewsbury. From there he wrote to Dorothy telling her 'how much I am unsatisfied with the proceedings here' and confessing that he is fighting not from conviction but for fear of being called a coward. His protest is pleasingly boyish:

> Neither is there wanting daily handsome occasion to retire were it not for gaining honour. For let the occasion be never so handsome, unless a man were reduced to fight on the Parliament side, than which, for my part, I had rather be hanged, it will be said without doubt that a man is afraid to fight. If there could be an expedient found to save the punctilio of honour, I would not continue here an hour. The discontent that I, and many other honest men, receive daily is beyond expression.

Some months later Spencer's friend Falkland put forward a similar argument when reproached for exposing himself unnecessarily to danger. He pointed out that 'it concerned him to be more active in enterprises of hazard than other men; that all might see that his impatiency for peace proceeded not from pusillanimity or fear to endanger his own person.' Spencer argues as a gallant boy, Falkland as a mature and thoughtful man; he is not concerned with a punctilio of honour but with his own credibility as a persistent advocate of peace.

Henry Spencer fought at Edgehill, the first pitched battle of the Civil War. The night before the battle he entertained Prince Rupert in the Spencers' family home at Wormleighton, a house which was to be burnt later in the war, legend says by his own side to prevent the Parliamentarian army turning it into a fortified post. After Edgehill Spencer and many other Royalists expected the King to march direct on London; instead, Charles turned off to Oxford and established his winter quarters there. At Oxford Spencer found his father-in-law, Lord Leicester, still impatiently awaiting the King's command to proceed to Ireland, a command which never came. Presumably because Althorp lay too directly in the path of the opposing armies Dorothy and the children had settled at Penshurst. The winter lull in the fighting gave Henry Spencer an opportunity to visit them there and to see his second daughter, Penelope, born on 19 November.

Meanwhile Dorothy's old admirer Edmund Waller, now a member of the House of Commons, had remained in London as a supporter of the Parliamentarians. Being not altogether happy with the company in which he found himself he kept in touch with a group of Royalists in the city and also, it seems, with the Court at Oxford. There was so much to be said for and against both sides that even at this late stage in the struggle it was possible for a man to hesitate before committing himself one way or the other. Waller, however, was not a victim of honest doubt but a prudent time-server who believed in keeping in with both sides; writing of his political principles or lack of principles his biographer says, 'He was a little too inconstant to them and was not naturally as steady as he was judicious.' Now he became entangled in a devious and obscure scheme to form an association to oppose the payment of taxes for the prosecution of the war and to petition Parliament to make peace. Side by side with what came to be known as 'Waller's plot' there seems to have been a second and more dangerous plan to seize the Tower and other strong points and to open the City gates to the Royalist forces. News of these plots leaked out; the leading conspirators were caught and put in prison, and three of them were hanged.

Waller's quick brain and total lack of principle saved him from a similar fate. He was ready to tell all, and perhaps rather more than all, that he knew about the supposed plots and to betray the names of his fellow-conspirators, and he was also quick-witted enough to insist on his right as a Member of Parliament to be tried not by a Council of War but by the House of Commons. There he defended himself so ably that he escaped with a sentence of temporary banishment and the enormous fine of £10,000. The fact that he was cousin to John Hampden and kin to Oliver Cromwell probably told in his favour. Cromwell frequently visited Waller's mother, whom he addressed as 'Aunt' although the relationship was not

in fact so close. This formidable lady was a fervent Royalist, and she would berate
him so fiercely that often he would jokingly throw his napkin in her face. When he
came to power he allowed Waller to return to England, and the two men became
firm friends, Waller writing a rather fulsome poem to mark the occasion of
Cromwell's death in 1658 (he was to write an equally fulsome one in celebration of
Charles II's restoration two years later).

When spring came the armies returned to the field. Henry Spencer had lent the
King £10,000 with little expectation of ever seeing the money again, and he was
rewarded by being made Earl of Sunderland in June of that year, 1643. After the
storming of Bristol he returned to Oxford where he was in hopes that Dorothy and
the children might join him, but instead he was obliged to rejoin the King's forces
and to take part in the ill-advised siege of Gloucester. Ever since the beginning of
the war he had kept up a constant correspondence with Dorothy and now he wrote
her a particularly charming letter:

My Dearest Heart, Just as I was coming out of the Trenches on Wednesday I
received your letter of the 20th of this instant, which gave me so much
satisfaction that it put all the inconveniences of this siege out of my thoughts. At
that instant, if I had followed my own inclinations, I had returned an answer to
yours; writing to you, and hearing from you, being the most pleasant
entertainment that I am capable of in any place; but especially here, where, but
when I am in the Trenches (which place is seldom without my company) I am
more solitary than ever I was in my life.

He goes on to tell her that he is living in 'a little private cottage', where of an
evening Falkland sometimes came to dine bringing with him their mutual friend,
the theologian Chillingworth. In the seventeenth century a learned man was a
jack-of-all-trades; Chillingworth was with the army not as a parson but as an
engineer. The Royalist forces lacked siege weapons; and he had been ordered to
design a giant sling to hurl rocks at the city walls in the manner of the Roman
catapult. However, when the three friends were together the talk was not of slings
and sieges but of theology, a subject at which the amateur Falkland easily
outwitted the professional Chillingworth. 'I think it not unwise of him to change
his profession' Sunderland told Dorothy; 'and I think you would have been of my
mind if you had heard him dispute last night with my Lord of Falkland in favour of
Socinianism, wherein he was by his Lordship so often confounded that it really
appears he has far more reason for his engines than for his opinions.'

When the King was forced to abandon the siege of Gloucester Sunderland returned to Oxford and from there wrote Dorothy a long letter ending with a few affectionate, lighthearted sentences:

Pray bless Poppet from me, and tell her I would have writ to her but that upon mature deliberation, I found it to be uncivil to return an answer to a Lady in another character than her own, which I am not yet learned enough to do. I cannot, by walking about my chamber, call anything more to mind to set down here and really I have made you no small compliment in writing thus much; for I have so great a cold that I do nothing but sneeze, and my eyes do nothing but water all the while I am in this posture of hanging down my head. I beseech you to present his service to my Lady who is most passionately and perfectly yours
Sunderland.
My humble service to Lady Lucy and the other little ladies.

This letter was to be his last. Knowing that his life was almost daily at risk he had already made plans for the event of his death, settling large sums of money on Dorothy and their daughters, and trying, though unsuccessfully, to buy Holdenby* House near Althorp 'that she might have it after him who, should he die now, would be destitute of a good house'. Now he hurried from Oxford and rejoined the King in time to take part in the bloody but indecisive battle of Newbury which was fought on 23 September 1643. Time and again the Cavalier horsemen charged, only to be driven back by musketeers and pikemen of the London Train Bands. In one of these charges Falkland was killed instantly, in another Sunderland fell mortally wounded. Thus the two friends died together. Falkland lies in an unmarked grave at Great Tew; Sunderland was buried on the field of battle but his heart was cut out and placed among the graves of his Spencer kin at Great Brington.

Dorothy was heavily pregnant; and wisely Lady Leicester took upon herself the task of telling her of her husband's death. The messenger who had brought the news described the scene to Lord Leicester—'Falling on her neck she spoke such comfortable words to her, and in so affectionate a manner as I am confident it was not possible for any divine or orator, with all their study and pre-meditation, to have been able in so short a time to have charmed so great a grief.' He added a sad little postscript—'I shall not need to tell your Lordship that neither of their

* This is the correct spelling, but 'Holmby' is the more usual one.

Ladyships took much rest that night.' Dorothy was fortunate in having remarkably wise and loving parents. Now Lord Leicester wrote her an affectionate letter telling her that he knew that she must grieve, but reminding her that her husband would have been bitterly distressed to think that she grieved immoderately—'Remember how apprehensive he was of your dangers and how sorry for anything that troubled you.' A few days after that letter was written Dorothy gave birth to a son who was named Henry after his dead father.

The year 1643 held other troubles for the Sidney family beside the tragedy of Henry Sunderland's death. Lord Leicester found himself in difficulty with both sides at once. The Parliamentary authorities issued an order confiscating his estates while, after two years of fruitless waiting, the King dismissed him from his post as Lord-Lieutenant of Ireland and appointed Lord Ormonde in his place. Philip and Algernon, his two sons who supported the Parliament side, succeeded in having the order of confiscation rescinded; but the King remained deaf to all protests. Though Leicester was without doubt in Clarendon's words 'a man of honour and fidelity to the King' Ormonde was in fact by far the better choice for the work of governing Ireland. Like Charles himself Leicester was a person unsuited to the times in which he lived and to the position in which he found himself. Like Charles he was a man of learning and culture, a sincere Christian and a loving husband and father, but, again like Charles, he was hopelessly irresolute. Leicester was fortunate in that he could retire to Penshurst and devote himself to his books and his family; Charles had no such option.

For the next eight years Dorothy and her children remained at Penshurst. There was therefore no hostess to greet Charles I when he came over to Althorp during his imprisonment at Holdenby House, the home which Henry Sunderland had tried to buy for Dorothy. The King attended Great Brington church when he wished to make his Communion, and he seems to have been free to amuse himself in the grounds at Althorp for he was actually playing bowls there when Cornet Joyce arrived to snatch him from the custody of Parliament into the hands of the Army. 'Where, Sir, is your warrant?' asked Charles, who could be a stickler for legality. For answer Joyce silently pointed to his troop of 500 horse.

From Holdenby and Althorp the road ran straight to the scaffold outside Whitehall. Although Dorothy's two brothers, Algernon Sidney and Lord Lisle, were both appointed members of the Commission set up to try the King neither of them took part in the actual trial or signed the death warrant. The King's execution on 30 January 1649 deeply shocked and saddened Lord Leicester, and six weeks later he was further grieved by the death of 'the sweet little boy,

'Sacharissa'. The Chatsworth version of the painting of Dorothy Sidney, wife of the first Earl of Sunderland, by Sir Anthony van Dyck, *c.*1642. There is another version at Althorp.

Three of the children of Charles I. Detail from the painting by Sir Peter Lely, *c.*1646. On the right of the painting is James, Duke of York, aged fourteen; in the centre is Princess Elizabeth, aged twelve; on the left is Henry, Duke of Gloucester, aged eight. At Petworth House.

Harry Spencer, my grandchild, five years old from October last'. This child, born so soon after his father's death, had been the special consolation of his widowed mother and the pet of the whole family. Harry died not at Penshurst but at Leicester House in London, and there, the very day after his death, further trouble fell upon the unhappy family. Dorothy's aunt, Lady Carlisle, was with her sorrowful sister and niece when an officer burst into the house and arrested her on a charge of complicity in a Royalist plot. She was imprisoned in the Tower, but soon released, thanks to the influence exercised by her two nephews and other powerful friends. She had, however, been in grave danger, for three of those imprisoned with her were executed.

In the summer of this tragic year 1649 Lord and Lady Leicester found themselves charged with the care of two homeless and unhappy children. King Charles's family, like the families of so many of his subjects, had been broken up and scattered by the Civil War. When Charles went North in the Spring of 1642 he had taken the Prince of Wales with him. Meanwhile Queen Henrietta Maria left England, ostensibly to escort her daughter Mary Princess of Orange back to Holland but in fact to attempt to raise money and supplies for the Royalist forces. The three younger children, James, Elizabeth and Henry, were left behind in London, and on the outbreak of war they fell into the hands of their father's opponents. James succeeded in escaping to Holland, but Elizabeth and Henry remained in the custody of Parliament. They were placed in the care of Dorothy's uncle, the Earl of Northumberland, who took them to live at Syon House near Brentford. After the King's execution these two children, the only members of the Royal Family remaining in England, might have been made to serve as a focus for the loyalty of Royalist supporters. It was therefore decided to move them farther away from London and to send them to live with Lord and Lady Leicester at Penshurst.

From the children's own point of view there could not have been a better choice. For Princess Elizabeth in particular the next few months were to be a time of healing and comparative happiness. Henry, Duke of Gloucester was an attractive eight-year-old who easily made friends with those about him, but for his sister life was more difficult. A plain and delicate child, at the age of six she had been parted from the mother she was never to see again and put to live with people who, however kindly, were yet her father's enemies. Now, at thirteen, she had been subjected to a strain which might well have proved too much for an older and more mature person. When Charles had been carried off from Holdenby House and held at Hampton Court as prisoner of the Army he was allowed to see and make

Penshurst Place. Early nineteenth-century engraving by Tomlinson after a drawing by J.P. Neale.

friends with his children at nearby Syon House, who, because of the long separation, were almost strangers to him. This family reunion came to an end with his flight to the Isle of Wight and his imprisonment in Carisbrooke and later in Hurst Castle. For fifteen months Elizabeth and Henry had seen nothing of their father when on the afternoon of the day before his execution they were taken to St James's Palace to bid him farewell. The King behaved towards his children with the utmost gentleness and understanding, trying as far as he was able to soften the shock of parting. Elizabeth however, was his one remaining link with his family, the person to whom he must confide his last thoughts and messages for them; and he was forced to place on this grave little Princess a trust which overburdened her beyond her years. At first she cried so bitterly that he feared she could not take in what he said—'Sweetheart, you will forget this.' 'I shall never forget it while I live,' she answered, and promised to write everything down. He charged her with detailed messages to his two elder sons and to the Queen and with various more

[34]

general injunctions before he took Henry on his knee and spoke to him in simple direct language which a child could understand. He then kissed and blessed them both and said a last goodbye. When the two children left the Palace Elizabeth was weeping so desolately that onlookers shook their heads, saying that she would die of grief.

This was the girl who arrived at Penshurst on 14 June 1649 together with a dozen servants and a great stock of furniture and plate from Whitehall Palace. In spite of all this royal paraphernalia Lord and Lady Leicester had instructions not to address the Prince and Princess by their proper titles and to make no difference between them and their own children and grandchildren. Lady Leicester, however, insisted that they should be treated with the deference due to their rank and take their meals apart from the other members of the household. This touch of respect did not prevent the royal children from becoming part of the family circle. Dorothy established a particularly close relationship with the shy, withdrawn Princess Elizabeth who shared her own liking for books and learning. The thirty-three-year-old widow and the thirteen-year-old girl understood each other well enough; the one mourned a husband killed in battle and a young child more recently dead, the other, a father beheaded on the scaffold. From that last traumatic interview with the King and the shock of his subsequent execution Elizabeth was never to recover but now she began to improve both in health and spirits in the warmth of Dorothy's motherly love and sympathy.

Her happiness was to be brief. When her brother Charles landed in Scotland in the summer of 1650 the Council of State, fearing that Elizabeth and Henry might be made the centre of a Royalist rising in England, ordered them away from the comfortable family home at Penshurst to the bleak security of Carisbrooke Castle in the Isle of Wight where their father had been held prisoner for many months. Elizabeth was filled with horror at the prospect. She said goodbye in floods of tears, giving Lady Leicester a fine diamond necklace. To take a sensitive, sickly girl away from the care of sympathetic friends and to shut her up in a chilly fortress haunted by memories of the father she so sadly mourned was equivalent to pronouncing her death-sentence. Within a month of her arrival at Carisbrooke Elizabeth was dead, officially of a malignant fever but according to the unhappy mother who had not seen her for eight years, 'from grief at finding herself brought to the same castle where her father had been in prison, and in a place where she had no assistance in her malady.' The last accusation was unjustified; the Governor of the Castle had tried hard but failed to get competent medical help for his charge. In that last illness Elizabeth talked constantly of her friends at Penshurst and most particularly of Dorothy, whose presence might have been of more real help to the dying child than the efforts of any doctor.

The Royalist cause went down in final defeat at the battle of Worcester in September 1651. That same month Dorothy and her children returned to Althorp after an absence of seven years. The Civil War was over, leaving curiously little bitterness behind it. Royalist families did not find life altogether easy, but for the most part they escaped serious molestation, especially if they were great territorial magnates such as the Sidneys and the Spencers. Dorothy seems to have been in no way short of money judging from the fact that she undertook a scheme of repairs and alterations to Althorp, her most notable achievement being what John Evelyn describes as 'the incomparable staircase', built between 1653 and 1662, and still one of the most magnificent features of the house. Her chief concern, however, was the upbringing of her son, Robert Earl of Sunderland, a remarkably clever boy. For his tutor she chose Thomas Pierce, a Fellow of her husband's old college Magdalen, who had been ejected from Oxford by the Parliamentary Commission because of his Church opinions. Many of these ejected clergy found shelter at Althorp where Dorothy provided them with lodging and sustenance and protected them against further persecution.

In spite of her many commitments at Althorp Dorothy managed to pay frequent visits to Penshurst where her presence was more than usually welcome. Lord and Lady Leicester were in much grief and distress of mind. Between 1648 and 1651 their three unmarried daughters, Mary, Elizabeth and Frances, had all died of what appears to have been consumption. In 1650 a fourth daughter, Isabella, had insisted on marrying Lord Strangford, much against the wishes of her father. The marriage turned out badly, becoming a source of endless trouble to her family, and not least to Dorothy, who nevertheless remained obstinately blind to Isabella's shortcomings. 'My lady Isabella, that speaks and looks and sings and plays so prettily,' writes the perceptive Dorothy Osborne, whose letters are an invaluable source of information for the history of the other Dorothy, 'why cannot I say that she is as free from faults as her sister believes her?'

Dorothy's brother Algernon was another cause of anxiety. A virtuous, stiff-necked individual, full of principle but lacking in charm, he was for ever in trouble with the authorities. As a rigid republican he disapproved of Cromwell as much as ever he had disapproved of Charles I and he made no secret of his opinions. In 1656 he went so far as to mount a production of *Julius Caesar* at Penshurst, himself playing the part of Brutus. His speeches were so clearly aimed at Cromwell that Algernon's elder brother, Lord Lisle, wrote a furious letter to Lord Leicester,

The staircase at Althorp – 'the incomparable staircase' as John Evelyn described it – built between 1653 and 1662. Engraving by Woolnooth after a drawing by E. Blore, in *Aedes Althorpianae* by T.F. Dibdin, 1822.

reproaching him for having permitted this insult to the Lord Protector, 'a public affront to him, which doth much entertain the town.' Algernon Sidney, however, went unmolested, and on Cromwell's death he returned to his old place in Parliament.

In times of trouble and anxiety Dorothy had always stood as a support to her family, a pillar of strength and good sense. Now she herself added to their dismay by announcing that she was about to marry again. Everywhere the news was greeted with astonishment and consternation. Her devotion to her husband had become proverbial; even now nine years after his death, it seemed almost blasphemous to suppose that she could contemplate putting anyone else in his place. During her widowhood Dorothy had had many admirers and received many offers of marriage. The motive which induced her to pick Robert Smyth out of this

[37]

Dorothy Osborne (1627–95), who married Sir William Temple in 1655, and whose correspondence tells us much about Sacharissa. Painted by Caspar Netscher, 1671.

throng of suitors remains a mystery. Rich, handsome, and of good character, he was a possible, but not a very probable choice for the Countess of Sunderland. He had admired and courted her for so long that his devotion had become a standing joke among their friends; Dorothy herself laughingly declared that she had taken him out of pity. This jest enraged Dorothy Osborne, who strongly disapproved of the marriage—'It was the pitifullest saying that ever I heard and made him so contemptible.' But whether from pity or from genuine love or from that last outburst of sexuality which seizes so many women in their late thirties and forties Dorothy Sunderland accepted Robert Smyth and married him at Penshurst on 8 July 1652. The fact that the wedding took place there and not at Althorp suggests that her family were at least not disapproving but, perhaps significantly, Lord Leicester was not among the 'much company' present.

[38]

Almost nothing is known about their life together as husband and wife. Although Dorothy spent some time at Boundes, Robert Smyth's beautiful home near Penshurst, Althorp remained her headquarters, at least until Robert Sunderland came of age in 1662. The only child of the marriage was a boy whom Dorothy always referred to as 'my son Smyth'. We do not even know the date of Robert Smyth's death; he fades away without comment. The few existing references to this middle-aged marriage come from Dorothy Osborne's letters; and she is not altogether an impartial witness. Dorothy Osborne and William Temple were married in 1655 after a seven year courtship. During that time in spite of the opposition of both families they had remained faithful to one another and had kept up a regular correspondence. Dorothy's enchanting letters fortunately survive, a valuable source of gossip and information but not, in this case, an absolutely reliable one. William Temple had been among Sacharissa's many admirers and he kept her portrait in his room even after he was pledged to Dorothy Osborne—'I have sent you my picture because you asked for it but pray let it not presume to disturb my Lady Sunderland's.' In Dorothy Osborne's letters a touch of tartness understandably creeps into all references to Dorothy Sunderland—for so she remained, keeping her title. 'We do abound in stories about my lady Sunderland and Mr Smyth,' Dorothy Osborne writes in an undated letter of 1663, 'with what reverence he approaches her, and how like a gracious princess she receives him, that they say 'tis worth going twenty miles to see.' Later, however, she admits that she has heard that the two are very happy together and that in private wife and husband were on more equal terms.

But, whether or not the marriage was a happy one it had done Dorothy Sunderland no good in the eyes of the world. She lost the remarkable reputation for virtue and sense that she had gained by keeping herself a widow. To quote Dorothy Osborne yet again, 'It was then believed that wit and discretion were to be reconciled in her person that have so seldom been permitted to meet in anyone else. But we are all mortal.' In the seventeenth century those whom St Paul described as 'widows indeed' were people to be greatly respected. By marrying Robert Smyth Dorothy Sunderland had tumbled off her pedestal.

Perhaps for that reason, more probably because of a chance lack of evidence, for the next twenty-five years she vanishes into the shadows. Among her contemporaries Dorothy was renowned as a letter-writer; but unfortunately most of her letters have disappeared and almost all those which survive date from 1679 and 1680. We know nothing about her reaction to Charles II's restoration in 1662, an event which must have given her much joy as the triumph of the cause for which

[39]

Sir William Temple (1628–99), diplomat and author. Painting by Sir Peter Lely, *c*.1660.

her husband had fought and died. It also brought with it a more tangible and quite unexpected source of satisfaction; the large sum of money which Henry Sunderland had lent to Charles I was returned to his estate by the new King. The Restoration, however, did not put an end to all the family difficulties in which Dorothy was involved. The King acted with considerable leniency towards his father's enemies. Naturally he showed no mercy towards the regicides; but the only person unconnected with the trial and execution of Charles I to suffer the death penalty was Sir Harry Vane, like Algernon Sidney an extreme Republican. Algernon Sidney himself was exempted from the general amnesty and might have met the same fate had he not chosen to remain abroad, where he lived in exile for many years, 'forsaken of my friends and known only to be a broken limb of a ship-wrecked faction.'

Of Dorothy's three children the eldest, Dorothy, her father's Poppet, in 1656 married Sir George Savile, afterwards Marquess of Halifax, a notable character who was to become 'a perfect and constant good friend' to his mother-in-law. Even at the age of fifty Sacharissa was not short of admirers, one of the most ardent being George Savile's brother Henry, a fat, jolly character much given to making jokes about his own bulk and professing great devotion to Dorothy, his tongue ever so slightly in his cheek all the while. When, for instance, by some mischance, he damaged one of her fingers he wrote letter after letter protesting his penitence—

[40]

Sir George Savile, later Marquess of Halifax (1633–95), political philosopher, who married Sacharissa's younger daughter, Dorothy. Detail from painting attributed to Mary Beale.

'though your Ladyship should have so much mercy as ever to forgive me, I will never pardon myself whilst I live, or at least it shall be the last thing I do upon my death-bed.' Because she cannot use her finger for writing he offers his services as secretary, and refers to her great reputation as a letter-writer—'I shall raise the whole commonwealth of writers against me, to give them my style after having disabled the most eloquent pen in England.'

Henry Savile, Dorothy's son Robert Sunderland, and her brother Henry Sidney, formed a trio of inseparable friends. In early childhood Robert Sunderland and Henry Sidney, nephew and uncle but exactly of the same age, had been brought up together at Penshurst. Henry grew up to become a diplomatist, a courtier and a rake. He made love to the Duchess of York, Anne Hyde, and in consequence lost his post as Groom of the Bedchamber to her husband. As a diplomatist he made a success of his position of British envoy at the Hague at a time when relations with Holland were complicated, to say the least. This able and amusing charmer was Dorothy's favourite brother whom she loved far more dearly than the upright and humourless Algernon or the bad-tempered Philip. The third member of the triumvirate, her son Robert, in 1665 after an inexplicable delay, married the beautiful Lady Anne Digby, younger daughter of the Earl of Bristol. At the time the marriage seems to have pleased Dorothy, but as she is discretion itself on the rare occasions when she mentions her daughter-in-law it is impossible to know whether or not she ever saw through the pious professions of that curiously double-faced woman.

We do not know where Dorothy was living at this time. She must certainly have left Althorp after her son's marriage even if she had not already done so. She went back there on occasional visits but she was more frequently to be found at Rufford, the Savile's house in Sherwood Forest, where there was a growing family of grandchildren to delight her. Wherever she might be she was always accompanied by her younger daughter Penelope, a lively, entertaining girl who, sadly enough, died unmarried in 1667. Three years later came another and most unexpected blow; Dorothy Savile, now Dorothy Halifax (her husband had been created a Viscount in 1668) died very suddenly on 16 December 1670. Two years later Halifax married as his second wife Gertrude Pierrepont, of whom it was said that 'her mind seems to have been congenial to that of her lord, and her understanding and wit were still exceeded by the goodness of her heart and the purity of her taste.' If this eulogy is correct she probably made a good stepmother to Dorothy's four little grandchildren, and certainly Dorothy did not allow this second marriage to break the strong link of affection between herself and Halifax. Being a tactful woman, in her letters to him she enquires after 'my little friend' Lady Betty, his only child by Gertrude, almost as often and as warmly as she does after her own beloved granddaughter, 'dear Nan.'

To Dorothy her son was a much less congenial character than her son-in-law. Both men had embarked on a political career and both men, to use Halifax's own expression, were trimmers, Halifax from prudence, Sunderland from lack of principle. Prudent in other respects Sunderland certainly was not; it cannot have been pleasant for Dorothy to hear that he had lost £5,000 in one night of high play. Unfortunately no letter from Dorothy to her son has survived. Of her extant letters by far the most important are written either to her favourite brother Henry Sidney or to Lord Halifax. The first of this group of twenty-four letters is addressed to Henry Sidney and dated 2 September 1679, while the remaining twenty-three all date from the year 1680. Though the letters are so few and cover so short a period of Dorothy's life they lift the mists which have obscured her for so long and they give us some idea of her gifts as a letter-writer.

At the age of sixty-two Dorothy is already an old woman, 'mightily troubled with pain in my limbs when I offer to stir.' In March 1679 Halifax had reported to his

Opposite: Charles II (1630–85). Painting by Sir Peter Lely, *c.*1675. Probably the portrait seen by Celia Fiennes in 1698 in the collection of the Duchess of Grafton.

[43]

brother Henry Savile that 'my old lady Sunderland hath been very ill and is not yet out of danger'; but though her physical health is poor her mind is as clear and as active as ever; and she is deeply involved both in family affairs and in politics. The two in fact meet and mingle since nearly all the prominent statesmen of the day are related to her either by blood or by marriage. Though she describes herself as 'a poor old dolt in the corner' she is obviously still an attractive woman; everyone who is anyone comes to see her and she hears all the gossip that is worth hearing.

Living in a little house near Whitehall Dorothy was neighbour to her old admirer, Edmund Waller, who was as much in favour with Charles II as he had been with Cromwell although his poetry was falling out of fashion. Elderly and greyhaired, he was still very much of a lady's man; 'his whole business,' Dorothy writes, 'is to watch where my lady Betty Felton goes and to follow her.' To his Sacharissa he was sometimes less than gallant. When she asked him in jest when he proposed to write some verses in her honour as he had done in the old days at Penshurst he replied, 'When, Madam, you are again as young and as beautiful as you were then.' That ill-mannered retort betrays the sting of an old hurt. Dorothy, however, still found him very good company and frequently invited him to her house.

In her letters to Henry Sidney Dorothy has much to say about their brother Algernon who had been allowed to return to England in 1677 in order to see his dying father. After Lord Leicester's death he remained in England, entangled in a lawsuit with his brother, the new Lord Leicester, over the terms of their father's will. The matter dragged on for years, causing deep division within the family. Although Henry Sidney was at odds with his elder brother over this issue the two remained good friends, but not so Algernon—'My Lady Hervey says to hear him and you talk 'tis a wonder you should disagree in anything. As to the other brother, she wonders nobody shoots him.' Dorothy handled this prickly character with tact. Hearing that he was ill she sent to enquire; and touched by this show of interest he came several times to see her, renewing their old affectionate relationship:

> My brother Algernon has come three times and I believe will continue it, for he seems very well pleased with it. We have not said one word of any difference and I never contradict him.

But though she did not contradict him she could and did laugh at him:

> Mr Algernon is busy, about what God knows. Last night he was called out of my chamber; I asked my man by whom, and my man said, 'A Quaker'.

Whether she is writing to Henry Sidney or to Halifax Dorothy is carefully non-committal in any reference she makes to her son Robert Sunderland or to her daughter-in-law. In order to further his political ambitions Sunderland was paying court to the King's mistresses, entertaining Barbara Castlemaine at Althorp and politely flattering Louise de la Keroualle, Duchess of Portsmouth: 'For our friends at court, Lord Sunderland is as well as anybody; how long God knows,' is Dorothy's only comment on her son's behaviour; and when she tells Halifax that 'Waller told me with a great oath that my son was sick of the Duchess of Portsmouth and would be glad with all his heart to be rid of her,' she expresses no personal relief at this doubtless welcome news.

The letters themselves still make good reading. Although Dorothy Sunderland has not the literary gift of Dorothy Osborne she can turn a charming phrase—'Your kind letter does so delight me, I would fain say something that would be that portrait of my heart, but I am so dull'—and she can bring a person or an event vividly to life. To a historian of the period much of her subject matter is extremely interesting. The great issue in 1680 was the Exclusion Bill, the attempt on the part of Lord Shaftesbury and 'the country party' to exclude the Roman Catholic Duke of York from the succession to the throne and to substitute for him Charles's illegitimate son, the Duke of Monmouth. Dorothy's letters, full of speculation, news and gossip, give the day-to-day background to this tense situation. She took a particular and personal interest in the course of events because both her son and her son-in-law were deeply involved. Sunderland publicly supported the claims of the Duke of York while privately toying with the idea of putting forward the Prince of Orange as a possible Protestant heir. Halifax, 'a man of subtle wit and intellect, who never chose his side before it was necessary to choose, and never did himself harm by his choice', had prudently retired to Rufford, and firmly refused to be drawn from there although Sunderland, who badly needed his support, did his very best to lure him back to London. Meanwhile Dorothy was keeping him in touch, sending him affectionate and amusing letters telling him serious items of news and also 'little things which I have been told', straws that might show which way the wind was blowing. She described, for instance, the behaviour of James, Duke of York, at the time when the outcry against him was at its loudest—'His Highness smiles, dances, makes love, and hunts.' She had unqualified faith in her son-in-law's political wisdom and judgement—'I am never so pleased than when I am told these things will be done, that my Lord Halifax will approve, for then I am sure that it is good for the nation.' Her letters invariably end with some expression of the warm love she felt towards him—'My dear lord, be a little kind to your poor

[45]

old constant passionate lover of you,' or again, 'I long to see your Lordship most violently, and love and pray for you as well as I can.'

All through the summer of 1680 London was in a turmoil; and there were even fears that civil war might break out once more. The position was so critical that Halifax, disturbed for Dorothy's safety, suggested that she should come to Rufford to escape from the possible danger of an outbreak of violence. She, however, refused to leave her home. 'That you have, my dear Lord, but a thought of my seeing sweet Rufford again, gives me a dream of happiness,' she wrote on 29 July. 'I believe there will be nothing here suddenly to fright those who have more reason to love life than I have.' Underneath her serenity and kindness, her lively interest in people and events, lay a vein of profound sadness; life had not been so kind to her that she would wish to have it prolonged.

In October Halifax at last came up to London in time for the meeting of Parliament. The Exclusion Bill passed the House of Commons only to be rejected by the Lords, thanks entirely to his efforts. He spoke brilliantly in face of a very strong opposition—'Having a great deal of wit, judgement and eloquence he made so fine and powerful a defence that he alone, for so all confessed, persuaded the whole House.'

Dorothy's last two surviving letters are dated 19 November and 25 November, only a few days after the rejection of the Exclusion Bill. Although she is writing to her brother Henry her chief concern is with her son-in-law—'I am full of my Lord Halifax.' She is delighted by his triumph in defeating the Exclusion Bill but horrified at the subsequent attempt by his opponents to revenge themselves by ousting him from his place on the Privy Council, an attempt in which Sunderland himself was involved in spite of his relationship with Halifax and their professions of friendship. 'My son was there at one time—that is the thorn in my side—though in everything else they agree. But it cannot be as I would have it so long as my son is well with Lord Shaftesbury.' She had reason to grieve; of her four Spencer children three were dead, and the only surviving one, ignoble heir of a noble father, was a cause of more sorrow than satisfaction. Her very last letter ends with the melancholy admission, 'Some things lie heavy at my heart.'

Those sad words written, Dorothy disappears from history. She lived another four years, time enough to see Halifax the most powerful and respected man in the kingdom and Sunderland temporarily out of favour but soon back in office as Secretary of State. She is never again mentioned in contemporary diaries or correspondence; nowhere is there any record of the date and place of her death. According to an entry in the parish register she was buried in Great Brington

Louise de Kéroualle, Duchess of Portsmouth and Aubigny (1649–1734). Painted by Sir Peter Lely, probably in 1671, following a house-party at Euston Hall, described in Evelyn's diary, at which she became the King's mistress.

[47]

Edmund Waller. Painting after
John Riley, *c*.1685.

church on 25 February 1684, but no monument or inscription marks her grave.

Edmund Waller outlived Dorothy by three years, dying in 1687. Although perhaps not permissible it would be pleasant to think that his last and most lovely poem was inspired by the sight of his Sacharissa in her old age:

> The seas are quiet when the winds give o'er;
> So calm are we when passions are no more.
> For then we know how vain it was to boast
> Of fleeting things, so certain to be lost.
> Clouds of affection from our younger eyes
> Conceal that emptiness which age descries.
>
> The soul's dark cottage, batter'd and decayed,
> Lets in new light through chinks that Time hath made:
> Stronger by weakness, wiser men become
> As they draw near to their eternal home.
> Leaving the old, two worlds at once they view
> That stand upon the threshold of the new.

[48]

'The Little Girl in Green'. Painting by Sir Peter Lely, *c*.1650. Mystery has always surrounded the identity of this girl, though in treatment the picture is very close to that of Lely's idealised paintings of children of the Sidney family. Sir Oliver Millar identifies her as one of the sisters of the second Earl of Sunderland, probably Lady Penelope, a lively girl who was a constant companion of her mother until she died suddenly, unmarried, in 1667. At Chatsworth.

THE SUNDERLANDS

'The Character of a Trimmer.'

The Marquess of Halifax

'A Trimmer' – Robert Spencer, second Earl of Sunderland (1641–1702). Painted in classical attire in Rome by Carlo Maratta (1625–1713). The Earl leans on a slab representing 'Love overcoming Time', an allusion to his courtship of Anne Digby. At Althorp. There is also another painting of Robert Spencer, by Sir Peter Lely, at Althorp.

[49]

'A man whose actions had been so scandalous during his whole life that he never had any way to excuse one crime but by accusing himself of another'—in this damning phrase Lord Norris described the son of Sacharissa and the true-hearted Henry Sunderland. Robert, second Earl of Sunderland, was that rare phenomenon in the Spencer family, a bad man. He was disloyal to three kings, heartless to his own relations, a character apparently without scruple or honesty. Of all the admirable qualities which he should have inherited from his Spencer and Sidney ancestry he possessed only two, genuine artistic appreciation and a good brain, which, however, in his case was often nullified by poor judgement.

It might be argued that in his frequent changes of front, or to put it more bluntly, his treasons, Sunderland was only pushing the general practice to extremes. In his day loyalty was an unfashionable virtue. Stiff-necked individuals such as Algernon Sidney all too frequently ended up on the scaffold; and Sunderland was not of the stuff out of which martyrs are made. Nevertheless, the appearance of such an atypical figure in the Spencer family remains a puzzle to those who believe in the influence of heredity upon the formation of character.

In a typical passage Macaulay blames Sunderland's faults on his upbringing and education:

In him the political morality of the age was personified in the most lively manner. Nature had given him a keen understanding, a restless and mischievous temper, a cold heart, and an abject spirit. His mind had undergone a training in which all his vices had been raised up to the rankest maturity.

Sunderland's biographer, J. P. Kenyon, echoes this judgement by suggesting that Sacharissa's second marriage to a man 'of comparatively poor standing and unexciting personality' may have meant that the boy lacked the guidance and control of a strong hand. This second marriage, however, was a curiously unimportant episode in Sacharissa's life. She remained Countess of Sunderland in fact as well as in name; her home was at Althorp and her Spencer children seem to have meant much more to her than the shadowy Smyth or her son by him. There is evidence to show that she devoted an unusual amount of care and consideration to the upbringing of young Sunderland. Little is known about the character of Dr Thomas Pierce, whom she chose as tutor for the boy; but it seems unlikely, to say the least, that a man who had given up his Oxford Fellowship and his means of livelihood rather than abandon his religious principles would encourage his pupil in ways of double dealing and deceit. 'The shameless Sunderland', 'the unscrupulous career politician with a strong instinct for survival' remains an inexplicable freak in the long line of Spencer politicians and statesmen notable for their loyalty and lack of self-interest.

When he was seventeen Sunderland spent some time abroad under the supervision of Dr Pierce. This introduction to the treasures of France and Italy awakened in him a love of art and architecture and developed his natural taste and discrimination. His preference was of course for what was then contemporary art; and it is to him that Althorp owed its fine collection of baroque pictures. After the Restoration he returned to England and went up to Oxford, where he struck up an improbable friendship with William Penn, later famous as the Quaker founder of Pennsylvania. When Penn was sent down for fomenting a riot against the re-establishment of Anglican ritual Sunderland left Oxford as a gesture of sympathy.

In 1663 an eminently suitable marriage was arranged between Sunderland and Lady Anne Digby, daughter of the Earl of Bristol. The settlements were signed, the trousseau prepared, and the date fixed, when the prospective bridegroom absconded, giving no reason for his flight beyond the statement that 'he was resolved not to have her'. He spent the following year abroad in company with various friends, including his uncle and contemporary Henry Sidney, buying pictures, having his portrait painted, and apparently undergoing a change of heart since in April 1664 he returned to England and two months later married Anne Digby.

Looked at from a distance of three hundred years the new Lady Sunderland is a puzzling character. Queen Anne detested her as a cheat and a hypocrite, 'the greatest jade that ever lived'. The diarist John Evelyn, on the contrary, described her as 'a wise and noble person' and 'a lady of great soul', believing her loudly voiced concern for religion to be entirely genuine. She was generally thought to have committed adultery and incest—the relationship is within the prohibited degrees—with her husband's uncle, Henry Sidney. If this was indeed so Sunderland did not repay her in kind. Bad though he may have been he was not debauched; gambling was his particular vice, and neither wine nor women held much temptation for him. Set against this rumour—and whatever its nature may have been certainly her relationship with Henry Sidney was a very close one—is the fact that the marriage which had begun so unpropitiously ended up as a remarkable success. Anne apparently loved and certainly cherished her husband, doing all she could to further his career. In their later years the two drew very close to one another; he became more and more dependent on her for comfort and support, missing her sadly whenever they were separated. She bore him seven children, four of whom survived to grow up but not to live happily ever after.

In the early years of his marriage Sunderland spent much time and money repairing and beautifying Althorp. He procured an Italian architect to rebuild the exterior in brick with stone dressings and to redesign all the interior rooms leaving only the Long Gallery untouched because it made so admirable a setting for the collection of pictures which was his especial pleasure and interest. The gardens and grounds he altered according to plans drawn up by Le Nôtre, the famous French landscape-gardener. Now that he had so greatly improved his family home Sunderland delighted in entertaining large parties there, the guests including King Charles II's illegitimate son, James Duke of Monmouth, his brother James Duke of York, and his mistress *en titre*, Barbara Castlemaine. Such people could help forward the political career on which Sunderland was now embarking under the aegis of Lord Arlington, a member of the little group known as the 'Cabal'. Arlington found for him various diplomatic posts, including, for a short time, the Embassy at Paris, all of them more high-sounding than genuinely important. Now Sunderland embarked on the innumerable changes of front which make his foreign policy such a tangled thread to unravel. Fortunately it is not necessary to catalogue here in any detail the many times he switched from France to Holland, from Louis XIV to William of Orange, with occasional flirtations with Spain thrown in for good measure.

Such behaviour was by no means unprecedented; in foreign policy duplicity was the order of the day. Where Sunderland differed from his fellows was not so much in his methods as in his motives. Danby, for instance, a notoriously crooked dealer, was fundamentally on the side of Roman Catholicism and therefore of France. Charles II himself could twist and turn with the best of them, but throughout his devious course he was guided by two *idées fixes*. He was determined to remain on the throne, disliking nothing so much as the idea of once again 'setting out on his travels', and he was equally determined to uphold the theory of legitimate and hereditary succession. Though he had no great liking for the Duke of York and loved Monmouth as he loved no one else, he would not hear of his bastard son ousting his brother from the succession to the throne nor would he consider legitimizing Monmouth. Sunderland, however, was the archetypal Mr Facing-Both-Ways. His changes of front were dictated by nothing except self-interest; and because his judgement was poor they often appeared to be as devoid of reason as they were of principle.

With the passing of the Test Act in 1673 the Roman Catholic Clifford lost office and with him went Arlington. The Cabal was broken; and power passed to Danby,

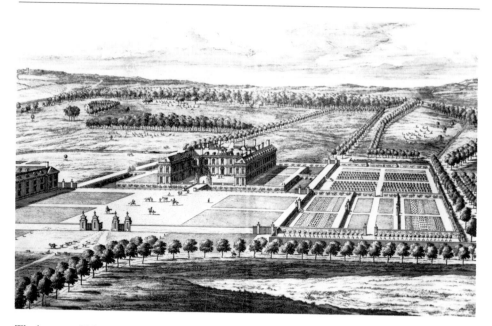

The house at Althorp, as refaced by an Italian architect for the second Earl of Sunderland, with the gardens laid out according to plans drawn up by Le Notre. Engraving after Knyff.

a man of many names, beginning as Sir Thomas Osborne and becoming successively Viscount Osborne, Viscount Latimer, Earl of Danby, Marquess of Carmarthen, and finally Duke of Leeds. Sunderland could have followed Arlington into opposition but characteristically he chose to remain a hanger-on at Court, hoping for a lucrative post to come his way since his finances were as entangled as his politics, thanks chiefly to his propensity for gambling. So short of cash was he that he actually 'touched' his own chaplain for £100 while Lady Sunderland borrowed money from John Evelyn. At last he received an appointment as Envoy Extraordinary charged with the impossible task of salvaging something from the wreck of an unratified French treaty. He had always loved Paris but he now found that city less attractive than he had done in earlier days, and he was pursued there by personal difficulties. His heir Robert, shockingly spoilt by Lady Sunderland, who doted on him as 'the prettiest boy in town', had at the age of fourteen become quite ungovernable. The Huguenot tutor

[53]

James, Duke of York, later King James II (1633–1701). Unfinished painting by Sir Peter Lely.

whom Sunderland had left in charge of this outrageous child made a special journey to Paris to complain that his own efforts at discipline were constantly thwarted by the boy's indulgent mother. Somewhat naturally, Sunderland took his wife's side in the quarrel with the result that young Robert went from bad to worse, piling up a load of trouble for himself and his parents in the years to come.

In 1678 Sunderland's prospects suddenly brightened. Danby's position had been much shaken by the agitation over the supposed Popish Plot and by the discovery of his own secret dealings with the French; and in an effort to strengthen his unpopular minister Charles II appointed two new Secretaries of State. One was to be Sir William Temple, who in fact never took up the post; the other was Sunderland. His appointment was regarded as a stopgap; a post of such importance, the equivalent of the modern Foreign Secretaryship, did not often go to a man of so little experience or standing in politics. But as sometimes happens Sunderland's comparative insignificance proved a positive advantage; nobody had much against him because nobody knew much about him. They did not long remain in ignorance; two years later he was a national figure with a reputation for double-dealing remarkable even in that generation of double-dealers.

Danby's resignation in March 1679 and his subsequent imprisonment in the Tower brought Sunderland at once to the front. From his own point of view he had received office at precisely the right moment. Government was now in the hands of the 'Triumvirate', Essex, Halifax, Sunderland. On the question of the Exclusion Bill, the great topic of the day, all three were apparently committed to support the Catholic James Duke of York against the demands of the Exclusionists, who wished to see him excluded from the succession to the throne in favour of a Protestant heir. When in August 1679 Charles II fell dangerously ill of a fever, with the connivance of Sunderland James, who had been living in exile in Brussels, returned to England. On the King's recovery he was once again exiled, but this time with more show of politeness, being sent to Edinburgh as High Commissioner. Meanwhile the Triumvirate collapsed; and power passed into the hands of the less-experienced 'chits', Godolphin, Lawrence Hyde, and the inevitable Sunderland. In public he was one of the Duke of York's most convinced and enthusiastic supporters; privately, he was toying with the possibility of pushing the claims of William Prince of Orange who was a Stuart on his mother's side and married to James's elder daughter Mary. If James were to be excluded from the succession William was in fact the most desirable Protestant substitute; but Shaftesbury and the Exclusionists chose to pass him over in favour of Monmouth.

All through the spring and summer of 1680 the battle raged, both sides manoeuvring to gain a better position. Parliament was called for October; and when it met an Exclusion Bill was to be introduced. Now Sunderland made an extraordinary error of judgement. Totally miscalculating the odds, he switched sides and came out in favour of Exclusion. Never did he make a worse mistake. The King sent a message to Parliament declaring his unwavering support of James as the rightful heir; and though the Bill passed the House of Commons it was thrown out by the Lords, thanks almost entirely to Halifax. In the uproar which followed the Bill's rejection Sunderland made a second miscalculation. The Exclusionists in the House of Commons bitterly attacked the man who had caused their defeat, bringing in an Address to the King 'praying that he would be pleased to remove George Earl of Halifax from his Council'. Although he was much in company with Shaftesbury Sunderland publicly opposed the Address, but privately he advised Halifax to resign office and retire into private life. The suggestion was both insulting and uncalled-for, part of a scheme to get rid of a man who stood in the way of his own advancement. Not surprisingly, 'Lord Halifax fell into such a passion that he went out of the room, and from that time they have hardly lived in any common civility when they met.' Quite unnecessarily Sunderland had made an enemy of his own brother-in-law, a man who was the most able and influential politician of the day.

In January 1681 Sunderland was dismissed from office in circumstances of some ignominy. His career was apparently finished. In the matter of the Exclusion Bill he had betrayed James Duke of York and it seemed impossible that James's brother the King, who had gone so far as to use the term 'Judas', should ever think to employ him again. His public life lay in ruins and his private affairs were in hardly better shape. He was desperately short of money and when he tried to improve the family finances by marrying his raffish son Robert to a rich heiress the girl's father refused to consider the match because of the young man's evil reputation. Yet within a year Sunderland was back in favour at Court and in January 1683 he was once again appointed Secretary of State.

This extraordinary rehabilitation of a man who could fairly be called a traitor was in great part due to the influence of Louise de la Keroualle, Duchess of Portsmouth. Sunderland had never been above worming his way into the King's favour by way of the King's mistresses. As a young man he had been on very friendly terms with Lady Castlemaine and when she was supplanted by the Duchess of Portsmouth he had been at great pains to curry favour with the rising star. Now his efforts in that direction paid a handsome dividend. In the closing years of his reign Charles fell more and more under the influence of the Duchess.

Algernon Sidney (1622–83), republican and brother of Dorothy Sidney. Painting after Justus van Egmont, 1663.

He was too tired and also too lazy to hold out for long against her constant pleading on behalf of her *protégé*; moreover, he himself was in need of a competent minister with a knowledge of foreign affairs and of the day-to-day business of diplomacy. So Sunderland came back, and remained in office till Charles's death in 1685.

During those years he was guilty of one peculiarly base sin of omission. In the spring of 1683 after the discovery of the Rye House Plot the Earl of Essex, Lord Russell, and Algernon Sidney were all three imprisoned in the Tower, accused of complicity in this attempt to murder the King. Essex committed suicide; Russell was beheaded, and later Algernon Sidney, whose trial had been delayed for some months, also died on the scaffold protesting his innocence. Although Sidney was his own uncle Sunderland never made the smallest gesture of help or kindness towards him during his long imprisonment or lifted a finger to save him from an unmerited death.

With the accession of James II Sunderland was generally regarded as 'a man lost'; and when James took no immediate steps against him it was supposed that his dismissal had merely been delayed. But, given even a temporary foothold,

Sunderland knew exactly how to make himself indispensable. He was adept at manipulating elections and packing parliaments, and he saw to it that the first Parliament summoned by James should be an unexpectedly loyal and complaisant body. Soon James, who four years previously had said of Sunderland 'He shall never play me such a trick again for I will never trust him', was speaking of him 'with great esteem, and as one who would be serviceable in the execution of his designs.'

Those designs amounted to nothing less than the conversion of England to the Roman Catholic faith; and because Sunderland was prepared to support this fantastic and impracticable policy it was he who now became James's chief adviser. Seeing which way the wind was blowing even before Charles II's death, with the connivance of his ardently Protestant wife in 1684 Sunderland had sacrificed one of his own children to the advancement of the Roman Catholic cause. The young Earl of Clancarty, head of a Catholic family and owner of vast estates in Ireland had been brought up in England by his Protestant mother. In order to remove the seventeen-year-old Earl from his mother's influence and to prevent the Clancarty property from falling into Protestant hands Sunderland, together with James's Catholic advisers, arranged that he should be invited to Court and coerced into a huddled-up marriage with Sunderland's daughter Elizabeth, a child of thirteen. This scheming profited nobody. The marriage was not consummated; Clancarty went off to Ireland where he led a wild and reckless life, while Elizabeth remained at Althorp, her beauty, youth and happiness all run to waste, destroyed by her father's futile machinations.

Sunderland himself had no religious convictions strong enough to stand in the way of his personal advancement. If it would be to his advantage to turn Roman Catholic a Roman Catholic he would become. He was, however, too shrewd to commit himself prematurely; and it is difficult to discover exactly how far he went in that direction. Certainly he attended Mass, but that might be explained away as bowing to the house of Rimmon. In 1688 he announced 'that he was now a sincere Catholic'; a year later he was declaring, 'I never abjured, I never received Communion their way, I never had a priest in my house.' When it suited his convenience he posed as a Papist; but there is no evidence to prove that he was ever formally received into the Roman Catholic Church.

As Duke of York James had been an unpopular figure, but when he succeeded his brother on the throne he was given a surprisingly warm welcome. Monmouth's rebellion only increased the general feeling of goodwill towards him though the brutalities of the Bloody Assize caused some dismay and disquiet. Within three years he had dissipated all this stock of loyalty which he had inherited from his more popular and pliant brother. An honest and obstinate man, James put principles above prudence, and he endeavoured to ram his own principles down the throats of his unwilling subjects. Toleration was a word which had no meaning for him nor did he believe in the wisdom of making haste slowly. And, instead of counselling prudence, Sunderland, his chosen adviser, urged James on so rashly that some have thought he was deliberately plotting his master's ruin. If this were indeed true it would make sense of much in Sunderland's career that is otherwise incomprehensible. Most historians, however, are not in favour of this theory, if only because, as David Ogg puts it, 'it is unlikely that Sunderland tried deliberately to ruin his master because he perceived that in this matter James would need no help.'

The Test Act confined office under the Crown to those willing to take Communion according to the rites of the Church of England; and a similar restriction existed in such bodies as corporations and universities. Parliament and the nation as a whole were prepared to adopt a slightly more tolerant attitude and to agree that the King's dispensing power allowed him to make certain exceptions to the Act; but this was not enough for James. He wanted freedom to appoint Roman Catholics to any and every position, civil and military, and rather than settle for less he prorogued Parliament in November 1685. It never met again during his reign.

With an extraordinary lack of political wisdom or even of plain common sense James now proceeded to put a Roman Catholic into every vacant post. In 1687 he turned his attention to the two universities. On the death of the President of Magdalen, Oxford, Sunderland, who was himself a Magdalen man, personally despatched the mandate ordering the Fellows to elect a Roman Catholic of the King's own choice. They refused; whereupon James expelled twenty-five of them and forced the remainder to accept his nominee. At Cambridge the Vice-Chancellor was deprived of his position because he would not grant a degree to a Benedictine monk. Not content with these high-handed measures James issued a Declaration of Indulgence granting full liberty of worship and suspending all religious tests. Since the Declaration applied to all Dissenters, Catholic and Protestant alike, James hoped that it would win him the support of the Nonconformists; but they were not so easily deceived. The alarm and dismay felt by all Protestants was heightened by the announcement that the Queen, Mary of Modena, who had already borne and lost several children, was once again pregnant. If the coming child were a girl the Protestant princesses Mary and Anne,

[59]

James's daughters by his first wife, would of course come before her in the succession; but if it were a boy the heir to the throne would be a Roman Catholic.

Always a gambler, Sunderland now risked his entire future on the sex of an unborn child. He informed James privately that he was prepared to declare his conversion to Roman Catholicism although he still refrained from making any public statement. Another member of the family had recently announced his conversion. Robert Lord Spencer had developed into a full-blown specimen of a drunken rake. Already he had been badly injured in an encounter with the London constables, but worse was to come. In March 1687 he marched into a church in Bury St Edmunds during a service, drew his sword and, cursing and swearing, tried to drag the preacher out of the pulpit. The enraged congregation hustled Robert out of the church, tore off his clothes, beat him severely and finally rolled him in the mud and muck of the open drain. His wounds were near mortal, and in this extremity he was rumoured to have sent for a Roman Catholic priest. Sunderland, however, remained unforgiving until the prodigal son recovered sufficiently to return home and inform his family that he had indeed turned Roman Catholic.

In May 1688 the King issued a second Declaration of Indulgence and ordered that it should be read in churches throughout the country. Archbishop Sancroft and six other bishops presented a petition asking that this order be withdrawn; in reply, James charged the seven bishops with seditious libel. Up to now Sunderland had encouraged rather than restrained James in his headlong course towards disaster, but now he suddenly saw the red light. He strongly advised against the prosecution of the seven bishops, but James refused to listen and committed the bishops to the Tower. Two days later on 10 June the Queen gave birth to a son. On 20 June Sunderland publicly announced his conversion to Roman Catholicism.

The gesture did him no good. For a short time he was high in favour with the King and Queen, the only people who believed his conversion to be genuine; but nevertheless James persisted in disregarding his wise and sensible plea for clemency towards the seven bishops, who were fast becoming popular heroes. On 29 June they were brought to trial. At first the jury disagreed; but finally the verdict was brought in—'not guilty'.

At once the nation went wild with joy and relief. For James the end was now very near. In July seven men of high standing, including Sunderland's friend Henry Sidney, sent a letter to William of Orange inviting him to England and pledging him their support. Meanwhile Sunderland's reputation had sunk to its lowest level yet. In the streets of London the crowds pursued him with shouts of 'Popish dog', and after attending the trial of the seven bishops he left the hall by a back door, believing his life to be in danger from the mob. Protestants despised him as a renegade, and Roman Catholic extremists disliked and distrusted him because he was now advocating a policy of moderation which they regarded as craven surrender. He was still necessary to the King as the one competent politician remaining at his side, but the position was precarious in the extreme.

For a while both Sunderland and the King remained obstinately blind to the threat of an invasion by a Dutch force under William of Orange; but by September William's preparations were completed and the danger was clear for all to see. At this crucial moment Sunderland collapsed. In explanation and extenuation it should be pointed out that he was under exceptionally severe strain, personal as well as political. When Robert Spencer had announced his conversion to Roman Catholicism the King had rewarded him by sending him on a trivial diplomatic mission to Modena. On the way there the profligate young man stopped in Paris where he indulged in such debauchery that his health gave way and he could get no further than Turin. There he remained desperately ill until he could drag himself back to Paris where he lay drinking himself to death. He died in this same fatal month of September. Perhaps even more distressing to Sunderland than his son's death was his alienation from the wife on whom he was coming to depend more and more. His announcement of his conversion to the Roman Catholic Church had been an outrage to her strident Protestantism. And although her religious principles were so evident her morality was much in doubt; London was humming with rumours about her supposed affair with Henry Sidney.

Not surprisingly, Sunderland's nerve broke. In his alarm he rushed hither and thither like a frightened rabbit. He made abject confession to his wife who, if unfaithful sexually, was always loyal and loving to her husband in other respects. She was quick to forgive him and to write to her supposed lover, Sidney, now living in Holland, asking him to find them some refuge from the coming storm. Meanwhile Sunderland was privately making the same request to Barillon, the French Ambassador. A minister in this state of panic was a hindrance rather than a help; and in October James dismissed Sunderland from the Privy Council and commanded him to hand over the seals of office as Secretary of State.

Sunderland's immediate reaction was to make a formal request to be granted asylum in France. It was refused. On 5 November 1688 William landed at Torbay. James led the Army out to meet him but on reaching Salisbury decided to retreat rather than give battle, the morale of his troops being so low. Every day someone of importance defected to William. Still Sunderland lingered in London, unable to decide where to take refuge and desperately short of money. James secretly left England on 11 December only to be caught and brought back again. (He finally escaped to France a fortnight later.) That same week Sunderland and his wife embarked in a ship which landed them in Holland, the very last country where any supporter of James might have expected to find shelter.

Sunderland had declared that he would be 'without resource' should William of Orange come to power, yet he seems to have been under William's personal protection during his stay in Holland. His exile was not uncomfortable. He spent a short time in jail but he was soon released on private orders from William. He and Lady Sunderland then found themselves 'a very pretty convenient house' in Amsterdam, where they were joined by their surviving children. Later they moved to Utrecht so that the fifteen-year-old Charles, now Lord Spencer, could attend the university there. At Utrecht Sunderland could be seen every Sunday walking at the head of his family to attend service in the Reformed Church, preceded by a servant carrying a huge Bible.

Meanwhile William and Mary had accepted the English throne where they were to reign as joint sovereigns; and Parliament had been requested to bring in a Bill of Indemnity and Oblivion. Sunderland was one of the few people specifically excluded from this generous measure and also from a subsequent Act of Grace and General Indemnity. A double traitor, he was the only man to be excluded both from these two measures and from the Proclamation of Pardon issued by James in exile at St Germain. Nevertheless by May 1690 he had returned to England and been received in audience by William before retiring in comfort and safety to his home at Althorp where for the time being he could devote himself to gardening and to his fine collection of pictures.

That Sunderland, the Papist convert who had served James as his most trusted minister, should now become the confidential adviser of the Protestant William who had supplanted James on the throne is one of the unsolved mysteries of history. Sunderland's own attitude is easily explained. By nature he was a gambler who felt no more loyalty towards a monarch or a policy than a punter does towards a horse on which he has placed a bet. If it does badly in a race he does not back it next time it runs but transfers his money to another animal. So Sunderland behaved with perfect logic though less loyalty towards Charles II, James II, William III and even Louis XIV; moreover, he was much given to hedging his bets. Unfortunately for him he was not only a backer but a jockey, and a jockey should not attempt to change mounts in the middle of a race.

William's reliance on Sunderland is much more difficult to understand. While in exile in Holland Sunderland had written and published a pamphlet entitled *A Letter to a Friend Plainly Discovering the Designs of the Romish Party and Others for the Subverting of the Protestant Religion and the Laws of this Kingdom.* Contemporaries believed that William trusted Sunderland because by publishing this pamphlet he had publicly and irrevocably burnt his boats where James was concerned; as Portland put it, 'He must serve the King faithfully because his whole future depends on the King's success.' But William knew very well that in 1680 over the Exclusion Bill and again in 1688 with his conversion to Roman Catholicism Sunderland had burnt his boats equally publicly and irrevocably, yet, to continue the metaphor, when the wind changed he had rebuilt his fleet and sailed into safe harbour on the opposite side. Slippery as an eel, Sunderland would never commit himself finally to anything or anybody.

It might be argued that William sought Sunderland's advice and wished to include him among his ministers because he believed in a broadly based ministry representing all parties and shades of opinion. Sunderland, however, had changed sides so many times that now he represented no interest but his own. Because William's involvement in the war against France obliged him to spend so much of his time away from England he might have felt peculiar need of a competent and experienced adviser. But was Sunderland any more competent or experienced than other available policitians? Certainly there was no question of a personal friendship with homosexual overtones such as existed between William and Keppel. William, however, was bisexual in his love-affairs; and Sunderland, who made a habit of cultivating the mistresses of kings, may have owed something to the influence exercised on his behalf by Elizabeth Villiers, Queen Mary's childhood friend who was also William's mistress. Whatever the reason, although the weight of adverse opinion kept him out of public office, from 1692 onwards Sunderland was William's *éminence grise*, in his own words, 'the minister behind the curtain'.

It was a position that suited him very well. He had always sat lightly to party ties, but now he emerged as a strong Whig. In 1693 he entertained a great gathering of Whig magnates at Althorp, and, acting on his advice, that same year William abandoned his own preference for a mixed ministry and entrusted the government to a Whig 'junta' which remained in power till the end of the reign. This period might be called the beginning of the modern system of party government because now for the first time it was thought necessary that the King's ministers and the House of Commons should be of the same political complexion. Sunderland had

[63]

always been adept at packing and managing Parliament and he now saw to it that the Whigs should be in a permanent majority; as he himself wrote, 'We have looked over and considered the list of parliament men, and agreed upon the best means of persuading them to be reasonable.'

Sunderland's success in manipulating people and parliaments did not depend upon personal charm but rather the contrary. He had always been noted for his black temper and his bitter tongue; and as he grew older his sarcasm became yet more biting and his outbursts of rage yet more terrifying. Admittedly he was witty, but at other people's expense and often in the worst of taste, and thus he made for himself many enemies even among the Whigs who owed so much to his machinations. Only William remained if not his friend at least his patron. In the autumn of 1695 he visited Althorp where he enjoyed such good hunting that he stayed on for three days after the arranged time. Presumably therefore Sunderland followed, or at least encouraged the sport that was a hereditary passion in the Spencer family.

In April 1697 William appointed Sunderland Lord Chamberlain and also made him one of the Lords Justices who acted as regents when he himself was out of the kingdom, Queen Mary having died in 1694. The King apparently wished to complete his supporter's rehabilitation by restoring him to some sort of public office; but the memory of past treacheries was still fresh in men's minds, and so great was the outcry that Sunderland was almost immediately forced to resign. This fiasco marked the end of his hopes for a renewed political career, although in the following year he made one final and futile attempt to return to public life. It failed, and he retired to Althorp, 'never more to trouble myself or anyone else with public business'.

Private business was indeed troubling enough to occupy most of Sunderland's leisure. His daughter Elizabeth was now living by herself in London. Her husband Clancarty arranged a meeting with her at her house and tried to persuade her to consummate their thirteen-year-old marriage. At first she refused but finally yielded, perhaps not altogether reluctantly. Meanwhile the house-porter had thought it his duty to hurry over to inform Elizabeth's brother, Lord Spencer, of Clancarty's arrival. With more haste than good sense Spencer collected a posse of soldiers, broke into his sister's room, found husband and wife in bed together, and dragged Clancarty off to Newgate prison. The scandal was immense, increased by the fact that Clancarty had already been proscribed as a Jacobite. The worst sufferer was the unhappy Elizabeth who was cast off by her own family. She personally approached the King to beg for her husband's life and freedom. When

Lambeth Delft pottery charger, depicting King William III, *c.*1690. Chargers of this type, now extremely rare, were made as a symbol of popular support for William of Orange, after his accession. There are others in existence depicting Charles II, Queen Anne and George I.

ANNE COUNTESS OF SUNDERLAND DAUGHTER
OF THE DUKE OF MARLBOROUGH
AND ROBERT SPENCER HER SON

her request was granted the graceless Clancarty went back to Ireland where he had a second wife waiting to welcome him.

Of Sunderland's other children Anne, the eldest and best-beloved, had married Lord Arran and died in 1690, aged only twenty-three. There remained the son and heir, Charles, Lord Spencer. He had made a very advantageous and happy marriage with Arabella, daughter and heiress of the Duke of Newcastle. 'Bel' was a general favourite and her death from smallpox in June 1698 was a great grief to all the family. To the Sunderlands, however, business was business, whatever the circumstances. Although Charles Spencer was prostrated with sorrow, with almost indecent haste his parents set about arranging a second marriage for him with Marlborough's daughter, Anne Churchill. Marlborough himself was very reluctant to give this beautiful and gifted girl to a man so sunk in grief that he could not feel for her as he ought or appreciate her at her true worth. Within a few months, however, this inconsolable widower was as much in love with Anne as ever he had been with Arabella; and the two were married in January 1700.

Sunderland was now an ailing and prematurely aged man. He was so far removed from politics that the death of William III meant little to him although he could hope for nothing from Queen Anne who had never made any secret of her hatred for 'the subtlest working villain on the face of the earth'. He outlived William by only six months, dying on 28 September 1702 in the odour of Anglican sanctity, and cared for till the end by his devoted wife. He has his rightful place in that pantheon of British worthies, the *Dictionary of National Biography*, where he is described as 'the craftiest, most rapacious, and most unscrupulous of all the politicians of his age.'

Though his career closely paralleled that of his father in character the third Earl of Sunderland more nearly resembled his great-uncle, Algernon Sidney. Like Sidney, he was a prickly person sadly lacking in charm; like Sidney, he described himself as a Republican, going so far as to tell his friends to address him as plain Mr Charles Spencer. He had his father's liking for devious twists and turns, but through them all he was guided by a thread of Whiggish principle; to take an obvious example, unlike most politicians of his day he never flirted with Jacobitism or made an approach to the King over the water.

Opposite: Anne Churchill, daughter of the Duke of Marlborough, who married Charles Spencer, third Earl of Sunderland. Beside her is her son Robert Spencer, later fourth Earl. Painting by Sir Godfrey Kneller, 1709–10, at Althorp.

When Charles Spencer was a boy in his teens John Evelyn had described him as 'a youth of extraordinary hopes, very learned for his age'. This early promise was not fulfilled; able and ambitious though he might be he was never among the first flight of politicians. His bad manners—he was rude to everyone from Queen Anne downwards—made him one of the most unpopular of men. Touchy, self-assertive, mannerless, he was his own worst enemy.

In one field, however, he was supreme. His precocious love of learning blossomed into an overmastering passion for books. He started collecting them in 1693, when he was nineteen, and by the time he was twenty-five he had become, with the possible exception of his political rival, Robert Harley, England's most notable bibliophile and the owner of what was described as 'an incomparable library'. He spent heavily on this collection, and he did so with unusual knowledge and judgement. At one time financial pressure forced him to mortgage the library to the Duke of Marlborough in return for a loan, but he would never consider selling although the King of Denmark offered him what was then the enormous sum of £30,000.

In his political career Sunderland owed much to his connection with the Marlboroughs through his second wife, Anne Churchill. Anne's father, the great Duke, was the man of the day, and his wife, the fiery Duchess Sarah, was Queen Anne's best friend and *confidante*. Though Sunderland was the least popular member of the Whig junta, through Sarah's influence he was the first to be given office by the Queen, in 1706 becoming Secretary of State. Four years later a foolish error of judgement brought about his undoing. Dr Sacheverell, a High-Church cleric, caused some consternation by preaching an inflammatory sermon denouncing Whigs, Low Churchmen, Dissenters, and Latitudinarians. The Queen's ministers, or rather, the majority of them, over-reacted to this piece of provocation and, urged on by Sunderland, impeached Sacheverell. The result was a startling outburst of religious fanaticism; pamphlets poured from the press, dissenting meeting-houses were wrecked, and rioters filled the streets. Sacheverell was found not guilty; and a month after his acquittal Sunderland was dismissed from office. Though Queen Anne disliked him almost as much as she had disliked his father she attempted to soften this bitter blow by offering him a large pension. Sunderland was neither a spendthrift nor a man greedy for money, and he haughtily refused this *douceur* declaring that 'if he could not have the honour of serving his country he would not plunder it'. From now onwards he kept in close touch with the heir to the throne, George, Elector of Hanover, but when the Queen died in August 1714, to his dismay and disappointment—he is said to have turned

[66]

dead white when the names were read out—he was not among the Lords Justices appointed as a Commission of Regency until the arrival of the new King. Instead, he was fobbed off with the Lord-Lieutenancy of Ireland, an appointment then regarded as a polite way of getting rid of an unwanted politician. (Incidentally, during his brief tenure of that post he never once set foot on Irish soil.)

Although he was to hold office under George I as Secretary of State and Lord Preident of the Council Sunderland never again enjoyed effectual political power. In 1721 he found himself involved in the financial scandal known as the South Sea Bubble, and though innocent of any peculation he was forced to resign. George I then appointed him Groom of the Stole which, although a Court post, was one of considerable political importance since its holder was in close and constant touch with the Sovereign. Sunderland, however, had little time in which to profit from his new position for he died suddenly on 19 April 1722. So unpopular was he that poison was suspected; but a post-mortem disproved that rumour.

In private life Sunderland seems to have been a devoted husband and a good if rather detached parent. Frances Spencer, his only child by his first wife, became Countess of Carlisle. The five children of his second wife, Anne Churchill, saw much more of their grandmother than ever they did of their father. Anne herself was an attractive and personable young woman and an ardent politician who was nicknamed 'the little Whig'. She worked tirelessly to further her husband's career, and she would charm those whom she wished to influence on his behalf by inviting them to talk to her while her maid brushed out her beautiful head of hair. All fashionable London was in tears when she died of pleuritic fever in the spring of 1715 leaving three sons and two daughters. To her husband she had written a moving letter:

> Pray get my mother the Duchess of Marlborough to take care of the girls and if I leave any boys too little to go to school, for to be left to servants is very bad for children and a man can't take the care of little children that a woman can. For the love she has for me and the duty I have ever showed her, I hope she will do it and be ever kind to you who was dearer to me than my life.

Sarah took the children to live with her but she did not continue ever kind to her son-in-law. Sunderland was not a man who could live without a wife, and eighteen months after Anne's death he married Judith Tichborne, a rich heiress who bore him three more children. Sarah was distressed by the marriage and deeply disturbed by the consequent financial settlements which she regarded as unfair to

[67]

Anne's children. She spoke her mind sharply to Sunderland, who replied in kind, being one of the few people who could stand up to her in a slanging match. The split between them proved final; they never spoke to one another again.

In spite of this quarrel the children remained with their grandmother; and when the great Duke died in June 1722, two months after Sunderland, she centred most of her interest and affection upon them. As might have been expected, the relationship was not an easy one; Sarah quarrelled as often and as fiercely with her nearest and dearest as she did with her declared enemies. Her eldest granddaughter Anne, who married Viscount Bateman, fell so much out of favour that Sarah blackened the face of her portrait and added the inscription, 'She is much blacker within.' The eldest grandson, Robert, became for a brief time the fourth Earl of Sunderland and died in 1729, much to the distress of Sarah, who rightly believed that his death was due to the blundering and brutal methods of treatment employed by his doctors. The next son, Charles, the fifth Earl, was in and out of favour but more often out than in. This was the grandson who was to inherit the Marlborough title and estates on the death of his aunt Henrietta, who had married Lord Godolphin and was now Duchess of Marlborough in her own right, the great Duke having left no male heir. Charles was something of a spendthrift. When he had been in her good books Sarah had given him a diamond-hilted sword which had belonged to his famous grandfather but later, hearing that he was in financial difficulties, she brought an action at law to force him to return it to her—'That sword my Lord would have carried to the gates of Paris; am I to live to see the diamonds picked off one by one and lodged at the pawn-broker's?' Sometimes, however, Charles could give as good as he got. At a party held to celebrate her seventieth birthday when she remarked how delightful it was to see all her branches flourishing round her he was heard to mutter 'branches flourish better when their roots are buried'. Otherwise his only claim to remembrance seems to be the fact that he employed an architect called Roger Morris to build the handsome stables which Sir Nikolaus Pevsner described as 'the finest piece of architecture at Althorp'.

Sarah's favourite among her grandsons was John Spencer. In her eyes this charming philanderer could do no wrong. If he behaved so badly that she lost her temper and ordered him out of the room he would reduce her to fits of laughter by vaulting in again through the window. He atoned for all his misdeeds by his show of demonstrative affection, lavishing small attentions upon her, giving her presents of fruit and game and honey, and delighting her by paying surprise visits to her home in Windsor Great Park. But better even than 'Johnnie' Sarah loved his

Sarah Jennings, Duchess of Marlborough. Painting by Sir Godfrey Kneller, at Petworth House.

The Hon. John Spencer (1708–1746) with his young son John, later first Earl Spencer, on horseback, and a page, Caesar Shaw. Painting by George Knapton, 1745, at Althorp.

sister Diana, 'Lady Di', and when this beloved child grew up she set about arranging a suitably splendid match for her. Among Diana's suitors was Lord Chesterfield, author of the famous *Letters to his Son*; but Sarah aimed at even higher game. Her ideas on this subject have a curiously prophetic ring about them. Anticipating the fate of a later and happier Lady Diana Spencer she planned a marriage with the Prince of Wales, Frederick, son of George II and Queen Caroline. The Prince was very willing; the girl was charming and would bring with her the colossal dowry of £100,000. For the Prince the match had the added advantage that it would greatly distress his parents with whom both he and Duchess Sarah were on the worst of terms. A date had actually been fixed for a secret wedding when the all-powerful First Lord of the Treasury, Sir Robert

'The Shooting Party', painting by John Wootton, 1740. To the left is John Spencer, grandson of the Duchess of Marlborough, whom he succeeded as Ranger of Windsor Great Park. Frederick, Prince of Wales, is seated. In the Royal Collection.

Walpole, got wind of the scheme and scotched it. Shortly afterwards in October 1731 Lady Diana married John Russell, brother and heir to the Duke of Bedford who had himself married Diana's cousin, Lady Anne Egerton.

The Duke was a degenerate character, a gambler, a drunkard and, it seems, impotent, since the marriage was never consummated. Anne dragged out a miserable existence until his death in 1732 when she announced her intention of marrying John Spencer with whom she had been in love for some time. At once Sarah was up in arms, having other plans for this favourite grandson. Anne gave way, and eight months later married the Earl of Jersey, a match which proved an extremely happy one.

Since John Russell inherited his brother's title and estates Diana was now

[71]

Duchess of Bedford and mistress of the great house at Woburn. She was naturally very anxious to produce a son and heir, the more so because she had already given birth to a boy who, to her deep distress, lived only a day. In the summer of 1735 she thought herself once again pregnant but she was tragically mistaken. The feeling of illness which she had believed to mark the beginning of pregnancy increased rather than lessened; and instead of growing big she became painfully thin. In August the doctors diagnosed galloping consumption; the beloved Lady Di had only a few weeks to live. She died a month later in September aged twenty-six.

Two years before Diana's death her brother Lord Sunderland had become Duke of Marlborough on the death of his aunt Henrietta. A year later in 1734 he left Althorp although he chose not to live at Blenheim, preferring a smaller house. The Sunderland earldom now became one of the secondary titles of the Dukes of Marlborough. The great library was divided, part going to Blenheim but the larger and by far the more important section remaining at Althorp. That house and estate now passed to John Spencer, who had greatly pleased his doting grandmother by marrying the bride she had chosen for him, Lady Georgina Carteret. Their children were the great delight of Sarah's old age. She enjoyed nothing better than having them to stay and playing at 'drafts' with them—'They both beat me shamefully; I believe really they like to come to me extremely.' When at last 'old Marlborough' died on 19 October 1744, aged eighty-four, life for the Spencer family became more tranquil but surely also a trifle dull, lacking the emotional storms and stresses with which she had filled their days.

His grandmother's death made John Spencer a very rich man. She had left him all her personal property so that now, as well as Althorp, he owned Holywell House near St Albans and a fine villa at Wimbledon with valuable land in both places. He did not live long to enjoy his wealth for he died in 1746 at the comparatively early age of thirty-eight, leaving everything he possessed to his twelve-year-old son, John.

The stables at Althorp, built for Charles Spencer by Roger Morris, and described by Sir Nikolaus Pevsner as 'the finest piece of architecture at Althorp'.

THE DEVONSHIRE
HOUSE SET

'She supplicates a vote and steals a heart.'
Westminster Election Squib

A gaming table at Devonshire House. Drawing by Thomas Rowlandson, 1791.

John Spencer's great inheritance was his undoing. 'I believe that he was a man of generous and amiable disposition,' his grandson wrote of him, 'spoiled by having been placed at too early a period of his life, in the possession of what then appeared to him inexhaustible wealth, and irritable in his temper partly from the pride which this circumstance had produced, and partly from almost continual ill-health.' But if John Spencer might have been a better character and achieved more in life had he not been born with a golden spoon in his mouth he was neither a bad man nor a failure; on the contrary, he won a fair measure of success in the fields of politics and scholarship, while as a sportsman he was in the very first flight.

By a curious provision in the will of Sarah Duchess of Marlborough he was deprived of the most obvious outlet for his energy and talent. She had left her property to her grandson John Spencer and his children only on condition that they took no active part in parliamentary life. John Spencer the younger was therefore obliged to confine his political activities to an endeavour to control the course of elections. This he did with such success that the great Lord Chatham rewarded him with a peerage, creating him Baron Spencer in 1761 and Earl Spencer four years later.

In the eighteenth century and for many years afterwards elections were rough and rowdy occasions when bribery was regarded as a matter of course. A curious document dated 23 October 1767 gives a vivid picture of the electioneering practices common at that date. It is signed by Spencer and various other Northamptonshire notabilities, who pledge themselves to observe certain rules during the election then in progress:

1) That mobbing of all kinds shall be discontinued by the above Lords and Gentlemen and all their friends until the Election shall be over.

2) That no house be open at any time or any ticket given for drink or liquor either by the above-mentioned principals, their friends or agents, except on seven days' notice to the Gentlemen who sign this paper.

3) That if on any occasion houses should be open after seven days' notice it shall be done by tickets for drink given to the male inhabitants, half-a-crown to drink to those who have promised one vote and a crown to drink for those who have promised two.

In one three-cornered election Lord Halifax, Lord Northampton, and Lord Spencer were each supporting a different candidate. Lord Halifax invited the voters to Horton Hall, where they ate enormously of the good food provided and

Spencer House, overlooking the Green Park in London. Built by Vardy between 1758 and 1765 for the first Earl Spencer, and for two centuries the London home of the family. Aquatint by Thomas Malton in *A Picturesque Tour through the Cities of London and Westminster*, 1800.

drank all his port. Lord Northampton did likewise at Castle Ashby; but Lord Spencer outbid both his rivals. When he entertained the voters at Althorp he stationed footmen at the main door holding plates of sandwiches. Each guest took one, and biting into it, found his teeth meeting on a golden guinea.

Although Lord Spencer does not seem to have been a notable scholar himself he was certainly a man of scholarly tastes since he bought a library of 5,000 volumes, mostly of Elizabethan date, belonging to Dr George, Master of Eton. These books, together with what remained of Lord Sunderland's collection, formed the nucleus round which the second Earl was to build up the world-famous Althorp Library. Spencer was also a collector of pictures, commissioning his friend Sir Joshua Reynolds to paint a series of family portraits of outstanding merit, and buying Italian paintings by such artists as Salvator Rosa, some to hang at Althorp and some to adorn the magnificent new house he was building overlooking the Green Park, which was to be known as Spencer House and to be for the next two centuries the London home of the family.

Politics, book-collecting and hunting are hereditary interests in the Spencer

[76]

George John, second Earl Spencer.
Engraving by H. Meyer after the
painting by John Hoppner, 1809,
which is at Althorp.

family; and it was at hunting that the first Earl excelled. The historian of the
Pytchley Hunt, Guy Paget, describes him as 'a model master of hounds' and adds
that 'he must rank with the immortal Hugo Meynell as the real founder of fast
riding to hounds.' Lord Spencer became Master in 1756, at the age of twenty-two,
and remained Master until his death in 1783. He was at great pains to improve the
breed of hounds, bringing in fresh blood from the Darley pack in Yorkshire and
buying up the whole of the famous pack owned by Lord Townsend. He spared
neither trouble nor expense in getting his bitches to the best stud dogs, if necessary
sending them in a post-chaise. As a pioneer of the new and fast method of hunting
he galloped so furiously that he sometimes overrode his own hounds, on one
occasion provoking the hunt-servant into calling out 'Damn it, my Lord, hold
hard, can't you?'

The famous Pytchley Hunt Club, founded about 1750, flourished greatly
during his mastership. Since, as Lord Jersey wrote, 'sportsmen as we are, we
cannot do without females' a few women were invited to join and given the
privilege of wearing the Pytchley white collar on their riding-habits. Lady Spencer
was of course among these favoured ladies. Like so many of his family, the first
Earl had had the good taste or the good fortune to marry an admirable wife. At
Christmas 1755 a party of 500 guests assembled at Althorp, among them Mrs

Georgiana Poyntz, Countess Spencer (1737–1814). Painting by Thomas Gainsborough, 1781. This, which is at Chatsworth, is a larger and sketchier version of the painting at Althorp.

Poyntz and her daughter Georgiana. This seventeen-year-old girl had already met the young John Spencer; and the two had fallen in love. A great ball was held the day after his twenty-first birthday; while the guests danced below, the two young people were privately married in his mother's dressing-room, afterwards rejoining the dancing separately, so that none of the dancers had any idea that such a ceremony had taken place.

This strange and secretive marriage proved very successful. 'They are really the happiest people I think I ever saw in the marriage system,' said the Duke of Queensberry, the notorious 'Old Q', admittedly not an authority on matrimonial bliss; '*Enfin, c'est le meilleur ménage possible.*' Georgiana was neither remarkably good-looking nor remarkably clever, but she had a charming disposition, a lively mind, a will of her own, and a keen sense of duty. She was also a genuinely religious woman. Her tastes were extremely simple. In an age when overeating and overdrinking were the order of the day she would breakfast off eggs, milk and fruit while the rest of the party were devouring ale and mutton chops; and her granddaughter complained that the dinners she provided consisted of nothing more solid than 'egg-shells and turnip-tops'. She was so frequently seen in a riding-habit that ladies who wished to appear similarly dressed would enquire if they might 'Spencer it', and this not because she was a particularly keen horsewoman but because a habit was a more plain and practical outfit than the cumbersome clothes then in fashion. Although she never rode to hounds, preferring to follow the hunt in a cabriolet, she shared her husband's interest in hunting and of an evening she would write down at his dictation an account of the day's sport in the 'Chace Book' which is still preserved at Althorp. Lady Spencer's own hobby was education; she founded schools wherever she might be living, supervising and sometimes teaching in them herself, and she assiduously visited schools run by other people so that she might study the new methods practised by such pioneers as Hannah More. It would have delighted her to know that her great-great-great-great-great-granddaughter Diana before becoming Princess of Wales worked as a teacher in a kindergarten.

Not only did Lady Spencer educate other people, but she gave much of her time to self-education. 'She had taken great pains with herself,' her grandson wrote, 'had read a great deal and though herself far from brilliant in conversation, had lived in the company of clever people,' adding the unkind comment, 'this gave her a reputation for ability to which she was not entitled.' Since those clever people included Dr Johnson, David Garrick and Sir Joshua Reynolds it must at least be admitted that she chose her company well. With Garrick she kept up a regular correspondence which has been published by her descendant, the seventh Earl Spencer. Garrick would address her as 'My best of ladies' or 'My most amiable Lady'; and one of her letters is endorsed in his hand 'Heavenly Lady Spencer to me.' She was a good and generous friend to him, as these letters make clear, and after his death she continued to befriend Mrs Garrick, writing frequently to her and sending her such presents as 'the finest and best turkey that was ever seen or tasted.'

Unfortunately with all her gifts and virtues Lady Spencer had one great failing. Her family were compulsive gamblers; 'I have known the Poyntzes in the nursery,' said Lord Lansdowne, 'the Bible on the table, the cards in the drawer.' Play was Lady Spencer's passion; in her day Althorp resembled nothing so much as a gambling house especially at Christmas time when the large parties assembled there would sit up till the small hours of the morning playing for alarmingly high stakes. This love of gambling she passed on to her two daughters, Georgiana and Harriet, with tragic effects upon their happiness and peace of mind.

As the attractive and forceful Lady Spencer outshone the shadowy figure of the first Earl so did these two beautiful and gifted girls tend to eclipse their only brother George John, who became second Earl Spencer in 1783, and who had the misfortune to be married to a lovely but formidable woman, Lavinia Bingham, of whom nevertheless he seems to have been sincerely fond. This quiet, sensitive and able man was in fact a person of much distinction both in private and in public life. He deserves to be remembered with gratitude by the Spencer family as the real founder of the magnificent Althorp library, and by the nation at large as the far-seeing First Lord of the Admiralty who had the wisdom and courage to promote the young Horatio Nelson over the heads of officers of more seniority but less genius.

On inheriting Althorp of necessity he set about the business of renovating the building, 'making the apartment we live in weatherproof, which it really hardly is at present and saving the house from tumbling down.' What began as much-needed repairs turned into a large scheme of alteration and renovation presided over by the architect Henry Holland, whose aim was to convert Althorp into a typically eighteenth-century mansion. He encased the exterior in unattractive white brick, a curious choice in a county famous for its beautifully coloured golden stone, and inside, as well as painting and papering over the last vestiges of the Tudor and Jacobean decoration, he remodelled the layout of an entire wing.

Where Althorp is concerned, however, the name of the second Earl will always be associated not so much with these building activities, important though they were, but with the wonderful library which was for so many years its special glory. As a bibliophile George John Spencer was beyond compare. Not only was he an enthusiastic collector but he was an unusually well-informed one. When a boy he had been placed under the tutorship of William Jones, a well-known Orientalist, who encouraged his scholarly tastes, and escorted him on two continental tours. Not, however, till he was over thirty did he devote himself seriously to the building up of a great library. In 1793 he had the opportunity to buy at a very low price the remarkable collection of Count Revicski, a Hungarian diplomat who was particularly interested in early printed editions of the Greek and Roman classics. This splendid acquisition determined the nature of the Althorp Library which was to be famous chiefly for its *incunabula* or early printed books. Revicski had sought

Georgiana, Countess Spencer, and her eldest daughter, Lady Georgiana Spencer, later Duchess of Devonshire. Painting by Sir Joshua Reynolds, *c*.1760, at Althorp.

Cristofon faccm die quacunqʒ tueris :·
Illa neмpʒ die мote мala non мoʒieus :·

мillesiмo cccc°
xx° anno :ᛋᛋ◌

out books in mint condition, having a great dislike of manuscript notes, no matter how interesting or important. Spencer continued this tradition, trying whenever possible to find a specially choice copy of any book he wished to add to the Library, and also collecting fine bindings.

To the Revicski collection he was later able to add the library of the Duke of Cassano-Sera, notable chiefly for examples of the work of early Sicilian and Neapolitan printers, and also the library of a Mr Stanesley Achorne, who specialized in English books and possessed several from the presses of Caxton and Wynkyn de Worde. Spencer himself was a keen and knowledgeable collector, searching for rare books all over Europe. After his retirement from political life in 1807 he devoted himself to the care and improvement of his library, supervising the business of cataloguing, and haunting bookshops and sale rooms in the hope of discovering yet more treasures. Though so enthusiastic a collector he was not in the least a selfish one. He was delighted if a chance came his way to benefit the library of a friend, and he scorned the practice of buying up copies of books he already possessed simply to prevent them from falling into the hands of rival collectors.

When George John Spencer died in 1834 he had collected what was regarded as the finest private library in the world. A hundred and fifty years later it has been described by a modern authority as 'one of the most important single collections illustrating the origin and development of Western printing ever formed.' Among the 40,000 or so books were over 3,000 *incunabula*, including 58 Caxtons, and many examples of the work of such printers as Wynkyn de Worde and the presses associated with Gutenberg. There were also over 800 Aldines, and many books from early Italian and French presses. One special treasure was a coloured block-print of St Christopher, dated 1423, the earliest piece of European printing that can be definitely dated. Among later books were a remarkable collection of Bibles, the first four Shakespeare folios, the very rare 1609 edition of the Sonnets, all the earliest editions of Chaucer, and splendid editions of Milton, Spenser, Bunyan, and Isaak Walton, to name but a few out of this vast galaxy of rare and beautiful books.

In politics Lord Spencer forsook the Whig traditions of his family and followed Pitt who in 1794 made him First Lord of the Admiralty, a position which he held

Opposite: Saint Christopher, coloured block print, dated 1423, the earliest piece of European colour printing that can be definitely dated. Formerly in the Althorp library; now in the John Rylands Library, University of Manchester.

[82]

until 1801. 'For him,' writes a naval historian, 'more perhaps than for any other English administrator, may be claimed the title of organizer of victory.' Spencer was in charge at the Admiralty when the battles of Camperdown and St Vincent were fought and won, but his first important concern on assuming office was not with the organization of victory but with the redressing of grievances and the suppression of mutiny. In April 1797 the men of the Channel Fleet at Spithead refused to put to sea. They behaved with admirable calm and restraint, asking only for such obviously overdue reforms as higher pay, decent food, better medical attention and some shore leave at the end of a voyage. Within a week the Cabinet had agreed to these reasonable demands, thanks in great part to Spencer's wise and generous attitude. A few days later another and more serious mutiny broke out at the Nore, to be repressed much more sternly but without any great harshness. For this too Spencer must be given much of the credit. His chief claim to the nation's gratitude, however, lies in the fact that he kept a watchful eye upon the career of Rear-Admiral Sir Horatio Nelson, and in April 1798, passing over the claims of more senior Admirals, gave him command in the Mediterranean and sent him out to win the Battle of the Nile. The news of this great victory was slow in reaching London, and meanwhile false reports came pouring in, one persistent rumour having it that an action had taken place in which at least seven British ships had been lost. Spencer was not a demonstrative man, and no one realized how great had been his anxiety until the day when the true story at last reached the Admiralty. On hearing that a great victory had been won without the loss of a single British ship the First Lord fell down in a dead faint.

All officers of the rank of captain or above were invited to dine with the First Lord on appointment to a new command; but except on such official occasions Lady Spencer made it a rule never to take any notice of a sea-officer's wife. When Nelson was bidden to dine before taking up the Mediterranean command not only did he upset all the table arrangements by insisting on sitting next to his own wife—he declared that he saw so little of her that he would not voluntarily lose one instant of her company—but he boldly told Lady Spencer that if she would show Lady Nelson some kindness and attention after his departure that would make him 'the happiest man alive'.

Three years later the Nelsons were once again invited to dine with Lord and Lady Spencer. 'Such a contrast I never beheld,' was Lavinia Spencer's comment.

Opposite: Georgiana, Duchess of Devonshire (1757–1806). Watercolour drawing by John Downman, 1787, at Chatsworth.

[83]

At table Lady Nelson pushed over to her husband a wine-glass full of walnuts which she had considerately peeled for a one-armed man. He thrust it aside so roughly that it hit a dish, whereupon poor Lady Nelson burst into tears. In the drawing-room after dinner she poured out the story of her wrecked marriage to a hostess who was more shocked than sympathetic. Nelson's infatuation with Emma Hamilton had already earned him a reprimand from Lord Spencer, who had bluntly told the hero that he had remained too long inactive at Naples, and hinted that if he did not return of his own free will he might find himself officially recalled.

Both his adherence to Pitt and his marriage to a woman whom they found unsympathetic tended to separate Lord Spencer from his two sisters. His name seldom occurs in their letters and he seems to have played a comparatively small part in their lives. A good and clever man, he lacked their special quality of brilliance. And of the two the one whose personality shone, and still shines, with an unquenchable glow is Georgiana, who was to become Duchess of Devonshire.

In 1774, at the age of sixteen, Georgiana was a tomboy with a mop of golden hair, wide-apart blue eyes, a tip-tilted nose, and a generously large mouth. She was not a classic beauty—some people have gone so far as to describe her as a *jolie laide*—but when she came into a room it was as if all the candles had been set alight. Although Lady Spencer had insisted on a strict and simple régime she had not kept her children secluded but had allowed them to mix with their parents' friends both in London and at Althorp. The Spencer girls were no strangers to society; yet Georgiana remained curiously unsophisticated. Not so Harriet, a quiet, critical child, less obviously attractive but more intelligent than her elder sister. Both were loving, warm-hearted and capable of dangerous depths of passion; but Georgiana was outgoing and spontaneous while Harriet tended to hide her emotions. Georgiana was to everyone's liking, Harriet an acquired taste. At thirteen, however, the younger girl was still in the schoolroom, her future not as yet a matter of serious concern, while Georgiana had reached an age when prudent eighteenth-century parents set about the business of matchmaking in real earnest. The most eligible young man in England had made an offer for Georgiana's hand; and she had already been called into her father's presence and told that she was to marry the Duke of Devonshire. Now, some six weeks later she was absorbed in the fascinating pursuit of catching butterflies in the garden at Wimbledon when her old nurse appeared, clouted her over the head and dragged her unwillingly indoors to be tidied up, dressed in her best, and sent downstairs for a meeting with her future husband.

[84]

William, fifth Duke of Devonshire
(1748–1811). Painting by Batoni, at
Chatsworth.

Lord and Lady Spencer believed that they had done their very best for their
daughter by arranging such a good match for her but they were loving parents who
would never have forced her into marriage against her will. Georgiana, however,
had no objection; she saw the whole plan in fairy-tale terms, herself a Duchess,
mistress of some half-dozen magnificent houses, lavishing gifts and favours on all
around her from the bottomless riches at her disposal. As for the silent and rather
clumsy young man who now confronted her, she liked him well enough and was
perfectly prepared to fall in love with him, never doubting that he on his side was
equally ready to fall in love with her.

Unfortunately love did not enter into the calculations of William fifth Duke of
Devonshire. He wanted a wife to adorn his dinner-table, entertain his guests, bear
him a clutch of children, and cause him as little trouble as possible. Although from
the worldly point of view the match left nothing to be desired the outlook for these
two young people was not a promising one. They were married on 7 June 1774,
Georgiana's seventeenth birthday.

[85]

Charles James Fox (1749–1806).
Painting by Sir Joshua Reynolds,
1784.

For a month all went very well; then the Duke abandoned the pretty attentions he had shown his wife during that honeymoon period and lapsed back into the silent and solitary way of life that came most naturally to him. The Cavendishes were a curiously inarticulate family. On one occasion when the Duke was travelling with his brother George the two young men were given a three-bedded room at an inn. First the Duke, and then Lord George, peered inside the drawn curtains of the third bed. Neither made any comment, but both undressed and slept soundly. Next day, some little time after they had left the inn, one of them asked the other, 'Did you see what was in that bed last night?' 'Yes, brother,' came the answer. No more was said. The third bed had contained a corpse.

Georgiana, on the contrary, had lived all her seventeen years surrounded by a group of highly articulate, demonstrative friends and relations who encouraged her to express rather than repress her overflowing affection and emotion. She found it impossible to adjust herself to the very different atmosphere which now enveloped her. On one occasion, in front of her mother and sister, she unthinkingly threw her arms round her husband's neck. Appalled by this open show of affection he brushed her aside and hurried out of the room. He had not thought to hurt her, but his action cut her to the quick.

Disappointed in her marriage Georgiana turned elsewhere for satisfaction. She was a faithful wife but a lonely one; and there were plenty of people ready to amuse a lonely and charming Duchess. Among them was the worldly-wise Lady Melbourne, the worst possible counsellor for an inexperienced girl. Aged seventeen and married to the only man who seemed impervious to her charm Georgiana was already the acknowledged queen of London Society. Giddy she may have been, but she was not at this stage involved in any sexual scandal; her passion for gambling was her greatest weakness. In her inexperience she had believed herself to be the mistress of inexhaustible wealth, but only a year after her wedding she found herself so deeply in debt that she was afraid to make confession to her husband. Lady Spencer stepped into the breach and asked the Duke to pay up which he did without hesitation. This however was the beginning rather than the end of trouble; from now onwards the problem of debt runs like a grim leit-motif through the pattern of Georgiana's life.

From the Poyntzes came this fatal taste for gambling; from the Spencers the interest in politics which was Georgiana's other great preoccupation. She was an ardent Whig; and the most prominent Whig of the day was Charles James Fox. Stout and heavily built, with bushy eyebrows and a black chin—'the black animal' was one of his nicknames—Fox was not a handsome man, but he was a magnetic character who fascinated everyone who came within his orbit. He never succeeded in becoming Prime Minister; his errors were many, his achievements small; yet even today his compelling personality springs to life in the pages of the history books where his more able and successful rival Pitt remains a name on a piece of paper.

These two attractive and generous-minded people, Fox and Georgiana, became firm friends and allies. Both of them loved parties and late hours; both of them gambled recklessly; both of them genuinely believed in the principle of liberty. For that reason Fox supported the American colonists in the War of Independence and later welcomed the outbreak of the French Revolution, on this issue parting company with that other great Whig, Edmund Burke. Meanwhile Georgiana made Devonshire House both a social and a political centre for the Whig party, where gambling, flirting and political discussion continued simultaneously into the small hours.

[87]

Richard Brinsley Sheridan (1751–1816). Pastel drawing by John Russell, 1788.

Among the *habitués* of Devonshire House was the young Prince of Wales, drawn there not only by the social gaiety but also by the Whig politics which were anathema to his father, King George III, with whom he was permanently at odds. Another specially welcome visitor was the rising young playwright, Richard Sheridan, whose masterpiece, *The Rivals*, had been the great theatrical success of the year 1775. This was not the company that Georgiana's mother Lady Spencer could approve of, and in fact she was constantly scolding Georgiana for her frivolous way of life and her unfortunate choice of friends, but nevertheless in 1779 she sent her younger daughter to live at Devonshire House. Harriet was now eighteen, and for the last three years or so she had persisted in refusing all the many offers of marriage that came her way. Perhaps her parents hoped that Georgiana might persuade her to adopt a more reasonable attitude towards matrimony. Harriet was an instant success in the Devonshire House circle, two of her more ardent admirers being the Prince of Wales and Richard Sheridan who nonetheless remained devoted to his lovely wife Elizabeth. She danced and gambled and talked

[88]

George, Prince of Wales, later King
George IV (Regent 1811–20,
reigned 1820–30). Painting by
Thomas Gainsborough, c.1795, in
the Royal Collection.

politics with zest and intelligence, but all the while she remained a curiously
private person. Then in 1780 she announced her engagement to Frederick
Ponsonby, Viscount Duncannon, son and heir of the Earl of Bessborough.

Unlike Georgiana Harriet went into marriage with no great enthusiasm and
with her eyes wide open. Shortly after she became engaged she wrote a revealing
letter to her elderly cousin, Miss Shipley:

> I wish I could have known him a little better first, but my dear papa and mama
> say that it will make them the happiest of creatures; and what would I not do to
> see them happy? . . . I will tell you exactly what I think about it, if you will
> promise never to repeat the nonsense I talk to you . . . There are many people
> whose manners and conversation I should like better as *flirts* only, *car
> assurément il n'a pa les manières prévenantes*, but when one is to choose a
> companion for life (what a dreadful sound that has) the inside and not the out is
> what one ought to look at, and I think from what I have heard of him, and the

[89]

Lady Elizabeth Foster, 'Bess',
mistress and later second wife of
the fifth Duke of Devonshire.
Painting by Sir Joshua
Reynolds, 1788, at Chatsworth.

great attachment he professes to have for me, I have a better chance of being
reasonably happy with him than with most people I know . . . I will not plague
you any more with my jeremiads for I am very low.

Harriet married Duncannon on 27 November 1780 and in August of the next
year bore him a son. Georgiana was still childless, to her bitter grief. Generous-
hearted as ever she tried to make some amends to her husband for his disappointed
hopes of an heir by interesting herself in the upbringing of his illegitimate
daughter by a milliner whose name, by an odd coincidence, had been Charlotte
Spencer. The child, whose date of birth is uncertain, was known as Charlotte
Williams and nicknamed Louchee. Georgiana placed her with a highly respectable
Mrs Garner and kept a watchful eye on her progress.

Her own childlessness made Georgiana feel special sympathy with a new
acquaintance to whom Lady Spencer had asked her to show some kindness.
Accordingly, when she and the Duke were staying in Bath in the early summer of
1782 she called upon Lady Elizabeth Foster, daughter of the eccentric Frederick

Georgiana, Duchess of
Devonshire. Unfinished sketch
by Sir Joshua Reynolds, *c*.1780,
at Chatsworth.

Hervey, Bishop of Derry and Earl of Bristol. Lady Elizabeth had left her husband and being short of money was living with her sister in cramped, uncomfortable lodgings. She had just parted from her two little sons, who were to be brought up by their father. Georgiana grieved for the bereft mother who knew exactly how to wring the last drop of pathos out of her sad situation. The Duke too seemed to find this new friend surprisingly congenial; and soon Georgiana was telling her mother that 'Bess' was their chief support in Bath 'else it would be shockingly dull for the Duke'. Thus began a triangular relationship which puzzled contemporary society as much as it puzzles posterity. As far as he could be in love with anybody the Duke was in love with Bess; the Duchess loved her hardly less dearly. As for Bess herself, she was delighted to have her bread buttered on both sides and to find herself as indispensable to the wife as she was to the husband.

When the Devonshires left Bath Bess went with them to Plympton, then to Althorp and finally home to Devonshire House. She now began to exhibit symptoms of consumption, and the doctors recommended a prolonged stay in a

Georgiana, Duchess of Devonshire, with her daughter Georgiana, later Countess of Carlisle. Painting by Sir Joshua Reynolds, 1786, at Chatsworth.

warmer climate. Georgiana was seized with a brilliant idea. Louchee's future was causing some concern; Bess should act as her governess and take her abroad, the Duke paying all expenses. The ill-assorted pair left England in December 1792, travelling through France, Switzerland and Italy to Naples. Bess found Louchee an unattractive companion but she consoled herself with several discreet flirtations, including one with Marie Antoinette's chivalrous admirer, Count Axel Fersen.

Meanwhile in England a near-miracle had occurred. In the ninth year of her marriage Georgiana was at last pregnant. Her daughter, Georgiana Dorothy, was born on 11 July 1783. Bess was in Geneva when this good news reached her, and she replied with a rapturous letter, 'Kiss *our* child from me . . . I am to be its little mama, Canis says so.' (In their private code the dog-like Duke was Canis, Bess, because of her pointed face, the Racoon, and Georgiana, most unsuitably, the Rat.)

Bess had some reason for claiming a special relationship with the baby since Georgiana always connected her pregnancy with the coming of Bess into their lives. She could have given no rational explanation as to how Bess's arrival could have brought about this much-desired event; she only knew that Bess had made the Duke happy and that when he was happy she herself had been able to conceive his child. Possibly she was right; conceivably Bess had succeeded in releasing some psychological or even physical tension in that inhibited man. More probably the idea was a pleasing fantasy which Bess applauded and encouraged because it played straight into her hands.

Unlike most fine ladies Georgiana suckled her child herself. The baby was her solace during the dreary winter of 1783–4, darkened for her by the death of her father and by growing anxiety over her ever-increasing debts. With the coming of spring she was once again absorbed in politics and the fortunes of Charles James Fox. In December 1783 George III had dismissed the Portland ministry in which Fox had served in an unnatural coalition with his old enemy, Lord North. William Pitt, aged twenty-three, now became Prime Minister. In March 1784 Parliament was dissolved, and a general election followed. Fox himself was one of three candidates standing for Westminster. The tide was running against him; some of his followers had already deserted to Pitt, and he himself was in danger of defeat. Ladies seldom if ever took part in elections; but Georgiana was not one to be deterred by convention. In the eighteenth century voting was not confined to a single day; and at Westminster the poll remained open for over a month. Everyone could follow the fluctuating fortunes of the candidates, and at first Fox's chances seemed small. The more the count went against him the harder Georgiana and Harriet worked to swing the voters over to his side. They organized transport to bring people in from outlying districts, and they caused much scandal and head-shaking by personally canvassing for votes. Here Georgiana scored a triumph; only the most churlish of voters could refuse the request of a young and attractive duchess. 'She was in the most blackguard houses in Long Acre by eight o'clock this morning' Cornwallis wrote on 9 April recording an effort that meant a real sacrifice on the part of a woman who usually lay in bed till noon or later. A—probably apocryphal—story has it that the price of a vote was a kiss. After all, today's candidates are expected to kiss babies; and in some circumstances it might be more pleasurable to kiss a butcher as Georgiana is reputed to have done.

The reaction of the common people of Westminster to Georgiana's arrival amongst them calls to mind the behaviour of the crowds who throng round another lovely young woman of the Spencer family when she appears at a royal walkabout. According to one of the many election leaflets 'the mob gaze and gaze and crowd until their senses are lost in admiration, and the pressure of those who push for the same pleasure drives them into areas, through windows, and rolls them along the kennel, bruised and be-mudded but not dissatisfied.' Georgiana had the rare gift of getting into immediate touch with individuals with whom she could exchange no more than a handshake or a smile. 'Her eyes were so bright that I could light my pipe at them,' exclaimed a navvy. That gift has not been lost. Two centuries later an old man made a similar remark. 'There were many hearts broken here yesterday,' said a Chelsea pensioner after Diana Princess of Wales had attended the Oak Apple Day celebrations in May 1983.

When the poll closed at Westminster the naval hero, Admiral Hood, had taken first place as he was expected to do. Fox came second, and since Westminster was a two-member constituency he too secured a seat. In delighted recognition of the part that Georgiana and Harriet had played in bringing about this victory the triumphal procession which wound its way from Westminster to Devonshire House was headed by a horseman bearing a banner inscribed 'Sacred to Female Patriotism'.

Thanks partly to Georgiana, Fox had scored a personal success; but his followers were out in the cold. Pitt was still Prime Minister and was to remain in power with one brief interval, for over twenty years. In the July following the election Bess returned to England and as a matter of course rejoined her friends, spending the summer at Chatsworth. By the autumn she was once again pregnant and so was Georgiana, both of them by the Duke. Bess retired to Italy while Georgiana remained behind to face a winter overshadowed by the inescapable problem of debt and by a scandalous rumour that she was engaged in a love-affair with the Prince of Wales.

This tale was almost ludicrously untrue. The Prince was head over heels in love with Mrs Fitzherbert and he came frequently to Devonshire House because he found Georgiana a sympathetic listener to the story of his difficulties over this virtuous Roman Catholic widow. Mrs Fitzherbert would have nothing short of marriage; and marriage was doubly impossible. No heir to the throne could marry a Roman Catholic; and by the Royal Marriage Act of 1772 no member of the Royal Family could marry without the Sovereign's consent, which would certainly not be forthcoming in this case. There was one terrible scene when the Prince attempted suicide. Mrs Fitzherbert was summoned in haste to his house in Carlton House Terrace, but refused to go unless Georgiana would accompany her.

The Westminster Election. Caricature by Rowlandson, 1784. The Duchesses are Portland, on the left, and Devonshire, on the right.

Together the two women went to see the Prince whom they found in a half-demented state, hitting his head against the wall and foaming at the mouth. He would not be pacified until Georgiana gave him one of her rings which he placed on Mrs Fitzherbert's finger as a pledge of his determination to marry her. The action of course had no binding significance but it served to quieten the hysterical boy.

On 16 August 1785 at Vietri in a squalid establishment which may have been a brothel, Bess gave birth to a daughter, whom she named Caroline. A fortnight later at Chatsworth Georgiana gave birth to the Duke's other child, and to everyone's disappointment, this baby also was a daughter. She was christened Harriet, and known in the family as Hary-o. In November a third girl was born, this time to the Duncannons, who welcomed her eagerly, their other children being boys. Like Bess's daughter she was called Caroline.

Meanwhile the Prince of Wales's affairs were coming to a crisis. After his attempted suicide Mrs Fitzherbert had wisely retired abroad to give herself a chance to consider her position in some peace and quiet. Now she discovered, apparently for the first time, that although a marriage with the Prince would be invalid in English law in the eyes of the Roman Catholic Church it would be a true marriage. The two consenting parties are the 'celebrants' in the sacrament of holy matrimony, the priest being present merely to give a blessing. She returned to England early in December, and immediately a difference became apparent in her relationship with the Prince. The two went about together so openly that his friends became alarmed and Fox wrote begging him to make the position clear. 'Make yourself easy, my dear friend,' the Prince replied; 'believe me, the world will now soon be convinced that there not only is, but never was, any grounds for those reports which of late years have been so malevolently circulated.' Taken literally these words might be read as no more than a refutation of the rumour that Mrs Fitzherbert was, or had been, the Prince's mistress. Fox, however, had questioned the Prince about marriage, and marriage only—'There was reason to suppose that you were going to take the very desperate step of marrying her'—and he was surely justified in reading this letter as a denial of any such intention. Four days later on 15 December 1785, without a word to Fox, the Prince secretly married Mrs Fitzherbert.

The Prince's duplicity landed his friends in deep trouble. Challenged in the House of Commons, Fox, with the Prince's letter in his pocket, felt that he could safely deny the existence of any marriage and when the truth was later proved beyond dispute, found himself branded as a deliberate liar. Like Fox, Georgiana

Maria Anne, Mrs Fitzherbert
(1756–1837), later wife of
George IV. Painting by Sir
Joshua Reynolds, *c*.1788.

could honestly say 'I declare I do not know that anything has taken place' but she
too was in difficulties. Lady Spencer, already horrified by the scandalous gossip
her daughters had brought on themselves during the Westminster election, now
begged Georgiana to show some discretion in her behaviour towards Mrs
Fitzherbert. 'In what light do you mean to appear?' she asked. 'Will you go about
with his mistress or do you mean to countenance such a marriage? At all events
how much better will it be for you to remain out of town until people are grown
accustomed to the thing, and till some respectable people, if any surely will do it,
have set you an example.' Then came the sad query, 'When, my dear Georgiana,
shall I see you out of scrapes that injure your character?'

Georgiana was in fact in another and much worse scrape than the affair of Mrs
Fitzherbert. The usually tolerant Duke had seen fit to take objection to her
friendship with a newcomer to the Devonshire House circle, the young Charles

[97]

Grey, Viscount Howick. Georgiana had, as yet, given her husband no real cause for jealousy; but added to this difficulty was the problem of her debts. In growing despair she had turned first to the banker Thomas Coutts and then to Calonne, once Minister of Finance to Louis XVI but now living in exile in England. Coutts had proved a real friend, lending her money and giving her good advice, but even he could not resolve her difficulties. Economy was essential; and economy was something foreign to Georgiana's nature. In order to curb her extravagance it was now suggested that she should leave the Duke and live quietly in the country for a while, either with her mother or with her brother and her very uncongenial sister-in-law. Georgiana was greatly distressed by the prospect; but Sheridan pleaded her cause and so did Bess who could not, for propriety's sake, remain with the Duke if his wife were banished. Though the relationship between husband and wife was badly damaged matters were smoothed over; and Georgiana refreshed herself with a visit to her mother where simple living and regular hours brought rest and relaxation to her overstrained nerves and tired body.

In the spring of 1788 Bess once more retired discreetly abroad. This time she bore the Duke a son, who was to be known as Augustus Clifford. The next year it was the turn of Georgiana and the Duke to be off on their travels, Bess of course going with them. They stopped first in Paris where they left Louchee with a Madame Nagel who already had in her charge a three-year-old girl known as Caroline St Jules. The streets of Paris were thronged with disorderly crowds but in spite of alarming reports they succeeded in reaching Versailles to pay their respects to Louis XVI and Marie Antoinette, whom Georgiana had known since childhood. Arriving at Spa to drink the waters which Georgiana hoped would set her 'breeding' again they were horrified by alarming news from Paris where riots had broken out and the Bastille had been stormed. The Nagels, however, wrote to reassure them that they need have no fears for the girls' safety since the situation appeared to be returning to normal. On 23 September Georgiana wrote to her kind friend Thomas Coutts telling him that she believed herself to be with child, and promising that if this were indeed so she would make a clean breast to her husband and tell him the full extent of her debts, something which hitherto she had never brought herself to do. Delighted at the prospect of a son and heir (nobody seems to have had much doubt as to the child's sex) and fearing that a rough sea-voyage might cause Georgiana to miscarry the Duke decreed that they must remain abroad until after the birth of the baby. Accordingly the party moved to Brussels, where they were joined by little Georgiana—'G.' to her relations—and Hary-o with their admirable new governess, Miss Trimmer, who was to be for many years

Charles Grey, Viscount Howick, later the second Earl Grey (1764–1845). Painted by George Romney in 1784, soon after the sitter left Eton.

a prop and stay to the whole family. Madame Nagel arrived from Paris with Louchee and Caroline, whose supposed parents had conveniently vanished into space. The little girl, said Georgiana, would fit well enough into her own nursery, being exactly the same age as Hary-o. Later Lady Spencer came out to join the party, which had swollen to enormous proportions with the addition of a doctor, a midwife and various maids, servants, grooms, and saddle-horses. In spite of the threat of revolution the child was to be born in Paris. On 20 May 1790 the whole cavalcade moved into a house at Passy; and next day Georgiana gave birth to a son.

The infant Marquess of Hartington was named William for his father and Spencer for his mother's family. Even now that she had given him an heir Georgiana could not bring herself to tell her husband the full extent of her debts. She confessed to Coutts that she owed £60,000, but the total sum was probably much higher. Meanwhile Lady Spencer had been moved to protest against Bess's

[99]

continued presence in the family. An extract from Georgiana's distraught reply clearly shows her extraordinary simplicity and candour and the generosity of spirit which refused to see faults in those she loved, taking all blame upon herself:

The Duke added just now that he could not help thinking it a most extraordinary circumstance that when a man and his wife both agree in living with a person, that you should be persuaded to imagine that there was a cause for complaint. In short, he added, granted Lady Spencer the fact, it seems almost as if she was hurt that you was [sic] not uneasy and made unhappy by it. I can only add, dearest M., that I was born to a most complicated misery. I had run into errors that would have made any other man discard me; he forgave me; my friend who had likewise stood between him and my ruin, was likewise his friend; her society was delightful to us, and her gentleness and affection soothed the bitterness that many misfortunes I had brought on us [sic]. And the mother whom I adore, whom I love better than my life, sets herself up in the opposite scale, forgets all the affection her son-in-law has shown her, and only says: I will deprive them of their friend or of my countenance.

These difficulties were bad enough but far worse trouble loomed ahead. According to the then current convention a wife must remain faithful to her husband until she had borne him a son, but afterwards she might do as she pleased. Georgiana had at last given the Duke a son and heir; for some time she and Charles Grey had been in love with one another; now they become lovers. By the late summer of 1791 she was pregnant with his child. The situation was a common one in the circle in which the Devonshires moved. Only the eldest of Lady Melbourne's sons—and he unfortunately died young—was Lord Melbourne's child; Lady Cowper produced several children by Palmerston; Lady Oxford's family, their surname being Harley, were known as the Harleian Miscellany. The Duke, however, was neither complaisant nor forgiving; Georgiana was to be parted from the three little children who she loved so dearly and banished abroad for an indefinite period.

The illness of Harriet Duncannon gave her a face-saving excuse for departure. Harriet, who had suffered a slight stroke, was showing signs of consumption. Accordingly in November Lady Spencer, Harriet, Duncannon and little Caroline Ponsonby set out for the South of France, where they were joined by Georgiana accompanied, of course, by Bess, whose presence was even more necessary to the wife than to the husband at this juncture. When the Duncannons and Lady

Henrietta Frances, Viscountess Duncannon, with her two children. Painting by John Hoppner, *c.*1787.

Spencer settled at Nice Georgiana and Bess went on to Aix-en-Provence, ostensibly to visit the shadowy Comte de St Jules. Faced with the possibility of death in childbirth, then a common hazard, Georgiana wrote a letter to her baby son:

> Marquis of Hartington.
> To be given him in case of my death when he is eight years old.
>   G. Devonshire.
> My dear little boy, As soon as you are old enough to understand this letter it will be given to you; it contains the only present I can make you—my blessing, written in my blood. The book which will be also given you is a memorandum [sic] of me you must ever keep. Alas, I am gone before you could know me, but I lov'd you, I nursed you nine months at my breast. I love you dearly. For my sake observe my last wishes. Be obedient to your dear Papa and Grandmama; consult them and obey them in all things. Be very kind to your sisters. Join with your dear Papa, when you can, in increasing their fortunes, and if you have the misfortune to lose your dear Papa, double your dear sisters' fortunes at least. Love always dear Lady Elizabeth and Caroline. Be kind to all your cousins, especially the Ponsonbys. Make piety your chief study, never despise religion, never break your word, never betray a secret, never tell a lie. God bless you my dear child, oh, how dearly would I wish again to see your beloved face, and press you to my wretched bosom. God bless you, my dear little boy.
>   Your poor Mother.   G. Devonshire.

With this letter she left a little note of blessing, written literally in blood.

On 21 February 1792 Georgiana gave birth to a daughter. Although she had been generosity itself over the Duke's illegitimate children, taking great pains with Louchee's upbringing, and readily accepting Caroline St Jules and Augustus Clifford as permanent members of the Devonshire House nursery, there was no hope that she would be allowed to keep her own baby. The little girl, known as Eliza Courtney, was to be despatched to Northumberland to be brought up by Charles Grey's parents. Georgiana herself was not to be allowed to return home; instead, the Duke ordered her to remain abroad with her mother and sister, a decree in which there was some good sense, since she and Bess might have found themselves in serious difficulties travelling unescorted through a country in the throes of revolution.

For a year or more the whole party wandered from place to place in Italy and

Switzerland. Of necessity Lady Spencer reconciled herself to Bess's presence, preferring that she should remain with Georgiana rather than live alone with the Duke. In Lausanne they visited Edward Gibbon, author of *The Decline and Fall of the Roman Empire*, who much enjoyed the company of 'the good Duchess of Devonshire and wicked Lady Elizabeth'. Georgiana's solace in what she rightly termed her banishment was the writing of charming, affectionate letters to little G., the only one of her children old enough to appreciate them. Then on 12 May 1793, came the longed-for letter from the Duke, bidding her come home. In haste she scribbled a line to G.:

> Dearest Love, my hurry of spirits has been too great to be able to write much, but the good news contained in this letter will make up for its shortness. In less than three months I shall embrace you—I shall see my dear, my dearest children—oh how good your dear Papa is.

On 18 September Georgiana was at last back in England. Miss Trimmer brought the children to Dartford to meet her. 'I have seen them, I have seen them, my dearest, dearest M.' she wrote ecstatically to Lady Spencer. At Devonshire House the servants were drawn up in line to greet her, 'everyone mad with joy', a condition doubtless enhanced by the glass of wine each had been given to drink in honour of the occasion. The Duke was all kindness, giving her a miniature of Lady Spencer as a present to mark her homecoming. At last she was forgiven.

Meanwhile Harriet Bessborough, as she had become on the death of her father-in-law, remained abroad, her health not having improved sufficiently to allow her to return to England. She settled at Naples with eight-year-old Caroline, while her husband shuttled between Italy and England where his father's death had involved him in much business. 'Be assured that I think of nothing but you,' he wrote to Harriet during one of these enforced separations. In the summer of 1793 he brought their six-year-old son William to Italy with him so that the little boy could spend some time with his mother. To all appearances they were a happy, united family; but a new element had entered Harriet's life. She had fallen in love. Although she had had many and persistent admirers she had never yet taken a lover, but now, like her sister, she surrendered to a man many years her junior. In Naples she met Granville Leveson-Gower, just down from Oxford, a young man handsome and attractive beyond the ordinary. A friendship began which developed into a love-affair lasting some twelve or fifteen years. She bore him two children, but so discreet was she that little is known about the dates or place of their birth. Her husband could not have been ignorant of the liaison, which was common gossip, but somehow she managed to hold his trust and affection. She did not expect him to countenance a *mariage-à-trois* like the one involving Sir William Hamilton, Emma Hamilton and Nelson, but instead she kept her family and her love life in separate compartments. Her success in so doing was the more surprising in that she was not a designing, cold-blooded woman like Lady Melbourne; although she was more subtle than Georgiana she was equally warm-hearted, and she loved Granville with an intense and selfless passion. Perhaps his many absences abroad on diplomatic missions helped to preserve appearances; it was comparatively easy for Lord Bessborough to overlook the fact that his wife had a lover if that lover was in Paris, Berlin, or St Petersburg.

Georgiana was temporarily leading a quiet life in the country and on returning to England in June 1794 Harriet did likewise. Both sisters had reason to try to economize since both were in debt, though Harriet less deeply than her sister. Georgiana was chiefly interested in the crowd of children growing up in nursery and schoolroom, her own three, Augustus Clifford, Caroline St Jules, who passed for a refugee French aristocrat, and Corisande de Grammont, a genuine French refugee whose brother also spent some time with the Devonshires. Louchee was not there, having been satisfactorily placed with the Chatsworth steward, whose nephew she ultimately married; but in 1797 Bess's two sons by her husband, John Foster, were added to the group after their father's death. Only one child was missing, although on her rare visits to London Eliza Courtney was allowed an occasional meeting with G. and Hary-o, and sometimes did lessons with them at the Chiswick villa which was Georgiana's favourite retreat. Though Eliza did not know of the relationship between them every now and again Georgiana would write a letter to the child whom she described in a set of touchingly bad verses as 'my sweet but hidden violet'.

When Devonshire House was reopened in May 1794 the whirl of London life began again; but Georgiana was not her old self. She had lost her looks and grown very stout, and she suffered more and more frequently from headaches. One of her eyes was badly inflamed; and it was feared that she might lose her sight. In 1796 an excruciatingly painful operation was performed which she bore with great courage. Harriet and her mother never left her side until the surgeons could assure them that 'something like sight would be restored'; but when she recovered she found herself blind in one eye.

In 1795 two important marriages had taken place in the Devonshire House circle. Disregarding his illegal marriage to Mrs Fitzherbert the Prince of Wales

[104]

had married Caroline of Brunswick; and Fox married his mistress, Mrs Armistead. Since he had been living with her very happily for some years, the actual marriage, which was not publicly announced till 1802, made little difference. Although her past had been somewhat lurid Mrs Armistead was a charming and unselfish woman who made him an admirable wife. Politically he was in the wilderness, and rather than spend profitless hours in the House of Commons he withdrew more and more frequently to his country home at St Anne's Hill where he could read the classics and enjoy the company of his loving wife.

In 1800 Georgiana presented the sixteen-year-old G. at Court and gave a great ball in her honour. By the end of the year G. was most suitably engaged to Lord Morpeth, whom she married in March 1801. In 1802 the Peace of Amiens put a temporary stop to the long war with France; and troops of English aristocrats flocked across the Channel to enjoy the pleasures of Paris and to catch a glimpse of the all-conquering Bonaparte. The Devonshires remained at home, but Fox, the Bessboroughs and the Morpeths all went over to France and so did Bess. Her going left Georgiana desolate. 'Do you hear the voice of my heart crying to you?' she wrote hysterically. 'Do you feel what it is for me to be separated from you?'

This cry of distress clearly reveals the extraordinary degree to which Georgiana had come to depend upon her husband's mistress. She herself was at this time in black depths of despair. Not only was she distracted by her ever-increasing money troubles and by anxiety over Hartington, 'dear Hart', who was growing increasingly deaf and developing 'habits of reserve, exclusion and timidity', but she was overwhelmed by a sense of guilt at the thought of her own sins and errors. (It never seems to have crossed her mind that the Duke might also have something with which to reproach himself.) In her distress she turned to a Dr Francis Randolph, whose sermons she had admired. She was not uncritical of him, describing him as all heart and no head, but she needed a father confessor and she wrote him a long and revealing letter. 'I am surrounded by difficulties and troubles in which I have involved myself, and have not the energy to meet and face my situation,' she told him. 'I have no healthy spot in my thoughts to rest on, except my dear children, and the fear of unworthiness to them distracts me. I assure you, so harassed and worried have I been that your letter, by directing my thoughts to an Almighty Being, has been the only moment of relief I have known, and I feel a most anxious and fervent wish to seek refuge with him.'

Part of her unhappiness was due to increasing ill health. She was plagued by more and more frequent headaches; and her eyes continued to trouble her. In

Lady Caroline Lamb (1785–1828), wife of Lord Melbourne. Painting by Miss E.H. Trotter.

September 1803 she suffered an alarming and very painful attack of gallstones. Harriet nursed her devotedly never leaving her day or night until she was well on the way to recovery. The next year saw Georgiana's financial difficulties come to a head; at last she was obliged to set about the business of counting up her liabilities and confessing them to the Duke. Harriet, who was her helper in what she called this '*grande affaire*', was horrified to discover how large were the sums of money involved: 'Sunday evening all will be laid before him; he expects five or six—and it comes to thirty-five!' A few weeks later she was writing, 'It is, alas, past forty.' Whatever the final sum might be Bess wisely advised Georgiana to make a clean breast of it. Her advice was echoed by Fox who was all too familiar with the problem of debt. Now he wrote urging her to 'conceal nothing, but make up the account against yourself as much as possible', and pointing out that otherwise she would soon find herself with 'new debts, new borrowing, and a new series of distress and misery'. Alarming though the amount undoubtedly was the Duke proved surprisingly helpful and sympathetic when faced with what he believed to be the total sum of his wife's debts. He made what should have been a satisfactory arrangement for their payment; but whether because Georgiana had not in fact brought herself to make a really full confession, or because in her extravagance she could not avoid contracting new debts this was not the end of what Lady Spencer described as 'the old and hopeless story of money difficulties'.

Georgiana had always been loving and maternal towards the curious assortment of children brought up in the Devonshire House nurseries, and now she found herself much involved in their love affairs. Corisande de Grammont had fallen in love with Lord Ossulston, and he with her; but his father, Lord Tankerville, objected to the match. Georgiana hoped that he would relent which he ultimately did three years later. There was talk of Georgiana's own Hary-o marrying her cousin Duncannon; but the young people did not seem enthusiastic, and in the autumn of 1805 Duncannon announced his engagement to Lady Maria Fane. In June of that year Duncannon's wild, enchanting sister Caroline married the Melbournes' eldest surviving son, William Lamb. The marriage caused some dismay to Harriet Bessborough, who disliked and distrusted the bridegroom's mother, and it deeply distressed Hartington who had taken it for granted that he himself would one day marry Caroline.

Meanwhile Georgiana's health was going from bad to worse. In March 1805 she had another attack of gallstones; and three weeks after Caroline's wedding Harriet was sent for to nurse her through a painful recurrence of her eye trouble. The one bright spot on the horizon was the political situation, and that from the point of view of Devonshire House appeared bright indeed. On Pitt's unexpected death in January 1806 Lord Grenville became Prime Minister. In his 'Ministry of all the Talents' Lord Spencer was Home Secretary; but even more interesting to Georgiana and Harriet was the appointment of Fox to the all-important post of Foreign Secretary. At last he had come in out of the cold. Georgiana gave a brilliant party in honour of his long-delayed triumph; but rejoicing was to be brief. Early in March she caught a chill and retired to bed shivering and feverish. Jaundice developed, but ill health was now so often her normal condition that no one was seriously alarmed except Lady Spencer. She had good reason to fear that physical illness might be greatly aggravated by mental anxiety for Georgiana had recently written to her begging urgently for the loan of £100. Harriet had as usual hurried to her sister's sick-bed; and Lady Spencer sent part of the required sum under cover of a letter to her. 'I am most uncomfortable about your sister, my dear Harriet,' she wrote. 'Some horrible calamity is hanging over her, I conclude. What can be done?'

[107]

Nothing could be done for Georgiana. Her condition fluctuated from day to day; on 23 March the doctors declared her out of danger, but on 27 March she fell desperately ill. The death struggle was long and painful. 'Anything so horrible, so killing as her three days' agony no human being ever witnessed,' Harriet wrote. 'I saw it all, held her through all her struggles, and saw her expire.'

When Georgiana died on 30 March 1806 brightness fell from the air. Six months later another light was extinguished. Fox had proved outstandingly successful as Foreign Secretary, and it seemed that the highest position of all was within his reach and that at this late hour he might yet fulfil the brilliant promise of his youth. It was not to be. In May he fell ill with dropsy. To spare him the long journey from London to St Anne's Hill he was lent the villa at Chiswick which Georgiana had so much loved and there he died on 17 September 1806.

Another friend of long standing had fallen on evil days. Sheridan's association with Devonshire House and the Whigs had done him little good, turning him from a dramatist of genius to a politician of the second grade. His lovely wife Elizabeth had died in 1793; and two years later he had married a young woman known as 'Hecca', daughter of the Dean of Winchester. From now onwards he went rapidly down hill. Drunken and decayed, he continued to pester Harriet with his attentions although both of them were now well into middle age. One day Harriet was sitting by the bedside of her daughter Caroline Lamb who was pregnant and very unwell. A despairing note arrived from Hecca; Sheridan was in a demented state and would not be quieted. As soon as she could leave Caroline Harriet hurried round to find him very drunk indeed, talking wildly and declaring over and over again that even now he loved her better than any other woman. For three hours Sheridan raved while Hecca wept and scolded until at last Harriet succeeded in locking him into his dressing-room and making her escape.

Harriet Bessborough's life at this period was not at all an easy one. Added to her deep grief for her sister was her anxiety over the state of affairs at Devonshire House. After Georgiana's death Bess had continued to live there; and it was becoming clear that the Duke would soon make her his wife. For Hary-o, forced to live in the same house as her father's mistress, the situation was already difficult enough, but should such a marriage take place her position would become intolerable. The problem solved itself in a manner deeply disturbing to Harriet Bessborough although on the surface she managed to preserve an admirable calm. She had always known that one day Granville would marry and she had even discussed the subject with him but she had not expected that he would marry her own niece. In the autumn of 1809 he set about paying court to Hary-o. That cool and critical young woman turned hither and thither in a vain attempt to avoid her coming fate; his charm and determination were too strong for her. Hary-o had known all about her aunt's love-affair and despised her for it; now she found herself falling in love with her aunt's lover. On 18 October 1809 the Duke married Bess; on 24 December Hary-o married Granville Leveson-Gower and lived happily ever after.

The blow to Harriet was very severe. She had loved, indeed, still loved, Granville wholeheartedly, and now she might well have repeated words she had written long ago in another context, 'You know I can never love anything a *little*, therefore you may judge how I suffer at this moment.' Life was not made easier for her by the spectacle of Bess reigning at Devonshire House and Chatsworth in the place of the sister she had loved so well; nevertheless when the Duke died unexpectedly in July 1811 she felt it her duty to spend some time at Chiswick sorting out financial problems and doing her best to comfort the disconsolate widow, who ultimately retired to live abroad.

Anxiety for her daughter Caroline Lamb added greatly to Harriet's burden of sadness. Though at heart devoted to her husband William and to their little boy Augustus, who was showing signs of mental deficiency, Caroline could not resist the thrill of falling in and out of love, and she had already had a violent flirtation with Sir Godfrey Webster. Now in an evil hour, she met Lord Byron. He was only too pleased to play up to her while she paraded her passion for all the world to see. They were not lovers—'Caroline,' writes Lord David Cecil, 'was of that cerebral temperament to which the pleasures of the imagination always mean more than the pleasures of the senses'—but had they been found in bed together the scandal could not have been greater. Lady Melbourne was furious and Harriet distressed beyond measure. Loving her daughter as she did she could not bring herself to act with the necessary firmness. She wished to see the affair brought to an end but she did not wish Caroline to break her heart in the process. The climax came one morning when Caroline, without a penny in her pocket, rushed out into the street and disappeared. All day long Harriet searched for her missing daughter who was finally brought home by Byron. He had found her hiding in a stranger's house in Kensington, planning with the proceeds of a ring she had pawned to take ship and run away, she knew not where.

The strain had been too much for Harriet; on her way home that evening she fell on the floor of her carriage insensible. The next day Caroline received a letter from the old housekeeper who had known her since babyhood. 'Cruel and unnatural as you has behaved,' she wrote, 'you surely do not wish to be the death of your mother

[109]

. . . you are the talk of every groom and footman about town.'

Even Harriet now felt that the time had come for firm and stern action. She and Lord Bessborough announced that they must visit their Irish estates, and, taking William Lamb and a very reluctant Caroline with them, they crossed to Dublin. Thankful to be at last rid of Caroline Byron embarked on an affair with Lady Oxford, meanwhile turning over in his mind the possibility of marrying Arabella Milbanke.

The year 1812 was a troubled time for Harriet. Not only was she deeply distressed by Caroline's vagaries but she was filled with anxiety for another one of her children. Her second son Frederick was serving with Wellington's army in the Peninsular War. When news came that he had been wounded his parents could not but be anxious although Frederick himself wrote that he hoped they would not be 'in a great fuss about this scratch of mine'.

Two years later on 14 March 1814 the dowager Lady Spencer died full of years and honour. Her death at the age of seventy-seven was only to be expected but it left a large gap in Harriet's life. The love between mother and daughters had been particularly deep and enduring; she was a pillar of strength to them both and in her they had found the order and stability which were lacking in their own lives.

The general rejoicing over the great victory at Waterloo was marred for the Bessboroughs by the news that Frederick had been seriously wounded in the battle. Immediately the whole family hurried over to Brussels to be with him and nurse him back to health. Not till August were they able to bring him back with them to England. For the next few years Harriet divided her time between London and her country home at Roehampton. The world as she had known it was rapidly disappearing. Old Lady Spencer, Georgiana, Fox and the Duke of Devonshire were dead, and her old admirer Sheridan, whom she continued to see in spite of the terrible scene in 1807 had only a short time to live. 'Sheridan has been here looking so ill I was quite shocked,' she wrote on 20 November 1815. 'He said in joke that he was dying. I believe he will find it a fact.' Harriet was right; Sheridan died eight months later and her brother Lord Spencer acted as pall-bearer at his funeral.

Three years later Harriet took upon herself the guardianship of an unwanted baby. Her namesake and distant cousin, Harriet Spencer, great-granddaughter of the Lord Sunderland who had become third Duke of Marlborough, was with child by yet another cousin, George Spencer Churchill, Marquess of Blandford. For a married woman the situation would not have been so difficult but for an unmarried girl an illegitimate baby spelt social ostracism and utter disaster. Compassionate and warm-hearted as ever, Harriet Bessborough came to the rescue. As soon as

Harriet Spencer's daughter was born she whisked the baby away, stood as her godmother, and assumed complete responsibility for her upbringing. Harriet Spencer was thus left free to marry a German suitor while the child she had hardly seen remained in the nursery at Roehampton. On Harriet Bessborough's death Caroline and William Lamb took charge of Susan Churchill, as the little girl was called, bringing her up in their home at Brocket and treating her with great affection and kindness. When Caroline died William, now Lord Melbourne, continued to hold himself responsible for Susan, who was generally known as 'Lord Melbourne's ward', her real parentage remaining a close secret.

In 1821 the Bessboroughs set out on a long continental tour, accompanied by their third son, Willy, his wife Barbara (born Ashley-Cooper), and their children, Charles and Henry. Sadly enough, little Henry fell ill and at Parma he died. Harriet had taken her full share in the nursing of the sick child and she admitted to feeling ill and exhausted. She knew, however, that Willy and Barbara were anxious to leave Parma as soon as possible and she concealed her more ominous symptoms. Believing that nothing was wrong with her serious enough to necessitate a change of plan the whole party moved on to Bologna and from there set out to cross the high Apennines on the way to Florence. At their first stopping-place Harriet was taken ill. The inn was very primitive, and in November the cold at that height was intense. It was decided that at all costs they must move on. A bed was made up for the sick woman in the travelling-carriage, and although she suffered painfully from the jolting at last they succeeded in reaching Florence. Here at least she could die in some comfort. She asked to be told the truth about her chances of recovery, and hearing that she must die, she summoned an English clergyman and received the Sacrament. For a few days she lingered on in great pain which she bore without complaint, then on Sunday, 11 November 1821, she died aged sixty. Her body was brought back to England, so that she might lie not with the Bessboroughs, nor with the Spencers at Great Brington, but as she had specially asked beside her sister in the Cavendish vault at Derby.

Harriet's death marks the end of an epoch. From now onwards the story of the Spencers moved out of an eighteenth-century and Regency ambience into a nineteenth-century and Victorian one, although Victoria was not to come to the throne for another twenty-six years. But although on the surface life might become more sober and decorous the change was not really so great as it is often supposed to have been. Fundamentally the Devonshire House set were serious people. They had standards in which they believed although they did not live up to them. Georgiana and Harriet, for instance, never lost their faith in the principles they had learnt from their mother, little though they might observe those principles in practice. On the credit side they were generous, kind, loyal, clever, and extremely entertaining; politically they were forward-looking, believing in the Liberal principle of liberty. On the debit side they piled up debts and produced bevies of illegitimate children, but they knew and admitted that these things were wrong, grieved for them, and accepted the consequences. Intellectually they were not dishonest; they did not call black white or even grey. To use old-fashioned terms they were sinners but repentant sinners. The epitaph which Georgiana wrote for herself applies equally well to them all. After describing with considerable perception but at too great length her own character, her many mistakes and errors, and the happiness she had found in the love of her friends and family, she ended the epitaph thus:

> The sentiments inspired by the thought of Death were these—
> Gratitude to her friends for their indulgence
>   And the hope
> That her remembrance would be harboured
>   With affectionate kindness
>   And forgiving love.
>
> And to her God she offered
>   Her deep contrition,
>   And the sorrows of her life,
>   And her presumptuous hope
> That the All-good long-suffering and All-seeing Power
> Who best would know the extent of her error
> Would although dreadful in His Judgements
>   Compassionate and appreciate
>   Her repentance.

Georgiana, Duchess of Devonshire, and her sister, Henrietta, Viscountess Duncannon, at a musical party. Watercolour drawing by Thomas Rowlandson, 1790.

[4]

ALTHORP OF
THE REFORM BILL

'The tortoise on whom the world rests.'

Lord Melbourne.

Lavinia, Countess Spencer, with her son, John Charles, Viscount Althorp, later third Earl Spencer.
Painting by Sir Joshua Reynolds, 1783–84.

The curiously assorted brood of children who filled nursery and schoolroom at Devonshire House had enjoyed a happy if haphazard existence. They lived surrounded by demonstrative and warm-hearted affection while the invaluable Miss Trimmer saw to it that they received a good formal education. Across the Green Park at Spencer House six children were growing up in a very different atmosphere. John, the eldest, called Jack by his parents but Althorp by the rest of the family, was born in 1782. Next came Sarah in 1787, Robert in 1791, Georgiana, known as Gin or Nig, in 1794, and finally two boys so near in age as to be treated like twins, Frederick or Fritz born 1798 and George or Hoddekin, in 1799.

Their lives were ruled, but ruled from afar, by the dominant figure of their mother. When they were young she neglected them, when they grew older she sought to gain and to keep complete control over them. Although she would occasionally give way to outbursts of passion, Lavinia Spencer was normally a reserved, aloof, unemotional person, with a tongue that cut like a knife. Nig, a pretty, timid child, lived all her life in terror of her mother; but it was Althorp who was the special butt of Lady Spencer's sarcasm.

Lavinia Spencer's interests were primarily artistic and intellectual; she drew admirably and she possessed an unusually quick and critical brain. Slowness was something that especially irritated her; and there is no denying the fact that Althorp was slow. From his earliest years both his father and his mother seem to have been convinced that the boy was a hopeless dullard. His passion for sport meant that he spent most of his time in the company of grooms and gamekeepers; and there his parents were content to leave him giving no thought to the development either of his mind or his manners. Such early education as he received was casual and unplanned; he learned his letters, for instance, from a Swiss footman whose command of English was very imperfect.

At the age of eight Althorp was sent to Harrow, an uncouth little ignoramus. At school he seems to have been comparatively happy. Surprisingly enough, he was not bullied by his seniors; 'the great boys' treated him with unusual kindness, one of them building him 'a very grand castle' and another teaching him to skip. He made friends easily among his contemporaries, and with his cousin Duncannon he indulged in the sort of ploys popular with most small boys, toy soldiers, bird's-nesting, model boats. On arriving at Harrow he was not surprisingly well below the average at school-work; but before very long his exercises were in demand among his fellows, who copied them out and showed them up as their own. (Rightly, his biographer points out that this was not very much of a compliment since no boy would be fool enough to show up a suspiciously good exercise.) All the time his

[114]

John Charles, Viscount Althorp, at the age of four. Painting by Sir Joshua Reynolds, 1786, at Althorp.

[115]

mind was turning to his home and to the parents whom he loved and respected although they had·treated him with so little comprehension or kindness. A few days after the death of his baby brother Richard in January 1791 he wrote home a letter so unusually long and interesting that his house-master felt moved to question him about it. 'Well, Sir,' replied the eight-year-old boy, 'it is the sort of letter I think I ought to write because if I write in a pleasant sort of way it will keep Dick from their thoughts, and so I should like to write as long a letter as possible.'

At home for the holidays, however, he was once more the ungainly, inarticulate hobbledehoy, perpetually nagged by his mother and the victim of her most unkind witticisms. In her beautifully modulated musical voice she would crush him with the type of remark best calculated to wound a slow but sensitive child. Even when he left Harrow and went up to Cambridge she continued to treat him as an idle, stupid schoolboy. So obvious was her scorn of his intellectual attainments that he was dumbfounded when, in his first year at the University, she informed him that she expected him to take a First Class in the coming examination. (This was not an examination like the modern Tripos open to the whole University, but a College examination, the only one which at that date noblemen were expected or even according to Althorp's biographer, permitted to take.) It says much for Lavinia Spencer's hold over her son that he immediately dropped his idle habits and for the two months that remained worked so hard that he succeeded in taking a high place in the First Class list. Perhaps she had a higher estimation of his abilities that she had ever admitted and realized that he needed some special spur to bring them into action. The ability was indeed there although he himself was the last person ever to recognize it, referring time and again to his 'very slender natural abilities' and bewailing both his want of information on subjects of general interest and his incapacity to express himself fluently either in speech or writing. In spite of this lack of self-confidence when he took another examination at the end of his second year he emerged top, showing a special aptitude for mathematics.

Unlike most noblemen—'tufts' they were called because of the golden tassel on their caps—Althorp spent a third year at Cambridge but, in the words of his biographer, 'by no means to the advantage either of his mind or his morals'. For the first and only time in his life he sowed a large crop of wild oats. With no examination in prospect and with Newmarket in easy and dangerous proximity he spent his time betting, racing, and running up debts so large that when he was forced to confess them to his father to his horror and astonishment he found that Lord Spencer was unable to clear them without borrowing heavily. The shock had a salutary effect on Althorp, curing him for ever of any taste for betting.

Aged twenty-one and now back at home with his family he found that he fitted badly into the place in society to which his rank entitled him. Plain and awkward in appearance, he lacked both manners and manner, and his speech was reminiscent of the grooms and prize-fighters with whom he chose to spend most of his time, declaring that 'he detested the life of a grandee'. That life, however, was the one for which he was destined. To fit him for it he was sent off on the Grand Tour of Europe, then considered an essential part of the education of a gentleman. From this experience he gained nothing except a lasting hatred of religious intolerance induced by the sight of Catholics oppressing Protestants abroad in precisely the same manner in which Protestants oppressed Catholics at home in England.

The next and almost inevitable step was entry into the House of Commons. In 1804 Althorp became Member for the nomination borough of Okehampton, moving from there to stand as candidate for Cambridge University in the election of 1806. In this contest, which was fought in an unusually friendly spirit, he defeated his old schoolfellow, Lord Palmerston, but was himself defeated, coming second in the poll to Lord Henry Petty. Lord Spencer's appointment as Home Secretary in the "Ministry of all the talents" almost automatically ensured that his son received some office; and Althorp became a junior Lord of the Treasury. Having given up Okehampton in order to contest Cambridge he now found himself a parliamentary seat by becoming Member for the Spencer pocket-borough of St Albans. Later in this same year of 1806 he fought and won Northamptonshire, a seat which he retained until his elevation to the House of Lords.

Out of loyalty to his father, whom he regarded with great affection and respect, Althorp had entered Parliament as a Tory, though he was later to boast that in those early days he had never given a vote against Fox. After the death of Pitt in January 1806 Lord Spencer returned to the Whig allegiance traditional in his family, and Althorp was free to follow his natural inclination which was towards the Radical wing of that party. For the present, however, he did not commit himself to any definite political creed and he continued to sit very lightly to his duties both at the Treasury and in the House of Commons. Most of his attention was given to prize-fights and above all, to hunting. After the House had risen he would ride all through the night in order to reach Northamptonshire in time for the next day's meet of the Pytchley, sometimes falling asleep in the saddle and allowing his horse to fall down under him. Even when awake Althorp was no great horseman. When out hunting he preferred to follow a pilot rather than take a line of his own. He had many falls, and so frequently did he dislocate his shoulder that

[117]

he trained one of the hunt servants to manipulate the bone into place straight away without leaving the field. His interest lay not so much in horsemanship as in hound-work; many years later he was to declare that the leading passion in his life had been 'to see sporting dogs hunt'.

Politics were all-important in London Society; and because of Lord Spencer's adherence to Pitt for a while there was little formal visiting between Spencer House and the 'grand Whiggery' at Devonshire House, where everyone was a devoted admirer of Fox. In any case, no love was lost between Lavinia Spencer and her sisters-in-law, Georgiana Duchess of Devonshire and Harriet Lady Bessborough; and although the Spencer, Cavendish and Ponsonby cousins met fairly frequently no really close intimacy existed between them. However, in the spring of 1807, a year after Georgiana's death, Lavinia Spencer, who could sometimes be as kind as she was cruel, invited Georgiana's daughter Hary-o to stay at Althorp, thus giving the girl a chance to escape from the unwelcome society of her father's mistress. Hary-o was a shrewd judge of character; and in her letters to her sister Georgiana Morpeth she gives a vivid picture of the Spencer family and in particular of Althorp. If her criticisms seem sometimes a little astringent it must be remembered that she was writing privately to a much-loved sister, and that she would have been horrified to think that her letters would be preserved for posterity to read—'burn this letter' is a frequent superscription. And if Harriet was critical she was never catty. She was clearly puzzled by the strange contradictions of her aunt's character. 'Lady Spencer continues in the most perfect good humour, and when she is it is difficult to be more delightful,' she writes in one letter. 'Her conversation is so improving without the least pedantry and so very entertaining and animated that I could listen to her for ever.' In another letter she complains of Lavinia Spencer's 'really unreasonable violence' which she sees as 'often entertaining, oftener disgusting', adding however that 'to me she is uniformly, I may say, *indulgently* kind.' Her opinion of her cousin Sarah is equally inconsistent. She describes Sarah as 'an angel', 'a most delightful creature', and as someone 'more improved by living more among young and *softened* people (I mean people whose tongues are not invariably two-edged swords) than I have time or spirits to explain'; yet only a few days later comes the sentence, 'Sarah would be impossible'.

Those words were probably intended to imply that Sarah would be impossible as a sister-in-law. The great Whig families, believing that good things should be kept within the family circle, greatly favoured marriages between cousins; and one of Lavinia Spencer's motives in inviting Hary-o to stay was a wish to see her safely engaged to Althorp. Such an idea certainly did not originate in the minds of the

Lavinia, Viscountess Althorp, later Countess Spencer (1762–1831). Painting by Sir Joshua Reynolds, 1782, at Althorp.

two people most concerned, who displayed only a minimal interest in one another.

Almost immediately Hary-o made up her mind that desirable though such a match might be from the worldly point of view, and much as she admired her cousin's many good qualities, she could not bring herself to contemplate 'a weary tedious existence with a man whose whole soul is engrossed in one most uninteresting pursuit,' that pursuit being, of course, hunting. Althorp, as Hary-o saw him, was an exact replica of the character called Flatus described by William Law in *A Serious Call to a Devout and Holy Life*:

Nothing was so happy as hunting; he entered upon it with all his soul, and leap'd more hedges and ditches than had ever been known in so short a time. You never saw him but in a green coat; he was the envy of all that blow the horn, and always spoke to his dogs in great propriety of language. If you met him at home in a bad day, you would hear him blow his horn, and be entertain'd with the surprising accidents of the last noble chase.

[119]

Charles King, Huntsman to the Pytchley Hunt, 1805–1818. Painting by Ben Marshall.

The perceptive Sarah wrote sadly to her sailor brother Robert, 'Though I do know and see that dear Althorp has in him much more than enough to put him high, very high, above all his fellow sportsmen, yet when he covers all that with a muddy red coat and does his best to forget it—oh, Bob, what a pity!' Hary-o was not oblivious of Althorp's good qualities, grieving to see 'a character that might have been distinguished both for all virtues and good understanding, dwindled into something less respectable than a groom.' She refused to contemplate such a man as a possible husband:

> Althorp as he might have been no *reasonable* woman could help loving and respecting. Althorp as he is now no reasonable woman can for a moment think of but as an eager huntsman. He has no more importance in society *now* (as he is, remember) than the chairs and tables.

The situation was further complicated for Hary-o by the unexpected arrival of her brother Hartington, with his friend Sir William Rumbold, who was credited with being her ardent admirer. 'This is not the place for real or sham *dénouements*,' she wrote in much perturbation to Georgiana Morpeth. No crisis, however, occurred; Sir William clearly regarded her as the most attractive woman in the party but he paid her no marked attention. She, meanwhile, was learning to appreciate Althorp better although she was constant in her determination not to be persuaded into marrying him. Althorp and his grandmother, the Dowager Lady Spencer, were two people who had much in common but yet persistently misunderstood and underestimated one another. Althorp admitted to being much influenced by his mother's open dislike of his grandmother, who in her turn made no attempt to hide her contempt for him and her preference for her other grandson Hartington. While agreeing that 'it is impossible to compare him with Hartington and not feel strongly all that he wants' Hary-o considered that her grandmother was unjust to Althorp:

> Dr Carr, whom my brother consulted about his deafness, said to my grandmother that he never was so struck with anyone in his life, and mentioned the sweetness of his countenance, kindness of his manner. He then looked very steadfastly at her and said, 'Lady Spencer, all this you have in your other nephew [sic] but repressed, checked—not one of you can know it—but if you were to see him as I do, you would know there were few—indeed, nobody like him.

If Althorp's grandmother was unappreciative his mother was actively unkind, forever mocking him and never making any effort to curb her impatience with his slowness. When he offered to read aloud to the assembled ladies she remarked waspishly, 'And who, my dear Jack, do you think would understand you if you did?' Another evening, as he sat down to play patience, she called out to Sarah, 'Sal, go and take those cards from your brother; I won't have them dirtied.' The son whom she treated in this manner was a man in his mid-twenties, a Member of Parliament who had served as a Junior Minister; it says much for his sweetness of character and genuine humility that he never answered her back or lost his temper. Though his mother was slow to notice any change in him Althorp was in fact beginning to develop an interest in matters other than sport. Books and reading took up a considerable amount of his leisure. 'He has been spending this summer just after his own heart,' Sarah reported to her sailor brother Bob in October 1808, 'with a little hunting to keep him in constant supply of exercise and eagerness, a great deal of study (for Papa is quite delighted with his account of himself in that respect) and good, useful, serious study to prevent his mind from growing quite rusty.' He taught himself to draw, though admittedly only pictures of horses and dogs, and he helped his father make a detailed catalogue of the classical section of the great Althorp library 'with notes about the different editions and copies, full of a sort of learning which neither you nor I understand, book-collectors' learning.' More surprisingly he, who had hitherto fled from London at the first opportunity, began to appreciate the pleasures of social life. 'He seems to enjoy himself amazingly this year in town,' Sarah wrote in 1809, 'and, to own the truth, I can't say I should very much wonder if it turned out that some little reason, some good motive or other, kept him.' The 'little reason' was believed to be Miss Tilney Long, a pretty girl and a great heiress. This tentative romance came to nothing; nevertheless, according to Sarah, Althorp continued 'to caper about for another week or two . . . he is, as usual, keeping himself down for his hunters by dancing most perseveringly.'

This year of 1809 saw the beginning of Althorp's real interest in politics. In the House of Commons he had naturally gravitated towards a group of young men who had grown up with him and who shared a similar background. His especial friend, Lord Milton, was heir to Earl FitzWilliam and a Northamptonshire neighbour, the other two, Lord Tavistock, the eldest son of the Duke of Bedford, and Harriet Bessborough's son Duncannon were his cousins on the Spencer side. All of them came from great Whig families, all were heir to famous titles and vast estates, all were very rich; Tavistock, Milton and Althorp were Masters of

Foxhounds, and Tavistock was even more of a fanatic about hunting than was Althorp himself. All four were high-minded and religious, and all four held strong Radical views. At this stage, however, the ties between them were personal rather than political.

A scandal in high places was to turn this loose-knit cluster of friends into a political group known as the Young Whigs. George III's son, Frederick Duke of York, was Commander-in-Chief of the Army. His mistress, Mrs Clarke, was accused of taking bribes from officers seeking appointments or promotion. Mrs Clarke's dealings were proved beyond shadow of doubt and her lover's complicity in them seemed almost certain; nevertheless the House was inclined to deal leniently with him, much to the fury of the Radicals. Althorp and his friends were particularly horrified, believing as they did in the importance of maintaining moral principles both in public and in private life, and inheriting all the Whig mistrust of the Royal Family. They were joined by other young men of similar views, and Althorp was chosen as their spokesman, in spite of the fact that although he had been in the House of Commons for five years he had never yet made his maiden speech. Now he had at last found a cause which roused and interested him, a subject which could vie with hunting in its claim on his attention; in Sarah's phrase 'he was all eagerness to hunt down both the foxes and the Duke of York'. His speech was described as 'totally devoid of affectation and full of ability'. The motion of censure was defeated; but public indignation was so great that the Duke was forced to resign.

In thus attacking a Royal personage Althorp had acted contrary to the judgement of those older men whom he had regarded as his political leaders, and of his father in particular. Lord Spencer, however, was a wise and understanding man; no rift opened between them, and they continued to keep in close touch where politics were concerned. 'I shall be glad to see you at Althorp to talk these things over with you,' Althorp wrote on 18 March in the middle of the uproar over the Duke of York. 'My political situation is very much changed within the last fortnight; my opinions, as you know, have long been the same, but till now I have never had the nerve to act upon them.' The fathers of other young Whigs were not so tolerant; they were horrified that their sons should openly declare themselves Radicals, followers of Whitbread and Samuel Romilly and allies of Brougham, with whom Althorp in particular now formed a lasting friendship. These Radicals were nicknamed 'the Mountain' after a famous group of French revolutionaries, and it was to the Mountain that the Young Whigs now attached themselves. They were hot against bribery and corruption; they could almost be called pacifists in

Wiseton Hall, Nottinghamshire, home of Esther Acklom, wife of Viscount Althorp. Early nineteenth-century engraving.

their hatred of war and of any display of militarism; and they were genuinely concerned with the condition of the poor and the grievances of the working people. They voted in favour of a Catholic Emancipation Bill which was heavily defeated, but as yet they had not come round to advocating parliamentary reform.

For the present, however, there was very little action that the Young Whigs could take in support of Radical ideals. Once again sport became Althorp's foremost interest. His friend, Evelyn Denison, later to become Speaker, heard him give a Homeric description of some famous prize-fights and declared that it was 'the one time in his life, in the House or out of it, that he ever spoke with eagerness and almost with passion.' Hunting remained his first love. As he himself admitted to Milton, 'I believe my head is at present much fuller of hunting than of political affairs.' In 1813 he succeeded his father as Master of the Pytchley, and for eight months of the year he made the business of a Master of Foxhounds his sole employment, as if, writes his biographer, 'he had no other vocation and could think of nothing else.'

[124]

Althorp was now over thirty and determined, it seemed, to remain a bachelor. But though he had no intention of marrying anybody somebody had every intention of marrying him. Esther Acklom was no great match for Lord Spencer's heir. Betty Askwith compares her to Trollope's Miss Dunstable though if the comparison seems unkind it should be remembered that Miss Dunstable made Dr Thorne an admirable wife. Esther was plump and not at all pretty but she was very rich, and she was also a young woman of courage and determination. At the age of fifteen when staying in Vienna with her mother she had stood up boldly to one of Napoleon's Marshals and forced him to give her party a *laissez-passer* out of the city. She was clever and well-read, and she was deeply in love with Althorp. Later he was to say that she was the only woman with whom he had never felt shy but when it came to a proposal it was she who had to make the first move. Sarah, who persisted in regarding her as 'a vulgar person and a spoilt child', maintained that Althorp had walked round and round the Park for two hours before he could bring himself to decide to marry her in order to pay off his debts. Whether or not this improbable story is true the fact remains that once married, the couple were supremely happy. Althorp was at least as much in love with his wife as she was with him. He behaved to her with the utmost gentleness and consideration, and she gave him all the warmth of affection and loving sympathy that he had never had from his own family.

Their home was to be Wiseton Hall in Nottinghamshire. The house was neither comfortable nor in good condition, but it was Esther's childhood home which she dearly loved; and for that reason her husband was prepared to spend £10,000 on repairs and alterations. He continued to hunt in Northamptonshire as Master of the Pytchley, where he showed excellent sport, and when at Wiseton devoted his time to farming while Esther took the derelict garden in hand. Four happy years passed, marred only by the absence of a child. Esther had miscarried once or twice, so that when she again became pregnant she was understandably nervous and careful of herself. Lavinia Spencer had always disliked her daughter-in-law, and now she gave her no sympathy. In a letter to Lord Milton, apologizing for being unable to make a promised visit because Esther, who was feeling unwell, could not bear him to leave her, Althorp wrote, 'you must not tell my mother the reason why I have not come to Milton as she does not make any great allowance for want of nerves generally and she is quite sufficiently inclined to find fault with Esther without having any additional reason.'

The main topic of this letter, which is dated 31 March 1818, is the proposal that

[125]

Althorp should become Leader of the Whig party in the House of Commons. 'Newport and Duncannon have pressed me very much to take the office,' he writes, 'and they say that most of the party wish it very much.' Clearly, in spite of his lack of brilliance, Althorp's strength of character and sweetness of temperament had already given him unusual influence in the House. Though he believes that 'the position of leader of such a party as the present opposition is the most honourable one a man can have', and admits that 'my personal influence in the House of Commons is perhaps more general than that of anyone of our party' because he has friends in all the 'sects', to use his own term, into which the Whigs were fragmented, he turns down the proposal on the ground of 'my total incapacity for the office'. He declares that he has 'the most decided objection to myself or anyone else being made leader unless he comes quite naturally to the situation', and he makes the sensible suggestion that as a temporary measure the leadership should be put in commission. In a committee 'by degrees of course someone would get a superior degree of influence and could then naturally take the post of leader.' Nevertheless, it is only with considerable regret that he turns down this flattering proposal—'I will not say that there was not a considerable struggle between my vanity and my reason before I came to this decision.'

In another letter to Milton telling him of Esther's pregnancy Althorp had written, 'I never saw her better in my life and I am therefore very sanguine as to the result.' Although there seemed to be no great cause for anxiety it was thought best to move to London for the birth of the child. There, on 9 June after a long and painful labour, Esther was delivered of a stillborn son. Two days later she herself died, leaving her husband stunned and desolate.

The loss to Althorp was an irreparable one. The light that had gone out of his life was never to be rekindled. He could count himself fortunate in that his marriage, though so brief, had been one of unclouded happiness, but that thought brought him no consolation. Years later, when congratulating a friend who was about to be married, his face suddenly darkened. 'The pain that I have suffered from the loss of my wife,' he stammered out, 'has been such that no happiness could compensate.' He shut himself up at Wiseton, where every corner of the house, every flower in the garden, held memories of Esther. Though he refused to allow any of his family to keep him company to their astonishment he invited his mother-in-law to stay with him and lavished endless care and attention on this difficult and unattractive woman with whom he had no bond in common except memories of Esther. For the rest of her life Mrs Acklom spent much of her time at Wiseton, and when they were not together he took the trouble to write to her every day.

[126]

At last, after months of hopeless grieving, he began to see a way through the darkness. Long afterwards, when Lord John Russell was prostrated by grief at the death of his wife, Althorp insisted that work was the only panacea for sorrow, a lesson he had learnt from his own experience of bereavement. Had he followed his inclination he would now have made farming and stock-breeding the business of his life. The work involved would have given him occupation enough; not only had he a herd of prize cattle and an estate of 2,000 acres at Wiseton but he was also tenant of Chapel Brampton, the home farm at Althorp. He had always been interested in the breeding of animals, and as Master of the Pytchley he had given much thought and care to the development of a lighter-boned, faster type of hound. Stock-breeding was now the one occupation that gave him some interest in the future. 'Of all my former pursuits,' he wrote a few months after Esther's death, 'it is the only one in which I can build castles in the air,' a sad little comment on the castles in the air he had been building round the children whom he would now never have. He used the same expression in a letter to Milton describing how he had travelled to Darlington for the sale of a famous North Country herd and there expended £900 on the purchase of three Shorthorn cows and a bull: 'I am enabled again to build castles in the air, and if the speculation turns out inprofitable from a pecuniary point of view I am quite sure that it will repay me in happiness.' He told his father that he intended to give much time and attention to his cattle and farms—'I hope by such quiet pursuits as these to bear the affliction I am suffering under with tolerable patience.'

But if Althorp's pleasure lay in farming and stock-breeding he knew well that his duty was to devote himself to political life, not in order to further his own ambitions—he had none—but to do the most he could to improve the lot of his fellow-men. The hunting which he so passionately enjoyed he now completely abandoned, partly as a sign of mourning for Esther, but chiefly because he knew that were he to continue with the sport it would inevitably absorb too much of his time and energy. He therefore resigned the Mastership of the Pytchley and nothing that his friends could do or say could persuade him to change his mind. In an endeavour to remedy the gaps in his education he gave himself to the study of divinity and economics, 'the first, to do myself good, the second, to do good to others.' Though he was a sincerely religious man his faith had brought him no comfort in the period immediately following Esther's death, but now he read the Bible assiduously. He was a humble and devout Christian, but he was also an inarticulate one; only here and there a chance reference or phrase makes clear that belief in God had become the mainspring of his thought and action.

[127]

Althorp had seen his life shattered to pieces, and he had had the courage and faith to begin to rebuild it in a new shape. Up to now he had not fully committed himself to politics. The tragedy of Esther's death proved a decisive turning-point. None of his friends among the Young Whigs were to achieve any important political position. Had she lived he might have chosen to follow their example, spending his days as a rich, benevolent, distinguished country magnate, enjoying a happy family life and dividing his time between sport, agriculture and local business, with only an occasional visit to Westminster to vote or speak on some issue of particular importance. Now he was to follow a different course and to find a place in history as Althorp of the Reform Bill.

The times however were not propitious for any Whig politician; and for the Radical section of that party in particular the outlook was a dreary one. The Tories had been in office since 1812 and seemed set to remain there indefinitely. In the House of Commons Althorp had nothing more interesting to occupy his attention than an Insolvency Bill designed to help small creditors such as shopkeepers, the 'little men' for whom he was always to feel special sympathy. He was further saddened by the death of a friend and fellow-member of Parliament called Elliot— 'never was there a more amiable, more friendly, or more kind-hearted creature in existence'—and by the suicide of the Radical leader, Samuel Romilly. His comment on Elliot's death shows how much religion had now come to mean to him: 'With only a moderate portion of religious feeling one must be satisfied that his death is only to be lamented by those whom he has left behind, for unless the Christian religion is a very different thing from what I suppose it to be to himself Elliot's death must be the greatest, the most inestimable blessing a created being can receive.' Again, when writing compassionately of Romilly, who committed suicide because of his wife's death, Althorp makes his own beliefs quite clear:

> I am not so very much surprised at such a catastrophe as I should have been had I not had the dreadful experience which I have. I think suicide in such a case not a very irrational step for a man to take who does not believe in the truths of religion, which I believe was the case with Romilly. The strongest support one has to bear the loss of one in whose society one's happiness depended is the conviction that the separation is only temporary, that the sleep, though long protracted, is as sure to have an end as the nightly sleep of everyone of our acquaintance.

John Charles, third Earl Spencer (1782–1845). Painting by Sir George Hayter, 1816, at Althorp.

Massacre at St Peter's , or 'Britons, Strike Home'. Caricature by George Cruikshank, published August 16, 1819.

This letter, dated 4 November 1818, is in answer to one in which Milton had reproached Althorp for concentrating exclusively on the care of Mrs Acklom to the detriment of his relationship with his own family. Since he planned to spend much of his time in the House of Commons he had taken a house in London for Mrs Acklom and himself, an arrangement which enraged Lavinia Spencer who had expected him to make his headquarters at Spencer House. (In fact, Mrs Acklom soon retired to Leamington Spa and Althorp returned to his old flat in Albany.) His answer to Milton's letter is worth quoting at some length. The sentiments may seem sententious and over-pious, but coming from Althorp, they have about them the ring of truth. At the very least, the letter shows that he took the claims of his religion seriously:

We are ordered if necessary to quit father and mother and every other relation to follow Christ. I consider this command in its application to us at the present day to mean that we are not to allow the claims of any relations, however near, nor of any other human being to interfere with the performance of our first duties to produce as much happiness or to alleviate as much misery as is in our power. The question therefore for me to decide is whether I shall perform this duty best by living at Spencer House or by living with Mrs Acklom, that is to say, by which line of conduct I shall produce the greater sum of human happiness and alleviate the greatest sum of misery. My Father and Mother have everything in their power; they have wealth, they have situation, high character, numerous friends and affectionate children . . . Of these advantages Mrs Acklom has only one and that the least of them, viz. wealth, and the difference to her of whether I live in her house or not, is whether she is to feel herself supported by a person attached to her or a solitary being in the world.

Althorp was never a pompous man, and he may have thought that his sentiments sounded a little high-flown for in the next sentence he explains and tacitly excuses them: 'In the grounds on which I decide you will have perceived that I have abstracted myself from all worldly considerations perhaps more than you will think right, but my prospects are so completely annihilated in this world that I only wish to make use of it as a stepping-stone to the next.'

In 1819 an event occurred which aroused the whole nation and Althorp with it, feeling as he did such a deep concern for the common people. The miserable condition of the working-classes inevitably produced discontent and disturbances. On 17 August a crowd of some fifty or sixty thousand assembled for a mass-meeting at St Peter's Field near Manchester. Yeomanry and Hussars were on the spot to see to the preservation of order. The magistrates lost their heads and gave orders to the troops to charge the crowd; 11 people were killed and about 400 wounded; and the occasion has gone down to history as 'the Peterloo Massacre'.

Alarmed by what they believed to be a real danger of Revolution the Tory Government brought in a series of repressive measures known as the Six Acts. Of these the most objectionable was an Act 'for the prevention of the assembling of seditious meetings' which was hotly attacked by the Radicals and by Althorp in particular. His opposition to this measure marked a further widening of the distance between him and the more conservative Whigs who, though protesting their belief in freedom of speech and assembly, were loud in condemnation of Radical support for those whom they regarded as revolutionaries.

Althorp had a happy knack of disagreeing with people and parties and yet retaining their confidence. He was liked and respected by every section of the Whigs in spite of his opposition to the Six Acts. In 1821 he served on a Parliamentary Committee to examine the question of the Corn Laws. Its first Report, almost entirely the work of the Free Trader Huskisson, was strongly in favour of abolition. Althorp was the only member for an agricultural constituency to vote in favour of this Report; but his support of a point of view totally opposed to their own in no way affected his popularity with his fellow agriculturalists and farmers.

George III died in January 1820. His successor, George IV, who was already separated from his wife Caroline of Brunswick, immediately upon ascending the throne asked his ministers to open divorce proceedings on his behalf. In June Lord Liverpool brought in a Bill of Pains and Penalties in the House of Lords. Proceedings dragged on for months, causing vast scandal. In a letter to Milton Althorp commented on this subject. His remarks are a model of good sense:

> I have no doubt that she is a woman of the most infamous character; all she has done since she has been in England would prove this if her previous conduct did not; but we must decide upon the evidence which is brought before us. If the evidence given against her is to be believed there is no doubt of her guilt but if it can be contradicted by anything like the degree stated by Williams it is impossible to believe one word of it and then she must be acquitted. And I really think some reasonable doubt will arise as to whether she has had an intrigue with Bergami or not. It is however, extremely difficult to imagine any other reason for his extraordinary promotion. . . . I would not, however, find her

Trial of Queen Caroline in the House of Lords. Engraving by Roberts after a drawing by George Cruikshank, 1820.

guilty merely upon this circumstance, but I should have very little satisfaction in voting her innocent unless this is very completely explained. . . . There is only one vote on which I am resolved and that is to endeavour to quash the business before the examination is entered into for there is evidently no public advantage to be gained by the enquiry and there is a great public evil in the repetition of all the obscenity which has recently filled the papers. . . . I therefore most fervently wish that the Bill may be thrown out in the House of Lords.

Althorp's wish was granted; the Bill did in fact pass the House of Lords but it was then withdrawn.

[131]

For the next few years Althorp devoted himself to politics. He was so frequently present in the House of Commons that it was believed that only the Speaker excelled him in regularity of attendance. Although he could never become a good speaker he was nearly always a well-informed one because he gave so much of his time to the careful and conscientious study of the subjects under debate. These duties kept him in London, a place he hated; but whenever possible he escaped to the country to cast a knowledgeable eye over his flocks and herds and to enjoy a day's shooting.

In February 1827 the face of the political scene suddenly altered. Lord Liverpool retired from office following a paralytic stroke; and George Canning took his place as Prime Minister. Wellington and the ultra-Tories refused to serve under Canning, thus forcing him to seek a coalition with the Whigs in order to form an administration. A section of Whigs, including Brougham and the Radicals, decided to give him their support, but Althorp and the Young Whigs refused to do so. Instead they allied themselves with Lord Grey, thus beginning a political partnership that was to be all-important in Althorp's career. The Young Whigs, and Althorp in particular, mistrusted Canning profoundly, believing him to be insincere in his support of progressive policies, especially Catholic Emancipation, Free Trade, and Parliamentary Reform. As early as 1821 Althorp had become a convinced supporter of Reform; as he remarked with better sense than grammar, 'No country ought to be governed in a way they do not like.' His own influence and popularity were steadily growing. Men of all shades of opinion had learned to trust 'Honest Jack'. 'I should like to hear what Althorp says about the state of politics,' one country gentleman wrote to Milton; and many people both in and out of the House of Commons would have echoed his wish.

Even those Whigs who had differed from Althorp and joined the Coalition recognized him as a person of influence and were anxious to conciliate him. Canning died within four months of taking office and was succeeded by the irresolute Goderich, 'as firm as a bulrush'. Huskisson, now a member of the Cabinet, invited Althorp to become Chairman of the important Finance Committee. Althorp accepted; but the Chancellor of the Exchequer, the ultra-Tory Herries, objected to the appointment. A storm blew up among the Ministers, whereupon 'Goody' Goderich, weeping copiously, tendered his resignation. For the first but not for the last time Althorp had involuntarily caused the fall of a Prime Minister.

After Goderich's departure the Tories still remained in office under the Duke of Wellington. The Whigs, so long fragmented into small factions, were beginning to realize the necessity for closer unity and better organization. The most crying need was for someone efficient and conciliatory who would act as Leader in the House of Commons. This position had of course been offered to Althorp in 1818 and again in a more formal manner in November 1827. On both occasions he had refused. At a meeting held in May 1830 the choice again fell upon him; and this time he accepted.

At first glance he appeared anything but a suitable person to fill such a position. The House of Commons is a place where speed of thought is all but essential; and Althorp's brain worked very slowly. He was a notoriously bad speaker; 'there is a better speaker than Althorp in every vestry in England,' wrote one of his contemporaries. Physically, he was certainly not a commanding presence. Ruddy-faced and thickset, he looked more like a farmer of the John Bull type than the aristocrat that he was by birth. But his brain, though slow, was a good one and his judgement excellent. Given time, he could more often than not come up with a wise and practical solution to any problem in hand. Moreover, he was a person who believed strongly in the necessity for party unity and who would work wholeheartedly towards that end. Even when he and the Young Whigs had formed what would today be called a splinter-group he had made every effort to minimize the split and, whenever possible, to work in concert with the rest of the party. If anyone could restore order and cohesion to the divided ranks of the Whigs it was he. Men liked and trusted him because they knew that he was without the slightest taint of personal ambition or self-seeking; 'In the close quarters of the House of Commons,' Trevelyan was to write of him, 'character carried the day.'

Althorp had not been Leader for more than a few months before it was suggested that he might perhaps fill a more important post. In November 1830 the Duke of Wellington resigned; the Whigs at last came into office, and Lord Grey became Prime Minister. Grey, who was never happy away from his native Northumberland, disliked the thought of being tied to London, 'the place I hate most'. He therefore suggested that Althorp might possibly take his place as Premier; but Althorp, who loathed London and loved the country at least as much as Grey did, firmly turned down this idea. Instead he became Chancellor of the Exchequer, of course retaining the leadership of the House.

The appointment struck many people as strange. 'Althorp as Chancellor of the Exchquer may be a good one,' Greville wrote, 'but nobody expects much from anything that is already known about him.' Although his first Budget was a failure, the position in fact suited him well enough; he had a natural turn for figures and a good head for business. Finance, however, was not to be his chief concern; for the next two years the best part of his time and attention was to be given to forcing the Reform Bill, or rather, three Reform Bills, through the House of Commons.

The credit for that achievement he shared with Lord John Russell. They worked in close co-operation; broadly speaking, Althorp was in charge of the House and Lord John of the Bill. Althorp was only too pleased to give Lord John the honour of introducing the Bill, which he did on 1 March 1831. It passed its second reading by one vote, only to be defeated in Committee. A general election followed which gave the Whigs a larger majority than they had previously enjoyed. A second Bill, almost identical with the first one, was introduced on 24 June. Now began a hard and exhausting struggle. All through July and August the Tories fought the Bill point by point. Night after night Althorp and Lord John were in the House, answering questions on every aspect of the Bill, going carefully into points of detail, and extricating themselves as best they might from what Althorp described as 'scrapes'. This fierce in-fighting demanded a quickness of thought and a gift for repartee which Althorp did not possess; and the effort to keep pace with minds which worked so much faster than his own put upon him a strain that was almost physically painful. Though he was at least as Radical in his views as Lord John his conciliatory manner made him much more acceptable to their Tory opponents. As Lord John's biographer writes, 'Althorp could soothe and Johnnie sting.' He had a firm grasp on the principles of the Bill and a remarkable knowledge of its details. His judgement was slow but very sure; and his lack of brilliance was far outweighed by his modesty and kindliness and his transparent honesty. A small episode illustrates the extraordinary hold he had upon the House of Commons. One evening, in answer to an able and argumentative speech by Croker, a determined opponent of Reform, Althorp stood up and informed the House that 'he had made some calculations which he considered as entirely conclusive in refutation of the honourable gentleman's arguments, but unfortunately he had mislaid them, so that he could only say that if the House would be guided by his advice they would reject the amendment.' Both sides of the House accepted this answer as perfectly satisfactory, and the amendment was rejected.

Every morning Althorp would go to his office immediately after breakfast and remain there dealing with Exchequer business until four o'clock, when he would return home for a hasty meal. 'Yesterday I went to see poor dear Althorp at his dinner,' Sarah wrote, 'and so hurried and uneasy a meal I never saw.' By five o'clock he was in the House of Commons, making statements and answering questions (one night he spoke as often as forty times) until the House rose, usually about midnight, when he would return to his rooms in Albany to sup off a bowl of arrowroot and a glass of sherry.

Charles Grey, second Earl Grey,
Prime Minister 1830–34. Painting
by Sir Thomas Lawrence.

Only a man of great physical stamina could for long maintain such a programme; and Lord John was delicate. On 10 August he collapsed, leaving the whole responsibility for the Bill on Althorp's shoulders. Lord John recovered quickly, but three weeks later Althorp himself fell ill, though he was only absent for two days. In September the Bill at last passed the House of Commons. To celebrate the occasion a group of Whigs gave a banquet in honour of Althorp and Lord John. When Althorp entered the room he was all but overwhelmed by the congratulations which poured in upon him from every side, members pressing forward to thank him as warmly as if he had done each one of them a personal service.

These celebrations were somewhat premature. On 7 October the Bill was thrown out by the Lords. Riots broke out in the country, and there were threats of a general refusal to pay taxes. When a mass-meeting at Birmingham passed a vote of thanks to Althorp and Lord John for their efforts in support of the Bill Althorp, who detested any recourse to violent or provocative measures, himself wrote to Thomas Attwood, the promoter of the meeting, to urge moderation upon him: 'I

The House of Commons in 1833, after the passing of the Reform Act. In the front bench, on the left, leaning forward, is the third Earl Spencer. Painting by Sir George Hayter.

beseech you, use all your influence, not merely to prevent any acts of open violence, but any such resistance to the law as is threatened by the refusal to pay taxes.'

Grey and his Cabinet decided neither to resign nor to whittle down the Bill. Althorp was the speaker chosen to announce to the House of Commons that the Government only remained in office in order to pass a measure no less far-reaching

[136]

and efficient than the defeated Bill. A third Reform Bill was introduced, and the whole business was to be done again complicated by differences over the possible creation of new peers. At first Althorp was against this desperate expedient but he came round to seeing it as the lesser of two evils, and he even threatened to resign if Grey did not ask the King to promise to create the number of new peers necessary for the passing of the Bill should it again be thrown out by the House of Lords.

Although the passage of this Bill through the Commons was easier than that of its predecessor by now Althorp was almost at breaking-point. So great was his hatred of London and so heavy the strain under which he was living that 'this most true and stout-hearted of God's creatures' thought it advisable to remove a pair of pistols from his bedroom lest he should be tempted to commit suicide. On 3 March he remarked to John Hobhouse, Whig politician and friend of Byron, 'I do not know whether I ought not to make matters easier by shooting myself.' 'For God's sake, not that!' Hobhouse exclaimed. 'Shoot anyone else you like.'

Inevitably the Bill was defeated in the Lords. On 9 May Grey resigned and a delighted Althorp retired to Wiseton to oil his fowling-pieces and to prepare for a happy season of sport and farming. But it was not to be. Wellington failed to form a Ministry, and Grey and Althorp were back again in office. William IV agreed to create new peers if necessary; and, bowing to this threat, Wellington and the majority of Tory peers abstained from voting against the Bill. On 7 June 1832 it received the Royal Assent. The battle was won.

In the reformed Parliament Althorp remained as Chancellor of the Exchequer and Leader of the House of Commons. In the first rôle his weakness as a speaker was a serious drawback. 'His financial statements, given out with endless humming and hawing, made his hearers quite nervous and uncomfortable,' R.H. Gronow wrote in his *Recollections*, but he added generous praise of Althorp in the capacity of Leader: 'He was possessed of great good sense, and was so upright and such a thorough gentleman that the reformed House of Commons, a difficult one to manage, had more confidence in him than they would have had in anyone else.'

Althorp was concerned with four important measures as well as the Budget which of course was his business as Chancellor. The first was an Irish Coercion Bill, which he introduced with reluctance, considering it to be too stringent. He had, however, high hopes of the second measure, the Irish Church Temporalities Bill, which abolished Church rates and cut down the number of Church of Ireland bishoprics from twenty-two to twelve, giving the revenues of the suppressed sees to charitable or educational purposes. The Catholic Irish had naturally resented the obligation to pay rates for the upkeep of an alien Protestant Church; and Althorp believed that the removal of this crying grievance would do much to lessen tension and to improve the general situation in Ireland. Both measures failed of their objectives. The Disturbances Act did nothing to put down disturbances, while the Irish Church Act had little or no effect upon the general atmosphere of mistrust and hatred which hung over Ireland like a pall. This Act had, however, one important and totally unpremeditated result. John Keble saw this harmless and indeed admirable measure as a serious encroachment by the State on the rights of the Church, and he made it the theme of his momentous Assize Sermon on National Apostasy. Unwittingly, Althorp had provided the spark which touched off the Oxford Movement.

His connection with another important movement was almost equally fortuitous. In 1833 Lord Ashley, later to be world-famous as Lord Shaftesbury, brought in a Ten Hours Bill limiting the hours of child labour in textile mills. Ashley was a Tory; the Government disliked his measure but, realizing that the question was a pressing one and that legislation of some sort was both necessary and inevitable, they decided to amend the Ten Hours Bill rather than bring in one of their own. On 18 July Althorp moved that thirteen be substituted for eighteen as the age at which the proposed restriction on hours ceased to operate. When this amendment was carried Ashley could only hand the Bill over to his opponents—'He found that the noble lord had completely defeated him; he therefore surrendered the Bill into the hands of the noble lord, but having taken it up with a view to doing good to the class intended, he would only say into whatever hands it passed, God bless it!' Although it fell far short of Ashley's intentions the Act did indeed prove a blessing to the factory children, limiting working hours for those under thirteen, introducing compulsory schooling, and establishing a body of inspectors to enforce its provisions. Althorp had no reason to be ashamed of the measure which bore his name although in fact it was Ashley's child.

Althorp's connection with a fourth important Bill was much less happy. By an irony of history this essentially kind-hearted man introduced into the House of Commons the new Poor Law Bill, one of the harshest measures ever passed by Parliament. In explanation and extenuation it should be pointed out that the pauperization produced by the existing system was a growing scandal. The Bill was aimed at the suppression of rampant abuses; and at the time few people realized how much suffering it would inevitably cause to the deserving poor. Some doubts seem to have crossed Althorp's mind for when proposing the abolition of

[138]

outdoor relief he remarked, 'We shall be charged perhaps with treating poverty as a crime; this is not our intention, but we cannot help its being a misfortune.' A misfortune poverty indeed became under the harsh provisions of the new Poor Law.

What makes the Whig ministry of 1832–1834 a unique phenomenon in British history is the fact that both the Prime Minister and the Chancellor of the Exchequer genuinely disliked office and yearned for a chance to retire into the pleasant obscurity of private life. 'My being in office is nothing more or less than a misery to me,' Althorp wrote to Brougham. 'I am perfectly sure that no man ever disliked it to such a degree as I do; and indeed, the first thing that usually comes into my head when I wake is how am I to get out of it.'

Even an ambitious man tenacious of political office might have found that membership of this particular Cabinet had considerable drawbacks. Brougham was a very trying colleague; and Althorp had stipulated that if he himself were to remain as Leader of the Commons his difficult friend must be removed to the Lords. This was done; but as Lord Chancellor Brougham was a constant thorn in the flesh to all the members of the Cabinet. Lord Durham, 'Radical Jack', was equally quarrelsome and contentious. He had married Grey's daughter, but that fact did not make him any the more polite or good-tempered. At one Cabinet meeting he reduced Grey to a state of near collapse while the kind-hearted Althorp sat with his face buried in his hands, unable to bear the sight of the Prime Minister wilting under this relentless bullying. Perhaps it was not altogether surprising that, in the words of Philip Ziegler, 'both Grey and Althorp courted defeat as a long-sought-for mistress.'

Their chance came in the spring of 1834, with the renewal of the Irish Coercion Act. Either through misunderstanding or through trickery—the matter is obscure—Althorp was deceived into believing that the more objectionable clauses in that act would be omitted, and he allowed this piece of misinformation to be passed on to the Irish leader, O'Connell. When the measure was introduced into the House complete with those clauses O'Connell rose in his wrath and accused Althorp of deliberate deceit. That most upright of men sat listening to this attack on his personal honour. 'The pig is killed,' he remarked to Lord John Russell, and forthwith sent in his resignation. Grey promptly followed suit. Their colleagues stood aghast; the Whig party was on the verge of collapse. Grey refused to be deflected from his intention of retiring permanently to his beloved home at Howick. Althorp, whose sense of duty was inconveniently strong, finally agreed to

[139]

THE BRADWELL OX.

The Bradwell Ox. Aquatint after the painting by H.B. Chalon, 1830. This aquatint of 'the greatest phenomenon of his species' was dedicated to the third Earl when Viscount Althorp. The illustration bears the Spencer arms.

absent himself from felicity awhile and to withdraw his resignation, but he would not be persuaded into taking Grey's place at the head of the Government, even as a temporary measure. Melbourne therefore became Prime Minister, and Althorp remained Chancellor of the Exchequer and Leader of the House.

Althorp was a lonely man; he had no one at home to whom he could turn for comfort and sympathy in these trials of political life. During the summer of 1834 he was seeing much of the widowed Lady Clinton, his cousin on the Poyntz side of the family. In September, with the warm approval both of his father and Mrs Acklom, he proposed marriage to her but she refused him. No other woman seems to have entered his life after Esther's death with the possible exception of a Mrs Wallace. She wrote him a series of wild, incoherent letters in which she addressed him as 'dearest benefactor'; and in his will he left her a large annuity. The obvious inference is that at some time or other she had been his mistress; but no evidence exists to prove what their real relationship may have been.

Althorp did not have to wait long for his release from office. During the brief time that remained to him in the House of Commons he saw its buildings go up in flame and smoke. On 16 October 1834 fire destroyed the Old Palace of Westminster. Watching the bungling efforts of the firemen fighting the blaze Members turned to their Leader as they had done in many another crisis, and begged him to take control. Althorp, however, refused to do so. 'I never saw a fire since I was five years old,' he replied with imperturbable good sense; 'and these men extinguish one every night. I suppose they understand what is to be done better than I do.'

On 10 November Lord Spencer died; and Althorp, henceforward himself to be called Lord Spencer, was translated into what he described as 'that hospital for incurables', the House of Lords. The bottom had fallen out of the Whig Ministry. To replace him as Chancellor of the Exchequer would not be difficult, but to find anyone with his gift for controlling the House of Commons was an impossibility. 'Without one showy accomplishment,' wrote Greville, 'without wit to amuse or eloquence to persuade, with a voice unmelodious and a manner ungraceful, and barely able to speak plain sense in still plainer language, he exercised in the House of Commons an influence, and even a dominion, greater than any Leader after or before him.' The slow-witted, slow-moving Althorp had become the one indispensable member of the Government: in Melbourne's phrase he was 'the tortoise on whom the world rests'.

Melbourne himself was prepared to try Lord John as Leader, but William IV would have none of him, being determined not to lose this heaven-sent opportunity to rid himself of the hated Whigs. 'Lord Spencer is dead, I hear,' he said to Melbourne. 'So is the Goverment; when the head is dead the body cannot go on at all. So you must all resign.' He therefore handed Melbourne a letter to be delivered to the Duke of Wellington, asking the Duke to form a Government.

Once again, through no wish or act of his own, Althorp had caused the downfall of a Prime Minister. As Brougham wrote to him, 'Because, and only because, you are removed from the House of Commons, the King turns us all out.'

[141]

To Spencer release from office was a foretaste of heaven, busy though he knew he must now be with the difficult and unpleasant task of restoring some order to the family finances. He was aware that for many years his father had lived far beyond his income, a state of affairs in which he himself had willingly acquiesced. 'Continue to live as you have been accustomed,' he had replied when Lord Spencer consulted him about possible economies. 'Let the task of retrenchment fall on me; I have no desire to keep up the state of a great nobleman and shall be prepared to live very economically.' How economically he was prepared to live he had now to demonstrate. Continuing to make Wiseton his headquarters he shut up Spencer House, sold off most of the Wimbledon property, and broke up the large establishment at Althorp, keeping only a few rooms open for occasional use. The deer-park he made over to more profitable grazing for sheep and cattle and the kitchen garden he turned into a market garden run by his head gardener.

The one extravagance he permitted himself was his herd of prize cattle; and here he would allow of no economies. His enthusiasm for these beasts was such that his addition to the magnificent collection of pictures at Althorp consisted of a series of portraits of his prize bulls. The farm at Wiseton was run more in the manner of an experimental research station than of a profit-making concern. Spencer was one of the early pioneers of Shorthorn cattle. The Wiseton herd was the largest and most successful of nineteenth-century strains, and it was in great part thanks to his efforts that this breed became the most popular one in Britain and remained so until the middle of the twentieth century.

In his liking for sheep and his knowledge of their ways he was perhaps a throwback to those early Spencers who had made their fortune as sheep-masters. He would spend long and happy hours seated on some grassy bank watching his flocks, recognizing each animal individually as a shepherd might, and conning over their good and bad points. His friend the Duke of Richmond was a high Tory who came round to supporting Reform. He was also a breeder of South Downs; and when the two men met they conversed together very happily about sheep rather than politics. Richmond and Spencer were co-founders of the Royal Agricultural Society whose motto was 'Science with Practice'. Spencer was at least as interested in agricultural science as he was in practical farming. As early as 1814 he had been studying the writings of Arthur Young in order 'to make myself a theorist in farming'. Now he fitted up a laboratory, and kept abreast of new discoveries in chemistry and biology. He experimented with different strains of seed and various nutritive compounds, and he raised rabbits for use in breeding experiments.

A Durham Ox, the property of Earl Spencer, exhibited at the Smithfield Show, 1835. Engraving by Walker after a drawing by W.H. Davies.

Believing as he did that 'the good that can be done by the application of chemistry to farming was incalculable' Spencer's great concern was to bring the benefits of agricultural science within the reach of the ordinary working farmer. He saw to it that the Royal Agricultural Society did not become a remote group of aristocrats and landowners but remained a farmers' society. Unless officiating as Chairman at its dinners he would sit not at high table but among the farmers with whom, of course, he was immensely popular. When inviting a duke to come to a meeting of the Smithfield club he wrote, 'We dine at the Crown and Anchor like farmers in boots.' He himself dressed like a farmer and thought of himself as one. When asked to become President of the Northamptonshire Farming and Grazing Society he declined, saying that he had joined as a tenant-farmer, not as the heir to the Althorp estate. A working farmer he certainly was; he would arrive at big agricultural shows before dawn and could be seen in his shirt-sleeves, pushing the animals into pens and sheds. He encouraged the development of these shows as occasions when farmers could exchange ideas, inspect new implements, and learn

[143]

about the most recent experiments in scientific agriculture. The show in the tiny village of Chapel Brampton which was of course his own personal concern drew visitors from as far away as Scotland.

Here on the Spencer estates conditions were very different from those prevailing in some other parts of the country.Although virtually all the tenants were on short yearly leases no problem ever arose as to security of tenure. Many of the farmers were members of families who had been in occupation of the same property for two or three hundred years. Down the generations the Spencers had become notable not only as able managers of their estates but as good and generous landlords; and what has been described as 'the sense of trust basic to the English landed system' had grown up and flourished between them and their tenantry. In this friendly atmosphere and busied with congenial country occupations Spencer came nearer to happiness than at any time since Esther's death; and no one could hope to lure him back to the treadmill of politics. Though he could no longer lead the House of Commons any other political office was open to him as a member of the House of Lords. On the fall of Peel's Ministry in the spring of 1835 his one-time secretary, Drummond, was sent to try to persuade him to take office under Melbourne. Spencer's reply was to point to the lambs gambolling outside the open window—'Nothing can induce me to leave them.'

Four years later in November 1838 he was offered the Lord-Lieutenancy of Ireland, a post held by two of his ancestors and more notably by one of his successors. Alternatively he was told that if he preferred he could become Governor-General of Canada. No such grandiose position could, however, lure him from his flocks and herds which at times took precedence even over the members of his own family. In May 1841 in order to reach Althorp in time to see the sheep just out of their wool after the shearing, he left London at dawn on the very day on which his sailor brother Frederick was expected home after a long absence abroad—'Of course all in good fellowship between them, only being *odd!*' commented his puzzled sister Sarah.

Spencer was never demonstrative of affection towards his friends and relations although he loved them well enough. 'We all know what depth of warm kindness there was in him,' Sarah wrote after his death, 'only he shut it up from most.' Like her mother before her Sarah could not resist the temptation to laugh at him and though her gentle humour could never wound that laughter may have raised a slight barrier between them. He was more at ease with Georgiana or 'Gin' who married Lord George Quin and died comparatively young. Her daughter Lavinia was Spencer's especial favourite in the family; with her and her alone, he could

[144]

relax and be openly affectionate as he had been with his beloved Esther.

One of Spencer's more intimate friends was John Grey of Dilston in Northumberland, father of the social reformer Josephine Butler. The two men corresponded about the Corn Laws and other economic questions affecting agriculture, matters on which they both held views far in advance of those of their fellow landowners and farmers. More frequently, however, their letters were concerned with the merits of Hector, Rhadamanthus, Duke, Flodden, Berwick, and the unaccountable faults in the progeny of these splendid bulls, Duke's son being born with a spot on the left side of his nose and Flodden's offspring tending to be not quite straight in the back. 'They used to laugh very much when they were together,' Josephine Butler told Spencer's biographer, 'and were like two boys in their eagerness about their pet bulls and rams.'

Not all of Spencer's time was given to farming and agricultural matters. Although Brougham would sometimes address him as 'Dearest of Graziers' or 'Dearest Man of Cattle' with this old friend Spencer would usually discuss more intellectual and abstract subjects. They wrote to one another frequently and at great length on such topics as the immateriality of the soul or the inspiration of the Bible. When dedicating his treatise on Natural Theology to Spencer Brougham declared that his friend had devoted much time and thought to the study of philosophy and religion.

So the years of contentment rolled by. Though he suffered from gout, an almost unavoidable disease among the gentlemen of that period, Spencer's good health and physical stamina had become proverbial. He seemed set to live to old age, yet in the summer of 1843 he made a curious remark to his nephew, George Lyttelton: 'I shall do this and that next year and the following year something else, and then I shall die.' This he said quite calmly as if he looked forward to the prospect which he saw before him with perfect equanimity and even with pleasure.

In December of this same year 1843 Spencer made a considerable stir when in a speech at a dinner at Northampton he declared himself to be in favour of the Repeal of the Corn Laws. He had never before stated his position so clearly; and even his phenomenal popularity with the farming community could not survive this public and unequivocal proclamation of views diametrically opposed to their own. He could not take the Chair at a meeting to promote the establishment of an Agricultural College at Cirencester, a project in which he was much interested, because his connection with it might damage its chances of success, and he was actually asked to resign from some of the Agricultural Societies to which he belonged. Of his own accord he withdrew from the Northamptonshire Society, as he told Milton, now become Lord FitzWilliam, in a letter characteristically optimistic and oblivious of self:

> I believe it was the only chance of enabling the Society to go on, and it is doing a great deal of good. The farmers have decided to carry it on and from what I hear from the leading men among them it is likely to prosper more than ever it has ever done, and they will still exclude all politics from it.

The excitement and interest provoked by his Northampton speech caused the supporters of Repeal, and among them FitzWilliam, to suggest to Spencer that if he would not take an active part in the Anti-Corn-Law agitation he might at least give them the benefit of his counsel and presence. In this same letter to FitzWilliam he gave his reasons for refusing this request:

> I do not think my presence in London would be of any use. When John Russell was with me at Althorp we had some little talk about Politics, and after a very short time agreed that I was so much withdrawn from the political world that my advice or opinion was not worth having. I suggested this and convinced him as I am convinced myself that it is the case. Then I have been so put forward in the newspapers lately that my going up to town for the meeting of Parliament would confirm people who do not know me in the belief which I think many appear to entertain that I really am going to put myself in the foremost ranks of the Anti-Corn-Law agitation, which would be extremely inconvenient to me and deprive me of any chance of regaining my influence in the agricultural world on which alone any power I have of usefulness depends. Taking the best view I can of my position I think the course I ought to take is to be as quiet as possible and not to let my name be mentioned as far as I can avoid it.

But although he refused to allow himself to become entangled in the Anti-Corn-Law movement, in June 1844, six months after writing to FitzWilliam, Spencer made one of his rare interventions in the House of Lords, speaking in support of the Maynooth College Bill, that measure which caused so much heart-burning to the young William Gladstone. For Spencer it was an opportunity to express once again his life-long belief in religious tolerance and his sympathy with the grievances of the Irish Catholics. In that same month the recently widowed Lady Holland, suffering grievously both in health and spirits, came to stay at Althorp.

'My host was so kind in his reception,' she recorded, 'so cheerful and pleasant all day long, that I really felt almost happy myself.'

Although he did not take a serious interest in racing Spencer liked to attend race-meetings and always entertained a party for the St Leger, an occasion which gave him a chance to see many of his local friends and neighbours. In 1845 he was for the first time appointed as Steward, and in order to be at hand if needed he decided to stay in Doncaster rather than at Wiseton. On the second day of the meeting he was suddenly taken ill with a disease which baffled the doctors. He rallied sufficiently to be able to return to Wiseton and to send a message to the parson to be read out at the Sunday service, 'Lord Spencer, having been delivered from the danger of immediate death, requests his fellow parishioners to join him in giving humble thanks to Almighty God.'

Death, however, was very near. Again he collapsed, and this time he knew there would be no recovery. He sent for his brother Frederick, who had been his heir since Robert's death from fever fifteen years previously, and with him discussed points of family business and went through his will. This done he insisted that Frederick should go to bed, refusing to allow anyone to sit up with him except one servant. During the night he called out to this man and when asked what he needed, pointed to a locket containing his wife's hair—'Give that to me. I promised her I would die wearing it.' He had never forgotten Esther or ceased to mourn for her. The light of his life had been extinguished by her death; yet to the hastily summoned doctor he could say, 'I have passed a happy life; I have been sensible of my faults; I prayed for grace and I received it,' and, once again, 'I am perfectly happy.' A look of joy was on his face when he died in the cold dark hours before dawn on the morning of 1 October 1845.

[5]

GEORGE SPENCER, FATHER IGNATIUS OF SAINT PAUL

'Spencer—my hand too coarse should fear to paint
The English noble and the Christian saint.'

Kenelm Digby.

Father Ignatius of St Paul. Engraving from *The Life of Father Ignatius* by Father Pius, Passionist, 1866.

When Jack Althorp was a boy no one had supposed that he would end up as the most respected politician of the day, a man who had twice refused the office of Prime Minister. An even more unexpected fate awaited his youngest brother. The metamorphosis of the Honourable and Reverend George Spencer into Father Ignatius of St Paul is one of the most surprising stories in the long history of the Spencer family.

Although no one suspected that he would become a Roman Catholic monk, from very early years George had known that he was destined to take Holy Orders, though of course in the Church of England. The prospect pleased him greatly. In 1810, when George was ten and his brother Frederick a year older, the two boys were told what their future careers were to be. Frederick was to become a soldier and George a country clergyman. Quiet, studious, and a lover of the countryside, George was as much pleased by the prospect before him as the more active, spirited Frederick was by the thought of army life. '*Il n'y a rien que j'aimerais autant que d'avoir un joli petit living, une maison à moi, où je puis vivre bien tranquille, et avoir soin de mon village,*' he wrote to his sister Sarah in very adequate French for a ten-year-old.

Sarah was the person in whom he naturally confided. From their earliest days she had delighted in mothering the two brothers whom she described as 'my two little sons, Fritz and George', reading to them, playing with them, riding with them, and giving them all the love and care which Althorp had so sadly missed in his childhood. She had a natural aptitude for teaching—'I know very well I was born to be a school mistress; I am never so completely pleased with any employment as that of hammering things into children's heads'— and she delighted in her task of instructing Frederick and George in the rudiments of History, French, English Literature and the Greek alphabet. After 1810 when they were both packed off to school she always looked forward with particular pleasure to the holidays and the return of 'the two dear boys from Eton'.

Thanks to Sarah George's childhood had been a happy one, but his schooldays were a time of almost unmitigated misery. The two boys were sent to board with a private tutor called Godley who lived about a mile from the school buildings. In order to preserve them from what George later described as 'the utter destruction of my morals' this pious and well-meaning man forbade them to linger with the other boys after school or chapel, but ordered them to come straight home to his house. Unfortunately their way lay across the playing-fields where in summer cricket practice would be in progress. The older boys had the right to stop any passing junior and fag him to field their balls. Poor George was on the horns of a terrible dilemma. If he refused to field he risked a nasty beating from the big boys, if he arrived back late he would be punished by Mr Godley. Frederick seems to have been made of sterner stuff, but little George, who described himself as 'a chicken-hearted creature, what in Eton language is called a *sawney*', went through daily agonies of alarm and fear. Yet he was not by nature cowardly. Like his eldest brother Althorp he had a bad seat on a horse, but while admitting that he was not really a good rider Sarah declared that when out riding he was afraid of nothing.

It was finally decided that Frederick should go into the Navy rather than the Army. At that period boys went to sea at a very early age, and he was therefore taken away from Eton, leaving George solitary and desolate, the one remaining resident pupil in the house. Pitying the boy's loneliness Godley treated him with unusual kindness and made him a constant companion. In later years George was to compare his own education unfavourably with that of the average Roman Catholic boy who would have been placed 'under the guidance of a tender spiritual father'. No complaint could have been less justified. A tender spiritual father was exactly what he had found in Godley who was himself a convinced Christian, and did his very best to foster any budding shoots of religion in his pupil. As Prebendary of Chester Cathedral he had to spend some time there each year 'in residence', and on one such occasion he took George with him to stay with his mother and sisters, devout ladies who lent the boy religious books and in his own words 'had no wish concerning me than to encourage me in becoming pious and good.'

Unfortunately the brand of Evangelicalism practised by the Godley family was not in favour at Althorp. For that reason George was removed from Godley's care and sent in September 1812 to an ordinary boys' house. Here his misery was extreme. Eton at that time was certainly a rough and tough place; George maintained that it was also a very immoral one. It is difficult to determine what exactly he intends to imply by his strictures; he hints at homosexuality—'a persecution as inveterate and merciless in its way as that which Lot had to bear at Sodom'—and he definitely mentions bad language; but the wicked deeds of which he actually accuses himself are not after all so very heinous. Egged on by his fellows, he robbed orchards as boys have done all down the ages, St Augustine of Hippo amongst them, and he stole ducks and hens from neighbouring farmyards, although as the son of a famous sporting landlord he seems to have stopped short of the far more reprehensible crime of poaching game.

In George's house there were very few juniors and the burden of fagging was therefore particularly heavy. This, however, was not his greatest trouble.

[150]

The school room, Eton College. Aquatint by Stadler after a drawing by Pugin in Ackermann's
History of the Colleges of Winchester, Eton and Westminster, 1816.

Doubtless he was a horrid little prig but he himself was not altogether to blame for
this. He might have been better prepared for public school life had he spent his
time as Althorp had done with grooms and gamekeepers rather than closeted with
the pious Mr Godley who in his eagerness to preserve his pupil's innocence had
succeeded in leaving him woefully ignorant. George simply did not understand the language the other boys used nor had he any idea as to what they were
talking about. He was one of those unfortunates who blush easily, and when
enlightened as to sin and sex in general he turned scarlet, much to the delight of his
tormentors. Night after night these boys would interrupt whatever employment
he might be engaged upon with his few chosen friends, wreck the room and

[151]

generally cause havoc. Even his fellow victims turned against him, blaming him 'for being so silly as to pretend ignorance of what their foul expressions meant for they could not believe it possible that I could really be so simple as not to understand them.'

In these circumstances it was not to be expected that George would make much progress in his work or find any real pleasure in cricket and the other sports at which he was later to become proficient. Instead he spent his time with a few boys as gentle and timid as himself, amusing themselves by catching minnows or building small shelters, childish ploys which they should have outgrown long ago. As George himself put it, 'my spirit was bent down when I was at Eton'.

If school was misery home was not so happy as it had been for Sarah was no longer there. She had officially 'come out' as long ago as 1805, making her curtsey to Queen Charlotte, and having her fill of balls, dinners, theatre-parties and that odd form of entertainment known as a breakfast which was in fact a garden party beginning in the afternoon and lasting well into the evening. Lavinia Spencer particularly enjoyed giving breakfasts in the beautiful gardens of Wimbledon Park (the house has vanished and the All-England Tennis Club now occupies the grounds), where some seven or eight hundred people would assemble to gossip, listen to the bands and dance on the lawns—'The numbers of people dressed in brilliant colours wandering about under trees and on the lawn and in the portico, the sounds of the different bands of music, the extreme beauty of the place, the profusion of roses and pinks in every part of the house and about it, and the sincere pleasure one saw on every countenance made it quite a delightful thing.'

Sarah much enjoyed these London gaieties, but she was equally happy at home at Althorp, reading serious books and teaching the village girls to do straw plaiting and satin stitch. 'All the girls here between eight and fourteen work at the straw work,' she proudly informed her grandmother, 'and they begin at their cottage doors at five o'clock in the morning.' Today a little girl set to work so early would seem a subject for concern rather than congratulation; but Sarah's contemporaries thought otherwise, perhaps because those of the poor who were not prepared to overwork almost certainly went underfed.

In 1812 Sarah was twenty-five, an age when an unmarried girl of her generation might begin to regard herself as an old maid. Although she had charming manners and a beautiful figure she was not a pretty girl nor was she what Hary-o called 'coming', an expression which might be rendered as 'come hither'. She was not unhappy nor had she any regrets for her one serious suitor, Sir Watkins Williams Wynne, who had taken himself off without making a proposal. When she was introduced to Althorp's friend, William Henry Lyttelton, she appeared rather scornful of this new acquaintance—'He is the most extraordinary mixture of brilliant wit, childish nonsense, frivolous small-talk, and a universal sort of scrambling information, which seems all to come out, whether he will or not, from an incessant flow of wild spirits. . . . I ought, to finish Mr Lyttelton's picture, to tell you that he dances out of time and is remarkably handsome.' She was, however, more interested in William Lyttelton than she would admit, or so at least some of her friends thought. When Lyttelton, distressed by his refusal by another lady, confided his woes to Lady Hood, she advised him to propose to Sarah—'I know she likes you and I am sure she would do it.'

Lyttelton promptly followed up this sensible suggestion. He invited himself to stay with the Spencers in their holiday house on the Isle of Wight, and there he fell in love with Sarah and she with him. They were married on 3 March 1812 and in the following June set out on a long tour of Sweden, Russia and Germany since the unsettled state of Europe precluded a more conventional honeymoon. They admired the beauties of distant Dalecarlia and the Swedish lakes, survived the rigours of a St Petersburg winter, and travelled home through a Germany where the ravages of war were still apparent. Returning to England just before Christmas 1814 they wandered from place to place before settling down to more than twenty years of married life.

In the year of the Lytteltons' return from abroad George was at last set free from the miseries of Eton. Perhaps disturbed by his lack of progress, perhaps sensing something of his unhappiness, his parents decided to take him away from school and to send him to a private tutor. He was told this joyful news immediately after his fourteenth birthday in December 1813, and although he had still to endure another year at Eton, knowing that a way of escape had opened he managed to find life there more tolerable. The man chosen as his tutor was Charles Blomfield, a country clergyman who later became well known as Bishop of London. Once settled at Blomfield's Buckinghamshire rectory George recovered his balance of mind and self-respect, developed his latent taste for books and book-learning, and returned to the religious practices which he had learnt from Godley.

In 1817 before going up to Cambridge, George spent a most enjoyable summer holiday with his family in the Isle of Wight. Now it was that he developed what he himself called a mania for cricket. His enthusiasm was the more surprising because it was his mother who had first suggested that he should take up the game. 'I remember generally,' he wrote years afterwards, 'that when anything in the way of amusement or serious occupation was suggested to me by her, or anything else but

The quadrangle of Trinity College, Cambridge. Aquatint by Bluck after a drawing by Westall in Ackermann's *History of the University of Cambridge*, 1815.

my own fancy, nothing more was required to make me have a distaste for it.' This time however the lure of the game proved too much for him, and he became, and remained for the rest of his life, a keen and skilful cricketer.

The only blot on this happy summer was a ridiculous 'affair of honour' which would have troubled nobody but the conscientious and over-sensitive George. He had developed a great liking for dancing, and at a ball he met the sister of one of his cricketing friends. Quite unintentionally, he caused some offence to this girl, whereupon her brother called him to account for his rudeness, threatening a duel. George consulted his father, who sensibly told him to write an apology and think no more about the matter. George, however, could not put it out of his mind. Much as he disliked the prospect of standing up to be shot at he almost equally disliked the disgrace of being thought lacking in courage, and for months he allowed this silly business to prey upon his mind and make him miserable.

On the whole the two years which George spent at Trinity seem to have been both pleasant and profitable. Later he was to bewail the 'great immorality' prevailing at Cambridge and this time he is more specific as to the meaning of that term. Apparently his college friends neither gambled, drank nor swore to any notable extent but, to quote his own discreet phrase, 'in our set any maintenance of chastity or modesty was altogether proscribed.' This statement is followed by two pages of contrite outpourings; and only at the end of these lamentations does the reader discover that George is not grieving for any lapse of his own but is bewailing the fact that he was kept from sinning by what he now believes to be unworthy motives.

George's career at Cambridge was in fact a reputable and reasonably successful one. True, he began by running up considerable debts, a predicament from which he was rescued by his kind brother Althorp, who had himself fallen into similar difficulties during his first year at the University. Apart from this one bout of extravagance he seems to have led a blameless life, amusing himself with cricket, tennis, and a little harmless whist and working harder than might have been expected. At first he deliberately idled, fearing that if he were seen to work the other men would despise him for a 'swot'. When he confessed this foolish notion to his mother she scolded him so roundly that, grown man though he was, he left the room in tears. He did very well in the College examinations and he even considered sitting for University Honours, but in the end he decided to avail himself of the privilege available to a nobleman's son, take an honorary degree and leave Cambridge at the end of his second year.

One evil legacy remained to George from his years at the University. Perhaps because of irregular hours, perhaps because, having no idea as to how to organize his time, he allowed spells of idleness to alternate with bouts of frenzied overwork, he began to suffer from attacks of biliousness, and, worse still, from fits of deep depression. He was never to get the better of this mental trouble and for the rest of his life he was to be, in his own words, 'a victim of the dumps'.

Cambridge was followed by a short spell of social life in London, made the more enjoyable to George by the presence of his brother Frederick, home on leave after a long period at sea. The hold which Lavinia Spencer had over these two grown men was an extraordinary one. She looked through their invitations, telling them which to accept and which to refuse; she expected them home at a fixed hour whenever they went to a ball or party, and if they were out too many nights in succession she made her displeasure perfectly plain.

In September 1819 George left England with his parents on the first stages of the Grand Tour. Travelling through France and Italy they reached Naples in time

St Mary's church, Great Brington. Drawing by George Clarke, *c*.1832.

to spend Christmas there with 'Nig', her husband Lord George Quinn, and their children. George was always to count the first few weeks of his stay in Naples as the happiest time of his life. He delighted in the sightseeing and social gaieties; but suddenly, without cause or reason, a cloud of depression, the blackest he had ever known, descended on him and blighted the remainder of his visit.

When his parents left to return to England George continued his tour, travelling all through Sicily and Italy, then going on to Germany and Vienna. Here a letter reached him telling him the elder of his two sailor brothers, Sarah's beloved Bob, had been killed in a duel in South America, and begging him to come home immediately to comfort his bereaved parents. At Calais he was met by the news that the story which was bringing him back to England was completely untrue and that Bob was alive and well. After a short stay at Althorp he set out again on his travels, this time to visit Nig who had settled with her husband and family in Switzerland. On the way there and again on the way back he stopped in Paris and visited the Opéra, where it chanced that on both occasions he saw a performance of *Don Giovanni*. In the improbable setting of the Paris opera house George experienced the first of the sudden conversions which were to alter the whole course of his life. As he watched the Don being dragged down into the flames of Hell he was visited by the appalling conviction that a similar fate awaited him unless he mended his ways, and there and then he determined to devote his whole life to religion.

At first George's change of heart made little perceptible difference to his way of life. After his return to England in November 1820 he made the best of both worlds, dancing, flirting, shooting and playing cricket, while at the same time preparing in real earnest for what one of his contemporaries described as 'this bother of ordination'. He visited his old tutor, Blomfield, now Rector of Whitechapel, where he met and talked with a group of clerics; he studied the art of sermon-writing by borrowing books from his brother Althorp who was in the habit of reading a sermon every Sunday afternoon; and he even went so far as to hire 'a dirty Jew master' to teach him Hebrew. These efforts received little or no encouragement from the Church authorities. When he wrote to the Diocesan Examiner enquiring what books he should read and what other steps he ought to take to prepare himself for Ordination that dignitary replied in tones calculated to damp any undesirable show of enthusiasm:

It is impossible that I should ever entertain any idea of subjecting a gentleman with whose talents and good qualities I am so well acquainted as I am with yours to any examination except one as a matter of form, for which a verse in the Greek Testament and an Article of the Church of England returned into Latin will be amply sufficient.

George Spencer was ordained deacon on 22 December 1822. Immediately he was put in charge of Great Brington, the parish in which Althorp was situated, this cure of some eight hundred souls having been left uncared for by an absentee parson. He continued to live at Althorp, an arrangement which mattered the less because the house was within easy walking distance of church and village and his parish was in some sense an extension of his family circle. Ever since childhood he had known and been known to the parishioners, nearly all of them being either Lord Spencer's tenants or workers on his estate. Every day, wet or fine, from dawn to dusk George was out visiting his people, an occupation which he described rather improbably as 'very amusing to me'. Finding that many of the village

[157]

children were unbaptized he saw to it that their parents brought them to him for baptism and he constantly urged the parishioners to come more frequently to Communion. Although he joined gladly enough in family gaieties at Althorp he gave up dancing and shooting; in short he became a model specimen of a pious and hard-working young clergyman.

At this period of his life George might have been described as a High Churchman of the type which the Tractarians were to mock at as 'High and Dry'. He was, however, always to be given to sudden changes of front; and now an evening's conversation with a theological scholar who chanced to be staying at Althorp was enough to convince him of the errors of High Church doctrine and practice and to turn him back again to the Evangelicalism which he had learnt from Mr Godley. This change was accompanied by the onset of serious doubts as to the truths of Christianity and of Anglican Christianity in particular. Like many eminent nineteenth-century characters, Queen Victoria and Lord Shaftesbury among them, George found the Athanasian Creed a great stumbling block. Try as he might he could not resolve his doubts, but he took refuge from them in good works and in the practice of asceticism. He attended hospitals and dispensaries in order to learn enough about medicine to be able to help his sick parishioners, doing so well that on one occasion he was able to set a broken thigh, and he began to practise fasting, although his efforts in this direction evoked cries of horror at Althorp. Naturally he attempted to keep his abstinence a secret both from the family and the servants, and on one occasion he concealed his breakfast tray in a cupboard, only to be betrayed by a penetrating smell of hot toast. Young men anxious to mortify the flesh seem to have found toast a particular stumbling-block; Sir James Stephen poked unkind fun at Hurrell Froude's 'contrite reminiscences of an undue indulgence in buttered toast'.

George Spencer was priested on Trinity Sunday 1824, and a few months later, the absentee incumbent having retired, he became Rector of Great Brington. 'It is quite comical to see him followed by his flock, and guiding them so gently, but so decidedly and so firmly as he does,' Lavinia Spencer wrote with unusual tenderness. 'He don't allow any deviation from the right path, but he only desires what he does himself. And his earnestness is truly persuasive; but when I see his authority amongst them it strikes me in the oddest way, for I can't believe that this excellent and grave character is the boy whom I remember so little a while since a little ragamuffin hobbledehoy.'

So ardent an Evangelical had George become that he corresponded at great length with like-minded Evangelicals in all parts of the country, and he even took it upon himself to reprimand fellow clergymen whom he considered lacking in zeal. On one occasion he landed himself in real trouble by reporting to his diocesan a parson who had refused to pay any attention to his remonstrances. Another bishop rebuked him kindly but firmly for his uncalled-for interference—'Amidst a great deal that is excellent and of right spirit in your observations there is a presumption and self-confident tone which is altogether new in you, and in my opinion not very consistent with real humility.'

George's parents were equally disturbed and disapproving. Lavinia Spencer, always one for firm action, dragged him to London in January 1826 and handed him over to Blomfield, now Bishop of Chester, as the person best capable of making him see reason. As George's biographer was to write, 'his obedience to directors of all kinds was remarkable; but the results were invariably contrary to their expectations.' Now, instead of allowing Blomfield to lead him back into the paths of High Church orthodoxy he lectured the bishop himself on the error of his beliefs, pointing out that he would have little hope of salvation unless and until he underwent the process of evangelical conversion. Blomfield must have been considerably taken aback when, on inviting George to preach one Sunday afternoon, he found himself listening to a fervent exposition of Evangelicalism, and heard the preacher tell his congregation that it was clear they were not accustomed to hear the Gospel fully and faithfully expounded. 'George, how could you preach a sermon like that?' was Blomfield's mild protest. 'In future I must look over your sermon before you go into the pulpit.'

When George returned from London still a convinced Evangelical and with his religious doubts unresolved both his parents wrote him letters of kindly advice. Lord Spencer, who remained a man of the eighteenth century as far as religion was concerned, warned him against 'the effects of too intense an application to the more difficult and abstruse points of religion which, if not under the corrective guidance of greater learning and experience than it is possible yet for you to have, might lead into the wildness of enthusiasm instead of the sensible and sound doctrine which it becomes an orthodox minister of the established Church to hold for himself and to preach to others.' Lavinia Spencer, not herself notable for gentleness, begged him to adopt a more gentle attitude—'It never can do to terrify into doing right'—and ended with the sensible caution, 'Do not permit yourself to judge uncharitably of the motives of others because their religious sentiments are not always floating on the surface of their words and actions.'

His family now came to the conclusion that matrimony might be the best cure for George's eccentricities; and George himself was in favour of the idea. He needed a mistress for the fine new rectory he had built at Brington and when on a visit to a clerical friend he chanced to meet one of his old flames he fixed on her as his intended bride. Driving to Althorp to ask his father's permission before proposing to her he underwent another of his sudden changes of heart. There and then he formed a resolution to remain permanently celibate, and, leaning out of the carriage window, he ordered the coachman to turn round and drive straight home to Brington.

There, in spite of his strict evangelical views, his parishioners found nothing to complain of in their Rector; on the contrary, they loved him for his obvious devotion to their interests and for his boundless charity. He tramped all over his parish with a bottle of wine in one pocket and a handful of coins in another to give to the sick and the poor. He would give his own clothes to a beggar, and he stinted himself of food, not simply because he wished to practise fasting but because he would thus have more to give away. Whenever he could he walked rather than rode, carrying his necessities in a knapsack, and when passers-by laughed at him, he would remark with a smile that he was merely following the practice of the Apostles. As Lord Spencer lamented, he was not likely to obtain any preferment in the Church, his Evangelicalism being a great stumbling-block, but he himself seemed perfectly content to remain a hard-working and reasonably happy Rector of Great Brington.

Suddenly, in December 1827, all this fell in pieces about him. His old doubts about the Athanasian creed revived with redoubled force, and he convinced himself that the only honest course would be to resign his living. His decision was as usual a hasty one—'I solemnly affirm that before last week I had no sort of idea of taking this step.' His mind made up, he wrote at once to his father and to Bishop Blomfield informing them of his decision. At last Blomfield's patience gave way. 'The letter which I have just received from you astonishes and confounds me,' he wrote, 'not that I ought to be surprised at anything strange which you may do, after what I have lately witnessed and heard; but I must say, in plain terms, that your letter is the letter of an insane person.' George, in his turn, dismissed the Bishop's reply as 'weak and flippant'.

Lord Spencer was a sensitive man who dreaded the idea of a face-to-face confrontation with his exasperating son. Instead he wrote a letter in which he stressed his own grief and disappointment should George abandon the career for which he had seemed so well suited, and begged him to consult yet another learned clergyman. George did so, but remained unconvinced, and finally sent in his resignation to the Bishop of Peterborough which, however, the Bishop refused to accept.

[160]

For two years George continued in a state of doubt and uncertainty. Previously he had approved of none but practising Evangelicals, but now he corresponded with people of every shade of religious opinion, including Edward Irving, founder of the Catholic Apostolic Church, and an anonymous correspondent in Lille, who purported to be a gentleman grievously troubled by the arguments in favour of Popery but who was in fact a Miss Dolling, a recent convert to Roman Catholicism. George himself showed some interest in that Church but he seemed moved by curiosity rather than conviction and in February 1829 he preached an anti-Popery sermon so violent as to call down a rebuke from Lord Spencer, a strong supporter of Catholic Emancipation. A rich young man called Ambrose Phillipps, heir to great estates in Leicestershire, had recently caused some stir by turning Roman Catholic at the early age of fifteen. George was much intrigued by his story, and wished to discover what argument might have persuaded Phillipps to take such an unusual step. Towards the end of 1829 the local Roman Catholic priest introduced him to the young man, still only seventeen. The two talked together for five hours, with the result that George was invited to spend some days at the Phillipps' family home near Loughborough. On 24 January 1830 he left Great Brington intending to return in time to preach the following Sunday. Sunday came, but George was not in the pulpit. That morning he had been received into the Church of Rome.

The Spencer family took this most surprising of all George's lightning changes with commendable calm. They were all too well aware of the unsettled state of his religious opinions; as Sarah wrote, 'Such has been his state of uncertainty and doubt and unfixity upon all but practical piety that we had no reason to be surprised by this last fatal change.' Lavinia Spencer put on mourning; but Lord Spencer, considerate and kind as ever, made clear to George that he would still always be welcome at Althorp as a son of the house, and gave him a capital sum of money as well as an annuity large enough to compensate for the loss of his clerical stipend. Althorp, who was himself a deeply religious man, took the matter more to heart, and for a time a rift opened between the two brothers. Their estrangement, however, proved merely temporary; and the unusually liberal-minded attitude of his family greatly surprised George's new Roman Catholic associates.

George was more fortunate than the many Anglican clergy who were later to go over to Rome in the wake of Newman and Manning. Not only did he not suffer financially because of his change of religion but, being a bachelor, he was not barred from taking Roman Catholic orders. With this in view he spent the next two years in the English College at Rome. Here he saw much of the Rector, Nicholas

Wiseman, afterwards Cardinal Archbishop of Westminster. George Spencer had that aristocratic self-confidence which is not in the least incompatible with Christian humility. If anyone rebuked him he took it with the utmost meekness, but he in his turn saw no reason why he might not rebuke all and sundry, even his superiors. A raw convert, newly arrived in the College and at the very beginning of his studies for the priesthood, he spoke his mind freely to the Rector, bidding him apply himself to something more practical than the study of Syrian manuscripts or treatises on geology. Wiseman took George's scoldings in good part; and indeed it was difficult for anyone to remain angry for long with this endearing eccentric.

George was priested in March 1832 and in July of that year returned to England to spend a summer holiday in the Isle of Wight with his family, who received him with open arms. Wiseman also happened to be in England; and Lord Spencer went so far as to invite him to spend the day at Althorp. In November George was appointed priest-in-charge of the newly opened Roman Catholic church at West Bromwich. Here he lived as a poor man among the very poorest of the poor. A seminary would not seem to be a place where it was easy to overspend, but in spite of his frugal way of life, when George left the English College in Rome he was seriously in debt. 'He has little idea as to the management of money,' Wiseman wrote to Bishop Walsh, Vicar General of the Midland District which included West Bromwich, 'and is easily imposed on and has the impression that all are as candid and sincere as himself.' When it was arranged that George should pay off these debts by quarterly instalments not only did he find it impossible to keep up the payments but he ran up considerable debts in England, not through extravagance but through sheer inability to refuse charity to anyone who asked it of him. To extricate him from these entanglements Bishop Walsh took over the management of the generous allowance paid him by his father, returning to him a sum sufficient only for necessities. His day-to-day life was very similar to his life as an evangelical parson at Great Brington. He spent much time in private devotion and nearly all the daylight hours he gave to the business of visiting his parishioners. As he had done at Brington he walked everywhere rather than incur the expense of a cart or carriage (saddle-horses were not for Roman Catholic priests). He gave his clothes away to beggars, and he stuffed his pockets with bottles of wine for the sick. Great Brington, however, had been a tidy, prosperous village where he was greeted everywhere with respect as Rector and Lord Spencer's son; now ragamuffin boys hooted at him in the streets, pelted him with mud and stones, and even attempted to rip the coat off his back.

George was completely unruffled by these trials. The doubts which had troubled him so sorely had vanished never to return, and in the Roman Catholic Church he had found a type of religion exactly suited to his temperament. The only problem which seriously disturbed him was his relationship with his family. All went well until Lord Spencer's death in 1834. As a matter of course the new Earl continued to pay George's annuity and welcomed him warmly to Althorp, but he forbade him to visit any of his old parishioners, fearing that he might attempt to unsettle their religious views. This, of course, was precisely what George had intended doing, but he was none the less distressed and hurt by the prohibition. The same problem soon arose at Hagley, where Sarah and her husband were now living. They had behaved to him with what in the 1830s was unprecedented broadmindedness. When in the summer of 1835 he had fallen ill through overwork not only did they carry him off to Hagley to be properly nursed but they attended to his spiritual needs as well as to his physical ones. When he was sufficiently convalescent they took him over to mass at Stourbridge, and went so far as to invite another Roman Catholic priest to stay in the house to keep him company.

George, however, could not match tolerance with tolerance. Profoundly happy in his new faith, his one idea was to try to bring other people to share in his happiness, and he even went so far as to try to convert his brother-in-law. The result was that at Hagley as at Althorp he was welcomed only on condition that he never opened his mouth on religious topics. This prohibition went so much against the grain that, regretfully, George decided that his visits to his family must cease. Separation from Sarah was particularly grievous to him; and he was deeply distressed when on William Lyttelton's death in April 1837 he could not go to Hagley to comfort the sister who had meant so much to him.

Much of the capital sum which his father had given to George went to help pay for new schools and churches. He was specially interested in the building of a church at Dudley and in order to collect funds for this project he went up to London to beg money from old friends and acquaintances. He even went so far as to approach the Duchess of Kent, undeterred by her staunch Protestantism or by her royal connections which, to tell truth, seemed no great obstacle to the son of a Whig peer. The Duchess received him in company with her young daughter, the future Queen Victoria. George was loud in praise of the kindness and courteous attention shown him by both ladies, although he did not say whether or not they gave him any money. He was always much given to wishful thinking, which maybe is another way of saying that he had unquestioning faith, and in later years he came to believe that the Duchess had died a convinced though undeclared Roman Catholic.

Augustus Welby Pugin (1812–52), artist and architect. Painting by an unknown artist, c.1840.

In 1838, almost casually, George Spencer began the work which was to become his overmastering occupation and interest. Acting on doctor's orders, in the summer of that year he went on a holiday to France with Ambrose Phillipps. There he met the Archbishop of Paris and in the course of conversation suggested that French Catholics might make a point of offering special prayers for the conversion of England. The Archbishop took up this idea with enthusiasm, arranging for George to address meetings of clergy and to visit religious houses in order to beg for such prayers. On returning home George pursued this quest with ever-increasing zeal, begging prayers from all and sundry. Since he was Lord Spencer's son his activities had a certain news value; and when comments began to appear in the newspapers the Roman Catholic bishops took alarm. They were all for the conversion of England but they wished to set about it in a tactful, discreet manner in order to avoid arousing anti-Popery prejudice. One bishop, Barnes, went so far as to forbid public prayers for this object. In his usual manner, George accepted the rebuff with Christian meekness and continued to behave exactly as he had done before.

About this time George had an odd encounter with the architect Augustus Welby Pugin, who was as anxious for the revival of the 'Gothick' style which he believed to be the only truly 'Catholick' one as ever George could be for the restoration of what he in his turn believed to be the only true Catholic faith. George himself cared nothing for the niceties of ecclesiology. One evening he took Benediction wearing a vestment of the Roman rather than the Gothick type. Pugin

Oscott College, Sutton Coldfield. Contemporary engraving, *c*,1840.

chanced to be in the congregation, and after the service was over he came storming into the vestry—'How do you think you will ever succeed in converting England if you persist in wearing such a cope?'

In May 1839, after seven years of hard but rewarding work at West Bromwich, George Spencer was moved to Oscott College, part school, part seminary for the training of priests. Here his special work was to be 'the spiritual care of the students, in order that he might shape their characters and infuse into them that apostolic spirit of which he had already given such proofs.' He also coached them at cricket.

Very soon the students at Oscott learnt to love George dearly, and to laugh at him a little. His commitment to religion was total, his faith childlike but spiced with a very gentle humour. Nothing surprised him; when someone expressed astonishment at happenings verging on the miraculous he replied, 'After all, our Lord's words do deserve a little attention.' (Years later, in similar circumstances,

[165]

his great-niece remarked, 'You should never be surprised when the Holy Ghost plays up.') His simplicity was baffling; and his other-worldliness could disconcert lesser mortals. One day out shooting a student accidentally hit an old woman who later died of her injuries. The student was much alarmed to receive a summons to appear at the inquest; and George attempted to console him, pointing out that as he had not intended to hit the woman he was innocent of any sin or crime, and should therefore regard reproof or punishment as a trial sent by God. 'But they might transport me,' the poor boy protested. 'Beautiful, beautiful—fine field for missionary work among the convicts!' Unattracted by this prospect the boy exclaimed, 'They might even hang me!' 'Glorious sacrifice—in satisfaction for your sins—glorious sacrifice!'

George Spencer's weapon was love, not logic. He was no scholar and not much of a theologian; when he was rash enough to engage in controversy with William Palmer of Worcester College at Oxford that learned Anglican made mincemeat of his arguments. George's dealings with Oxford and the Tractarians were not very happy. Professor Chadwick has described how he and Ambrose Phillipps 'bubbled over with unquenchable optimism about the goal of the Oxford Movement.' They were convinced that the Movement would not merely produce individual conversions but would result in the submission of the whole body of the Church of England to the See of Rome; and the reports which they sent to the Vatican seriously misled the authorities there. In point of fact George Spencer had little or no contact with the Tractarian leaders. He never saw either Keble or Pusey, while Newman refused to meet him at dinner, saying that he considered it wrong to dine with a 'schismatic'. In adopting this uncompromising attitude Newman was only following the example of his mentor Keble, who remarked of a friend turned Roman Catholic, 'I could not have him to dine; I should consider it scandalous in respect of the servants.' (Newman, however, agreed to meet George privately and behaved to him in so friendly a manner as to leave him positively bewildered.) The two men were to meet again several years later in curious circumstances. After his reception into the Church of Rome Newman went to Oscott to be confirmed. On arrival he was shown into a small room where he waited rather apprehensively for someone to come to greet him. The door opened; in walked Wiseman and the schismatic with whom he had refused to dine. Embarrassment was mutual.

In 1842 George Spencer paid his first visit to Ireland, a country he was to visit many times in the course of his quest for prayers for the conversion of England. He believed that since the Irish had suffered so much at the hands of the English their charity in praying for their oppressors would give a special value to their prayers. The Irish were perfectly willing to pray but on their own terms. On one of his later visits, after Pope Pius IX had attached an Indulgence to the saying of three Aves for the conversion of England, George was accosted in the street by an old Irish woman who told him with pride that every day she said those three Aves. Delighted to find such a strong supporter of his schemes, he suggested that she might persuade some of her friends to do likewise. 'What? Me ask people to pray for England?' came the indignant reply. 'I pray myself for the sake of the Indulgence, but I curse the English three times a day to be sure they get no good from my prayers.'

Two years after this Irish journey George Spencer again went abroad with Ambrose Phillipps. This trip, like their previous one, was planned as a holiday for the benefit of George's health, but it turned into a begging pilgrimage. The party were abroad for over three months; and wherever they went, France, Belgium, Germany, Italy, Austria, Switzerland, George busied himself calling on bishops and church dignitaries, talking with parish priests, preaching, which he could do reasonably well in four languages, and, in his own neat phrase, canvassing convents.

During this continental holiday George went into retreat with the Jesuits at Louvain and followed the Spiritual Exercise of St Ignatius, with the result that for the first time he seriously considered 'entering religion'. Hitherto he had always thought that parish priests rather than monks were the most effective instruments for the conversion of England, and that it was therefore his duty to remain a parish priest. For the moment he put the idea from him, but it recurred again when he made another retreat at a Jesuit house in England and for a second time followed the Spiritual Exercises. Having come to the conclusion that he must become a monk it only remained to choose the religious Order that he would enter. As usual, his decision was made at lightning speed. Naturally he inclined towards the Jesuits, and for a whole day he hesitated between them and the Institute of Charity, an Order specially favoured by Ambrose Phillipps; then in a flash he saw that neither of these Orders would be right for him and that he must become a Passionist.

By a strange quirk of destiny this Order, which was based on Italy and at this period consisted almost entirely of Italians, had been for some time actively engaged in the effort to convert England. Their Provincial, Father Dominic, was the priest who received Newman into the Roman Church. This aspect of their work may have commended them to George Spencer, who would also have been attracted by their reputation for strictness and austerity.

His decision to become a Passionist changed George's financial position. All the capital given him by his father had gone to pay for the building of the church at Dudley and for the buying of more land for Oscott College. There remained the three hundred pound annuity left him in trust and a second annuity also of three hundred pounds, which was conditional on the goodwill of his next of kin. When the third Earl died in 1845 Frederick succeeded, Bob having died at Alexandria in 1830. The news that George was about to become a monk was too much for Frederick to stomach. He saw no reason why in these circumstances he should continue to support Popery, and he stopped George's annuity but, being an upright man and disliking the idea of benefiting personally from the money, he gave it all away to charity. He also generously took upon himself the payment of forty-five pounds to a pensioner whom George would no longer be able to help. Since George's remaining annuity was already in the hands of his bishop he had his wish and entered the Passionist order *in forma pauperis*.

On 21 December George Spencer entered St Michael's Retreat, Aston, as a postulant and a fortnight later he was clothed as a novice. His experience there was not of a kind to give him an over-romantic view of the life of a Religious. The house contained only four professed monks, all of them Italian, and not one of them able to make himself understood in English. The middle-aged son of an earl who was henceforward to be known as Father Ignatius of St Paul, slept on a bed of straw, ate poor and scanty food, and suffered severely from cold, chilblains, and homesickness. He struggled with such domestic tasks as scrubbing a rusty iron staircase, and very badly did he do them, calling down upon himself many a severe rebuke. Towards the end of the first year of his noviciate the neighbourhood of Aston was invaded by a horde of penniless Irish peasants fleeing from the horrors of the Great Famine. Fever broke out amongst them; and, regardless of the danger of infection, the Passionist Fathers devoted themselves to the task of caring for the sick and dying. Father Ignatius caught the disease in its very worst form and was given up for dead, but against all expectation he recovered. It is pleasant to note that Frederick Lord Spencer, who disapproved so strongly of the Passionists and all their doings, nevertheless came generously to his brother's assistance and paid all the doctors' bills.

On 6 January 1848 Father Ignatius took his final vows and became a fully professed member of the Passionist Order. From now onwards he was to be chiefly occupied in taking missions in many different parts of the British Isles, a work which fitted very well with his self-chosen task of begging for prayers for the conversion of England. As a missioner he was a great success. Like his brother Althorp of the Reform Bill, the third Earl Spencer, Father Ignatius was a poor speaker. On one occasion when he was walking up and down in an abstracted manner before going into church to preach a sermon his Superior gently rallied him, 'Well, whatever are you thinking about?' 'I am praying that, if it be for the glory of God, my sermon may be a complete failure as far as human eloquence is concerned.' If any prayer could be counted unnecessary this one surely was. He was incapable of preaching a good sermon, but he had a genius for the informal talk; and this gift, combined with his ability to get into close and immediate touch with individuals made any mission he conducted a memorable and moving occasion.

Father Ignatius was a strange sight on his journeys up and down the country. He scorned any form of trunk or suitcase, packing his few possessions into two sack-like bags made of blue drugget. With these slung over his shoulder he tramped the roads, accepting any proffered lift and on the same principle eating what food might be given him or if none was offered, begging a meal at some roadside house. When obliged to take the train on longer journeys he invariably travelled third class. An irate friend, after searching in vain for this son of an earl through all the first and second class compartments exclaimed crossly, 'Why ever do you travel third class?' 'Because there is no fourth.'

Father Ignatius' clothes, usually second-hand ones, were threadbare, much patched, and very dirty. It was not customary for priests or monks to wear their distinctive dress out of doors, but hearing that the Oratorians had begun to go about in their cassocks he decided to follow their example and wear his Passionist habit all day and every day. Dressed in a long black cassock, an enormous cape embroidered with the emblems of the Passion, woollen shoes like bedroom slippers (a great grievance these, because but for his chilblains he would have much preferred to wear the traditional sandals), and on top of all what his sister described as 'an inordinate hat', he presented himself to Sarah Lyttelton, now acting as governess to Queen Victoria's children. Wisely, she had arranged to meet him at her own London house rather than at Buckingham Palace—'I don't want to figure in a paragraph, and so novel a sight in the Palace might lead to some such catastrophe.' She may have had another and more private reason for her choice of meeting-place. Cleanliness came a poor second to godliness in Father Ignatius' estimation; and after a previous visit he had paid her she had been obliged to open all the windows.

On this occasion she was delighted to find him 'better and happier than for years, and his manner, if possible, more strikingly gentlemanlike and calm than ever.' He asked Sarah to pray for 'unity in the truth', brushing aside her objection that he and she disagreed as to the meaning of truth and unity. Father Ignatius saw no reason why he should not ask Anglicans to pray for their own conversion. A few days after his visit to Sarah he called upon no less a person than the Prime Minister Lord John Russell. Lord John was not much given to prayer or to any outward show of religion. 'It conduces much to piety,' he was once heard to remark, '*not* to go to church sometimes.' However, he listened patiently to Father Ignatius, whom he had known long ago as George Spencer, and he was polite enough to say that 'anything which would tend to a diminution of the spirit of acrimony and of the disposition of people of opposite opinions to misrepresent one another's views, must do good.'

The following year, 1851, Father Ignatius tackled a much tougher subject in Lord Palmerston. The two men had first met thirty years previously when Palmerston had found George Spencer stranded at the close of a stag-hunt and had given him a lift home in his post-chaise. Now he listened to Father Ignatius with no great show of interest and not surprisingly replied 'with something sarcastic in his tone', saying that he had no wish to see England brought once again under the influence and domination of Rome. However, he was kindness itself on parting, remarking how glad he was to have had this opportunity of renewing old acquaintance.

In spite of the strength of the prejudice against Roman Catholics those who had known George Spencer were invariably delighted to meet Father Ignatius. Old friends who ran across him in the street would greet him with joyful cries of recognition. During the great outburst of anti-Popery feeling following the establishment of the Roman Catholic hierarchy in England followed by Wiseman's flamboyant and foolish pastoral, 'From out the Flaminian Gate', and Lord John Russell's equally foolish open letter to the Bishop of Durham, Father Ignatius was once or twice assaulted in the street by Protestant strangers provoked by the sight of his Passionist habit (in 1852 the wearing of such distinctive dress was formally forbidden), but as a general rule he was treated with the greatest consideration and kindness by people in every rank of society and of all religious persuasions. No one who knew this gentle, eccentric man could fail to remember him with admiration, amusement, and genuine love; in Dean Liddon's more formal phraseology, 'his memory can never be recalled without reverence and affection by those who had the happiness of knowing him.'

These feelings were shared to the full by those Passionists who came under his charge although in some respects his rule over them left much to be desired. At different times Father Ignatius was Superior of various Passionist houses, or Retreats as they were usually called, and for a while he filled more exalted positions, on the death of Father Dominic in 1849 becoming for a short time head of the English Province, which included Belgium, and later acting as Consultator or adviser to his successors in the office of Provincial. Admirable though Father Ignatius was at the personal and spiritual side of a Superior's work, as an administrator he was much less happy. Not only was he gullible and easily deceived; he lacked order and method, and he was incapable of dealing with money matters. Accounts meant nothing to him and accounts as he kept them meant nothing to those responsible for the Order's finances. His biographer describes him as 'a sage in spirituals but the very reverse in temporals', adding the comment, 'He had too little of the serpent in the Gospel sense to make a good Superior.'

Even when acting as the Superior of a religious house Father Ignatius spent much of his time away on missions or travelling about the world to collect promises of prayers for the conversion of England. His zeal for this cause took him all over the British Isles and into many European countries. In Rome he sought an audience with the Pope to ask for an Indulgence to be attached to such prayers, and in Austria he succeeded in obtaining an interview with the young Emperor Francis Joseph. When walking in the streets of Cologne on one of these journeys he ran across his brother Frederick, who at first had great difficulty in recognizing the oddly-dressed figure approaching him. 'Hello, George!' he at length exclaimed. 'Whatever are you doing here?' 'Begging,' came the answer.

So obsessed did Father Ignatius become by his campaign for prayers for the conversion of England that some good Catholics began to express doubts as to his sanity. Hearing of this, he sought to prove himself sane by writing to a Catholic newspaper a letter so long and so very odd that anyone reading it might well suppose the writer to be out of his mind. In fact, though perfectly sane, Father Ignatius was so simple and so saintly as to appear unbalanced when judged by ordinary worldly standards. Sarah's grandson, Albert Lyttelton, was just such another holy innocent; and a remark made about the great-nephew applies equally well to the great-uncle. Albert's sister, Hester Alington, a woman remarkable both for her wit and her sanctity, when asked to describe her brother replied, 'Well, he wasn't quite like other people,' then, catching herself up, added, 'Oh, not like *that*! I only mean that he couldn't tell the difference between this world and the next.'

For Father Ignatius the veil between the two worlds was wearing very thin. He was saddened by the death of his brother Frederick in 1857 but greatly cheered by

[171]

the kindness and affection shown by Frederick's son. John Poyntz, fifth Earl Spencer, was genuinely fond of his Uncle George, restoring his second annuity to him, visiting him at St Joseph's Retreat, the Passionist house at Highgate, and inviting him several times to stay at Althorp. On one of these occasions Father Ignatius attended a big dinner for the local Volunteers at which all the other guests were in uniform. After dinner at his nephew's request he stood up and made a rousing patriotic speech in which he referred to the Passionist habit which he was of course wearing as his own uniform.

The return to Althorp, the home which had been closed to him for so long, did much to cheer Father Ignatius's later years. Though not yet seventy he frequently spoke as if he knew that death was not far away. During a mission which he conducted at Greenock in September 1864 the priest who was his host noticed that although he would talk quite cheerfully of the twenty years of work still before him he could not altogether hide his physical fatigue or the mental depression which had dogged him throughout his life. Leaving Greenock he took another mission at Coatbridge, then on 1 October set out for Leith where he was to take yet another mission. On the way there he had to change trains at a junction close to Carstairs House, the home of his friend and fellow convert, Alexander Monteith. Although he had already arranged to spend a few days with Monteith in the following week he apparently now decided that rather than spend some hours at the station waiting for the incoming train he would walk up to the house and pay an unexpected call. In the park he met a little girl and enquired of her the way to the front door. Not long afterwards Monteith and a friend, when about to go shooting, were stopped by an agitated servant who told them that a priest lay dead in a path just off the main avenue. Hurrying to the spot, they turned the body over. The features were contorted beyond recognition but going through the pockets in search of some means of identification, they found that the dead man was George Spencer, Father Ignatius.

6

SARAH
LADY LYTTELTON

'Governess of England.'
George Lyttelton's name for his mother.

Sarah, Lady Lyttelton. Miniature painting by an unknown artist.

[173]

William, third Baron Lyttelton.
Miniature painting by Henry Bone.

Of the six Spencer brothers and sisters Sarah was now the only one left alive, and she was a widow. Her married life had been happy but uneventful. On returning from their adventurous honeymoon Sarah and William Lyttelton did not settle in a home of their own but for ten years wandered from place to place, sometimes renting a house for a short period, sometimes staying with relations. Their peripatetic way of life was the more surprising because Sarah devoted herself entirely to the business of bearing and rearing a family; and children are best brought up in a permanent home. Five children were born to the Lytteltons between 1816 and 1821, Caroline, George, Spencer, William and Lavinia. By Lyttelton standards this was a small family; but after giving birth to five children in as many years without benefit of twins Sarah seems to have decided that enough was enough, and contemplating the large brood produced by her sister-in-law, Caroline Pole-Carew, declared that she did not '*mean* or *wish* to have as many by half.'

This reluctance to increase her family beyond a reasonable limit was not due to any lack of affection or interest. Love of children was one of Sarah's most notable characteristics; her own five 'zitis', to use the private Spencer word, were her chief delight and occupation. Now at last she had full scope for her talent for teaching. 'Sarah is up to her ears in alphabets, copy-books and gamuts,' Lavinia Spencer wrote. 'Her babies are really uncommon fine ones, and very clever and sensible ones. And they will be admirably brought up for she thinks and does nothing else.'

As might have been expected Lavinia Spencer was a difficult mother-in-law. She found William Lyttelton a bore and she made no attempt to hide her feelings—'Lyttelton annoys me with an early visit every day, I really cannot bear it.' It was Sarah's business to keep the peace between her husband and her mother; and she must have found family disagreements particularly trying since she had no home of her own to which she could retreat. In 1826, however, William decided that he must take over the management of the family estate at Hagley in Worcestershire. His half-brother, the second Baron Lyttelton, who was mentally deranged, was becoming more and more incapable of managing his own affairs. He lived in the great house at Hagley, so Sarah and William planned to make their home in Rockingham Hall, a smaller house nearby. While this was being made ready for them they lived in the big house, which Sarah found a melancholy and somewhat alarming place, particularly when William was away and she left alone with the poor lunatic. Writing to her brother George to describe the beauties of the place she added, 'There in the midst of it all, tottering along on his melancholy evening walk, is the *owner!*—talking loud to himself, afraid of all human beings, and occupied only by gloomy delusions, unsatisfying wild pompous fancies.'

In November 1828 this unhappy man died, and William at last came into his inheritance. The house was in shocking condition, chimney flues so defective that at any moment the whole place might have gone up in flames, and the drains or lack of drains so bad that the rooms were filled with 'such a strong and prevailing stench that Sarah was all but sick'. These drawbacks did not prevent William and Sarah from entertaining Sarah's parents and her brothers George and Frederick in September 1829. A visit from Lavinia Spencer was always an alarming prospect. This time however, all went well—'even my mother was *nearly* as comfortable as at home,' Sarah wrote with obvious relief—while Lord Spencer, kindly as ever, expressed great admiration for the house and its surroundings.

In December of the following year came the news of Bob Spencer's sudden and unexpected death from fever at Alexandria. Sarah was heartbroken. She, who normally kept a stern control over her naturally strong emotions, fell down in a hysterical fit and wept long and bitterly.

When Sarah's eldest brother Althorp was labouring to force the Great Reform Bill through Parliament William Lyttelton loyally went up to London to attend the House of Lords and give the measure his support. This, however, was almost his last political appearance. From now onwards he devoted himself to the care and

[175]

Hagley, Worcestershire. Engraving by T. Matthews after a drawing by J.P. Neale, 1818.

improvement of his house and his estate and to local affairs. He adored Hagley—no lesser word would properly express his feelings—and he was perfectly happy to live the life of a country gentleman, noting down the weather, and recording the weight of his friends and family, going 'a-colonelling' with the local yeomanry, and serving on innumerable committees, including one set up to combat the great cholera epidemic of 1832 which raged particularly virulently in the neighbouring town of Stourbridge.

As well as busying himself with local affairs William Lyttelton gave an unusual amount of time and attention to the upbringing of his children. When the boys left home to go to school for the first time he personally escorted them to Eton or Winchester; and on these harrowing occasions it was the father rather than the son who broke down in tears. He was particularly distressed by the parting with Spencer, who following the tradition of Sarah's family, went into the Navy and at the early age of twelve left England on a three years' voyage. Sadly enough, all this devotion was not reciprocated; his children, who adored their mother, were not equally devoted to him. Towards the end of his life William suffered from increasing and painful ill health, which made him both irascible and alarming. His loud and frequent groans and grunts were terrifying to small children; and he lacked the art of endearing himself to the young, who much preferred their gentle and quiet grandfather, Lord Spencer.

William Lyttelton died in April 1837 at the comparatively early age of fifty-five, to be succeeded by his eldest son George, a character very much out of the ordinary. Partially deaf and in consequence painfully shy, he might have been expected to be miserable at school, but on the contrary, he loved Eton from the moment of his first arrival there and revelled in the opportunities to indulge in his twin passions for cricket and classical learning. So devoted was he to these two subjects that he would read Virgil while waiting to bat and would slip the volume into his pocket when going out to field so that he might read a line or two between the overs. Where cricket was concerned he never played either for Eton or for Cambridge but he did brilliantly at classics both at school and at the University. These remarkable intellectual gifts were combined with an almost embarrassing simplicity of character and a childlike Christian faith. Physically, he was plain, gangling, and clumsy, and he was totally lacking in social manner. 'If Lord Lyttelton were more aware of what he is about, whom he is talking to, if he were more master of his limbs and his tongue, and minded his stops, we should be able to get at the quantity of excellent stuff of all kinds which I am sure is in him,' wrote his critical but perceptive cousin Hary-o, now Lady Granville. This open-hearted man, normally the most cheerful of persons, borne up through sadness and trouble by his unswerving faith in God, was subject to bouts of blackest melancholia, far worse than the depression which haunted his namesake uncle, George Spencer.

The second son, Spencer, was the black sheep of the family. The exact opposite of George, he was a very handsome young man of no particular intellectual gifts who had inherited from his Poyntz ancestors an incurable passion for gambling. His career in the Navy was not a success; and from there he drifted into the Army, where he remained for a while, perpetually in debt and a constant anxiety to his mother. The third son, William, always known as Billy, was an uninhibited and on the whole a cheerful character although he too could suffer from black depression. He took Holy Orders and somewhat surprisingly developed what were then regarded as advanced views on religion. The rest of the family were strictly orthodox High Church followers of the Oxford Movement; and since to the Lytteltons religion was all important this divergence of views was a serious matter

[177]

which nearly cost Billy the living of Hagley. As patron George had scruples about appointing a parson who might teach unsound doctrine to his parishioners. The difficulty, however, was smoothed out; and Billy became a much-loved Rector of Hagley and a tower of strength to his brother who was, in his turn, devoted supporter of the church, attending weekday services, and if he had been out hunting arriving for evensong wearing an overcoat over his muddy pink coat and riding breeches. Billy's most memorable characteristic was his laugh; he would shout with merriment at the smallest jokes, especially if they were his own, and would burst out laughing again hours later, overcome by amusement at the recollection of his own humour.

In 1837, the year of his father's death, George Lyttelton, though only eighteen, fell seriously in love with the pretty and charming Mary Glynne, sister of Sir Stephen Glynne of Hawarden. Mary was uncertain of her own mind, and neither family was enthusiastic about the proposed match; but George never wavered, and by the autumn of 1838 it seemed as if his hopes might be realized. If George were to marry Sarah would have to leave Hagley; and the thought of this possibility may have been one of the reasons which impelled her to accept an appointment as Lady of the Bedchamber to the young Queen Victoria. She did not do so without serious misgiving: 'If I am able (which I dread and tremble to think I may not prove) to conduct myself tolerably well, to keep out of incessant scrapes from indiscreet words and irresolute blunderings, so that I can return from Windsor to my quiet and cross-stitch at Hagley with a tolerably easy conscience, I shall be thankful and surprised.'

At first Sarah found the formality of Court life very uncongenial but soon she came 'to feel settled into a proper stiffness'. For the most part her duties were those of a superior lady's maid, 'shawling and pinning Her Majesty and keeping track of numerous wraps, bags, bouquets and opera glasses.' Her worst moment came at the Prorogation of Parliament when it fell to her to pin the crown of England on to the Queen's head. All went well till after the ceremony when she had to remove the crown and replace it with a diamond diadem—'The last pin I could not find a place for in the diadem and ran it against the Royal head upon which she looked up with a comical arch look of entreaty.' As Lady of the Bedchamber Sarah was also in charge of the very young and rather flighty Maids of Honour, who found Court life too dull and circumscribed to be altogether to their liking—' "Lady Lyttelton mayn't I walk *for once* by myself on the slopes? I know it's against the rules, but what harm *can* it do?" Says Lady Lyttelton, "No, no." Then another time a gentle knock. "Lady Lyttelton, *may* I go out? My feet are *so* cold, poking up in my room

[178]

Queen Victoria at Windsor Castle. Lithograph by Lane after Chalon, published by T. Boys in 1838.

[180]

all morning! I will only go on the Terrace and keep quite in sight." Says Lady Lyttelton, "Yes, yes." '

The North Terrace at Windsor Castle was a favourite promenade not only for the Royal Family but for the general public. The scenes there often resembled the 'walkabouts' which have become so much a part of the routine of Sarah's collateral descendant, our Princess of Wales:

The crowds of people!—among whom the Queen walked, hardly able to get along at first, they press up to her so. *Il faut la voir*, tripping up to a thick-set row of men, women and Eton boys, as smiling and spirited as if *they* would do her no harm, till at last they fall back and make way for her. Her courtiers just tap them back as they get close.

Sarah admired the members of the Royal Family for 'their heartiness and their seemingly endless good-temper', but she could not resist poking fun at some of these plump personages:

We are all alone now, several ton weight of Royalty having departed. The day before yesterday we were twenty-eight at dinner, and considering that the Duchesses of Kent and of Cambridge, and the Princess Augusta of England and the Princess Augusta of Cambridge, besides the Duke of Cambridge, were of the number, it speaks well for the rafters and joists under the dining-room that we should not have gone through.

Sarah was in attendance on the occasion of the Queen's marriage to Prince Albert of Saxe-Coburg-Gotha on 10 February 1840. She saw very little of the actual ceremony, her view being blocked by the ample shapes of Lady Normanby and the Duchess of Bedford, but she watched the couple walk down the aisle as man and wife and noted the look of comfort and confidence on the Queen's face, 'very pretty to see'.

For Prince Albert Sarah had nothing but praise; the more she saw of him the more she found to like and admire. She was particularly impressed by his skill as a musician, and by the way in which he could express in his organ-playing feelings which at other times he must keep hidden. Towards the young Queen she was

Opposite: Albert, Prince Consort, at Windsor. Drawing by G.B. Champion, October 1839.

more critical, but she modified her judgements after a period of comparative peace and quiet had given her a chance to get to know Victoria more intimately:

> It makes me feel more towards the Queen—more of the admiration and wonder which some parts of her character excite, more of the affection which others naturally inspire, and more, alas! of the regret and compassion and hopelessness and helplessness which many circumstances of her education and present position and future fate fill one with.

In lighter mood she would sometimes refer to the Queen as 'the Zit', writing her private family word for a child with the royal capital letter. Her attitude towards the Queen was one of almost maternal affection—after all, Victoria was younger than her own daughter Caroline—salted with a gentle quizzical humour, poles apart from the uncritical adulation, almost to be called adoration, which her granddaughter Lucy was to exhibit some years later when serving as a Maid of Honour.

Sarah was particularly pleased and amused by the Queen's display of 'wifeism' towards Prince Albert, her efforts to learn more about the music and books which so much interested him and her sudden concern with the details of the country life which previously she had heartily disliked:

> She is learning trees and plants in a very pretty childlike manner, and told me quite gravely and low, half shy, 'That, Lady Lyttelton, is a tulip-tree, you see—a rare tree but yet hardy—we hope that it may succeed though it is rather large to be transplanted.' Last year she did not know an elm from an oak. 'Love rules the Court, the Camp, the Grove.'

What touched Sarah most of all was the Queen's submissive behaviour, the care she took never to assert her own authority, consulting the Prince's wishes even over so trivial a matter as the lighting of a drawing-room fire. The legend of Victoria's overbearing attitude which led to the famous quarrel when Albert locked his door and refused to open it until the Queen of England submissively described herself as 'Your wife', finds no confirmation from Sarah.

Life at Court could be very grand but it could also be very dull—'Our party grows more and more splendid—two Queens, a Royal Highness, and a Serene one drove out yesterday in a pony carriage and four, and were attended by a cortège of horsemen, among whom Lord Surrey appeared almost plebeian by comparison.'

[182]

Sarah could see the humorous side of this splendour only too well—'I got into a titter yesterday at the number of Kings and Queens; one had nothing else to make way for.' At times she found Royalty extremely boring, especially when the royal person in question was Queen Victoria's uncle, the Duke of Cambridge:

> To be sure how he did shout and cross-examine! But he never wants an answer, so it don't matter. . . . I was quite out of breath listening and could hardly stick in a word in answer here and there, and all as loud as a very sonorous voice can reach.

Courtiers could be as dull as their royal masters. 'Pray find out for me some of you, *who* in the world he *is*; what's his name, who's his wife?' Sarah wrote home apropos of Lord Poltimore. 'It might possibly enliven our intercourse a very little.' She found the company of one member of the suite of Prince Ernst of Coburg a particularly trying infliction:

> Count Kolowrath again my neighbour at dinner! My heart sank when he came—so very dull. We have quite reached *le bout de notre française et notre allemand*, and I can't help suspecting from a certain look in the corner of his eye and tip of his moustache that he quizzes me finely the moment we part.

Politicians made a pleasant change after such dull company. Some years later Sarah was to write of Sir James Graham, 'He made us a great break and refreshment to the brains, being a Minister and therefore, according to my general rule, very welcome at Court.' In October 1840 Sarah was much enlivened when Palmerston, Melbourne and Lord John Russell all visited Windsor, to be followed a few days later by Lord Clarendon. One passage in Sarah's letters makes clear that she was well aware of the curious relationship existing between Melbourne and the Queen—'I should think it would be hard to displace Lord Melbourne by any intrigue, constitutional or otherwise, while her present Majesty lives, unless he continues to displace himself by dint of consommés, truffles, pears, ices, and anchovies which he does his best to revolutionize his stomach with every day.' Sarah did not entirely approve of Melbourne, who was her cousin by marriage, but she could not fail to like him; at the beginning of his last long illness she wrote, 'I can't help feeling that I shall (if I survive him) wear my cousin's mourning with sincerity for the strange, inconsistent, but amiable man.' As for Palmerston, during a visit to Windsor in 1841, when he was fifty-seven, he astonished Sarah by

[183]

going swimming in the Thames before breakfast: 'He came in from this performance as fresh as a—no, I beg a rose's pardon!—but as an old river-god, to his customary hearty meal.'

On 21 November of this year 1840 the Queen gave birth to her first child, the Princess Royal, who was christened Victoria, and known in the family as Vicky. A year later came the birth of Albert Edward, Prince of Wales, called Bertie. The organization of the royal nursery was far from satisfactory; the head nurse was unequal to the task of supervising the staff under her control, and it was clear that a change must be made. The Queen and Prince Albert were anxious to find someone of rank and standing who would act as governess or supervisor, and in the spring of 1842 they offered the post to Sarah. She accepted it with much hesitation and only after consultation with her brother, Althorp of the Reform Bill, now Lord Spencer. She was troubled not only by misgivings as to her own ability but by the fact that the post of Governess, unlike that of Lady of the Bedchamber, involved almost constant residence with the Royal Family. This presented no difficulty as far as Sarah herself was concerned for George no longer needed her to act as mistress of Hagley. A year previously he had married Mary Glynne at a double wedding at Hawarden, the other couple being Mary's sister Catherine and William Gladstone. There remained the difficulty of Sarah's two unmarried daughters, Caroline and Lavinia. If their mother were to live permanently with the royal children they would be left homeless.

Within a year Lavinia, the younger and prettier of the two, had solved the problem by getting engaged to Mary's brother, Henry Glynne, the Rector of Hawarden. The elder, Caroline, was still unmarried and unlikely to remain so. A plain young woman, who had lost the sight of one eye as the result of a childhood accident, she had no success in society but consoled herself with a passionate attachment to her cousin, Kitty Pole-Carew. The two addressed one another as husband and wife (by nature a boss, 'King' Caroline, as her mother called her, was of course the husband) and so inseparable did they become that George's children who knew Caroline as 'Aunt Coque' ran the two into one person and addressed them collectively as 'Aunt Coquitty'.

In all probability Sarah had never heard or read the word 'lesbian', but she had an instinctive mistrust of passionate female friendships. 'As to Miss Estcourt, believe me I do not in any degree regret or wish away your friendship for her,' she wrote to Caroline apropos of another bosom friend, 'but I still do not repent of all I am often saying to the disparagement *in general* of great intimacies among young Ladies.' Kitty Pole-Carew was, however, in a different category to Miss Estcourt.

She and her sisters had lived more or less permanently at Hagley ever since their mother's death; and Sarah looked upon her almost as a daughter. Now she was glad to think that if she herself were to take the post of Royal Governess Caroline would not be left lonely but would have Kitty for companion. Sarah's salary would be sufficient to pay for the upkeep of a small house in London which she could use as her own headquarters and which Caroline and Kitty could make their permanent home. (In fact they were to spend much of their time following Sarah round from place to place and living in uncomfortable lodgings near Windsor or Osborne.)

With her daughters thus disposed of Sarah was free to embark on her duties as Royal Governess. However, before definitely accepting the post she was wise enough to make certain stipulations. She must be in sole and undisputed control of the nursery staff, 'the only chief to whom they can address themselves in all their affairs, wants, contrarieties or disagreements'. Where the care of the royal children was concerned she must have permission from the Queen and the Prince 'to ask questions, to discuss doubtful points, and even to maintain her own opinions by argument, without reserve.' Coming down to specific matters she must be present when any doctor attended the children so that she could know exactly what his report might be and what treatment he prescribed. Finally, subject to the Queen's wishes she must be in control of the children's dress. Sarah had strong and somewhat advanced views on children's dress, being all for simplicity and mocking at 'many a quiz of five years old, looking as little like a human being as Rob Roys and feathers and ringlets and long gaiters could make it.'

Even with these vital points settled to her satisfacton Sarah still felt considerable alarm at the prospect before her. She was a person curiously lacking in self-confidence, and she dreaded the responsibility which now fell upon her shoulders. She also realized that her work must inevitably cut her off from her friends and relations—'I must be looked upon as a sort of old and unholy nun, only to peep out at times.' The position of Royal Governess was, however, of much more interest and importance than that of Lady of the Bedchamber; and the salary was an added attraction, the Lyttelton family being permanently in financial straits. Sarah summed up her feelings on both these points when she wrote, 'I sometimes feel glad, as well as thankful, that I am doing what I used to fancy I wanted to do, really *working* for my bread—and yet it is not real work, and it is so much more than bread that I get for it.'

While the children were babies Sarah would have no opportunity to exercise her talent for teaching. Even when they grew older the Royal Governess would be concerned at least as much with organization as with education, for she was responsible for the general management of nurseries and schoolroom and the supervision of the nurses, nursemaids, housemaids and footmen employed there. But she was not to be merely an administrator. The Queen and Prince Albert were devoted and conscientious parents who sought to keep the upbringing of their children as far as possible in their own hands; but public duties claimed so much of their time that inevitably the Governess would be the person in closest day to day touch with the children and she would be in a position to exercise a strong influence upon the development of their characters.

When Sarah first took charge her main concern was with Vicky since the baby Bertie was of necessity left chiefly to the care of Mrs Sly, the new nurse who with Sarah's approval had replaced the inefficient Mrs Roberts. At first Vicky had greeted her new Governess with screams of rage, but she was easily won over and soon she was addressing Sarah by the affectionate nickname of 'Laddle'. 'My little Princess is all gracefulness and prettiness,' Sarah wrote. 'She is *over* sensitive and affectionate, and rather irritable in temper at present, but it looks like a pretty mind.' Poor little Vicky had much to irritate her temper:

Oh dear, I wish there were no portraits being done of the Princess Royal, and that all her fattest and biggest and most forbidding-looking relations; some with bald heads, some with great moustaches, some with staring, distorted, short-sighted eyes, did not always come to see her at once and make her naughty and her governess cross. Poor little body!

On public occasions, however, Vicky could be relied upon to behave admirably, which was no mean achievement for a child who was little more than a baby. Sarah described her on her second birthday 'desiring to be lifted up "to look at the people" to whom she bowed very actively whether in sight of her or not.' The little girl must have been a sight to affront Sarah's simple taste, 'prodigiously dressed up in garter blue velvet, Brussels lace, white shoes, pearls and diamonds.'

'She is more like a person of four years' old,' Sarah wrote of this alarmingly precocious two-year-old. Vicky was an emotional, sensitive child, unusually clever, with quick reactions and a temper that flared easily. She loved admiration and was already something of a coquette, but though she was not an easy child to control her faults were all on the surface. It was otherwise with the Prince of Wales. As a handsome, blue-eyed baby Bertie had a look of great intelligence; but as he grew older it became clear that he would never be able to compete intellectually with his sister. This heralded disaster since Albert set an extraordinarily high

'Vicky' – Victoria Adelaide Mary
Louise, Princess Royal. Engraving
by J.B. Hunt after a drawing by
A. Hunt on the occasion of her
Confirmation, 1856.

value on intellectual attainment while Victoria's great wish was to see her son grow up a replica of his father. Already Bertie was showing the social aptitude which was later to be one of his most notable characteristics. Sarah described him at two years old as 'most exemplary in politeness and manner, bows and offers his hand beautifully beside saluting *à la militaire*—all unbidden.' And for so small a child he could display quite remarkable self-control. In June 1844 the royal children attended a great military review. Bertie watched entranced until the firing began. This was too much for the nerves of a two-year-old. 'I afraid! Soldiers go popping! No more! I cry!' But, making a heroic effort, he refrained from tears and succeeded, outwardly at least, in emulating the calm of his sister who remained 'another Wellington, wholly unmoved.'

Very early in his life the curious dichotomy in Bertie's character showed itself. Now and again he would burst into uncontrollable fits of rage; but Sarah could also note 'his lovely mildness of expression and calm of temper'. Clearly he was neither slow-witted nor a fool; but by the time he was four she was finding him 'uncommonly averse to learning', and complaining of his inattention, interruptions and 'anti-studious practices' such as upsetting the books or crawling underneath the table. Nevertheless Sarah felt peculiar tenderness for this 'poor

Louis Phillippe being received at Windsor in October, 1844. Two-year-old Bertie, in skirt and pantaloons, holds one hand out to the French king. Vicky and little Alice stand behind. Sarah Lyttelton is amongst the attendant ladies. Painting by Franz Xavier Winterhalter in the Royal Collection.

little fair-haired child', Laddle's boy, as he called himself. She trembled when she thought of his future and her responsibility for his upbringing weighed on her mind—'Often indeed is my heavy burden increased to a crushing weight when I think of that child.'

During the seven years following the birth of the Prince of Wales five more children were added to the royal nurseries in quick succession, Alice (1843), Alfred (1844), Helena (1846), Louise (1848) and Arthur (1850). None of these was as dear to Sarah as 'Princessy' and 'Princey', but she seems to have had some special fondness for Alfred. 'Prince Alfred continues brilliantly intelligent and very attractive,' she wrote on 19 October 1848. 'He begins to read so as to understand at

[188]

once, and his dear calm penetrating blue eyes are so expressive and so earnest, he must turn out well,' a prophecy which unfortunately was not to be fulfilled.

From a very early age the royal children accompanied their parents on public occasions and were present when distinguished guests arrived on state visits. A charming picture by Winterhalter shows Louis Phillippe, 'King of the French', arriving at Windsor in October 1844. Two-year-old Bertie, in skirts and pantaloons, holds one hand out to the King while keeping tight hold of his mother with the other one. Vicky and little Alice stand close beside Queen Victoria and behind her is baby Alfred, long-skirted and carried by his nurse. Sarah Lyttelton appears among the attendant ladies.

After the pomp of state occasions came spells of comparative quiet at Claremont, 'dear, boring Claremont', and later at Osborne, the new house which Victoria and Albert were building for themselves on the Isle of Wight. Sarah was relieved to find that she was not expected to accompany the Royal Family on their visits to Scotland. She listened politely when the Queen assured her that 'Scotch air, Scotch people, Scotch hills, Scotch rivers, Scotch woods are all far preferable to those of any other nation in or out of this world' and telling her daughter Caroline of this outburst of enthusiasm, commented, 'the chief support to my spirits is that I shall never see, hear, or witness these various charms.'

Even when away from her and on holiday Sarah liked the royal children to keep to a regular timetable, and much as she admired Victoria and Albert, she allowed herself to become really irritated when they insisted in carrying off the children for a trip on the Royal Yacht—'they get so petted and neglected and irregular on these cruises in spite of much trouble taken by the Queen.'

The only other point on which Sarah clashed with her royal employers was religion. When the children were small the Queen kept Vicky's religious instruction in her own hands while handing Bertie over to Sarah. All Sarah's own children had enthusiastically embraced the tenets of the Oxford Movement. Although she did her best to keep up with these new ideas at heart Sarah preferred the old ways, enjoying a comfortable box-pew more than open seating and seeing no reason why she should make any special effort during Lent—'I can repent of my sins equally well in August.' To Victoria and Albert, however, her views appeared dangerously papistical, especially when she insisted that the children must kneel to say their prayers. On this point she flatly refused to give way. Finally a compromise was agreed upon; the children knelt when Sarah was in charge, but when Queen Victoria herself supervised their prayers they sat up in bed like good little Lutherans.

Vicky remained naughty but irresistible:

The Princess, after an hour's various naughtiness, said she wished to speak to me. I expected her usual penitence, but she delivered herself as follows, 'I am very sorry Laddle, but I mean to be just as naughty next time.'

In another letter Sarah reported a different conversation:

Princessy. 'H.O.M.E.L.Y.—homely. What does that mean, Laddle?'
L. 'It means not pretty, not *very* ugly, but not pretty.'
P. 'Who is homely?'
L. 'I think Laddle is homely.'
P. 'Oh, Laddle (very coaxy), but then you are kind, and I think you have a *very* sweet voice.'

Sarah wrote of this seven-year-old Princess that she 'might pass (if not seen but only overheard) for a young lady of seventeen in whichever of her three languages she chose to entertain the company.' Bertie seemed the more slow when seen beside his brilliant sister, but he showed no sign of jealousy and continued to love Vicky dearly. Sarah praised his 'kindness and nobleness of mind' and his unswerving regard for truth, a characteristic in which she saw a reflection of his mother. His self-confidence was not helped by the merriment which greeted his efforts to appear intelligent:

Prince of Wales asked the Queen, 'Pray, Mama, is not a pink the female of a carnation?' Poor darling! I am sorry he said it, for he got such shouts of laughter for all answer that he was quite abashed.

In Sarah's view his parents were too strict with the little boy and indeed with all their children. She herself believed that 'punishment does no good, perhaps only great harm, for one cannot tell if it is fully understood by the child,' an opinion which Vicky must have imbibed, even if only half consciously, for she quoted it almost fifty years later apropos of the upbringing of her own grandchildren.

As Governess Sarah habitually dined alone in her own room, but she continued to meet interesting and important guests at what she called her 'down-dinings'. She always enjoyed a chance to meet Lord Ashley, afterwards famous as Lord Shaftesbury, though on one occasion when she was put to sit next to him she was

Claremont – 'dear boring Claremont' – Aquatint by Havell after a drawing by J. Hassall in his *Picturesque Rides and Walks*, 1817.

somewhat taken aback by his choice of St Paul as a subject for dinner-table conversation. On another occasion she listened with no great pleasure to Macaulay, 'too insistent a torrent of long words, reminding one of Sidney Smith's remark, "Macaulay's conversation is charming. There are flashes of silence sometimes; they are *so* delightful." ' Sir Robert Peel stayed at Claremont in March 1846 at the height of the Corn Law crisis and the tragedy of the Irish famine. Sarah watched his behaviour at breakfast:

My breakfast was not quite happy. I could not help looking at the other end of the table and watching Sir Robert Peel. . . . And his pale looks, the total abstraction of mind, when, after whispering a discreet congratulation behind my chair,* he sat down and took a bit of roll in his hand, which was only turned about and hardly tasted, and the expression of his poor, ugly face as long as he sat there were sad subjects for my thoughts. He soon got up and went to the window, and seemed unable to *put on* anything like cheerfulness. It was the coming Session, the late 'Ministerial crisis' that were eating into him.

* George Lyttelton had recently been appointed Under Secretary for the Colonies.

[191]

Sarah herself was passing through an unhappy period. Lord Spencer—Althorp of the Reform Bill—had died in 1845. Although Sarah sincerely mourned this brother who had been a stay and support to the whole family, she did not grieve for him as she had grieved for Bob; and it was only gradually that she came to realize the full extent of her loss. Four years later, after going through a box of family letters, she wrote of the deep impression made on her by 'the beauty of two characters coming out on all occasions and in every trial—my father's and my eldest brother's; the latter *almost* the best, scarcely ever failing to be kind and true to the bottom.'

Sarah's eldest brother had always taken a kindly and helpful interest in her scapegrace son Spencer; and family tradition had it that on his deathbed he commended this tiresome young man as a sacred trust to his brother Frederick, who succeeded him as Lord Spencer. In 1846 Spencer Lyttelton, now aged twenty-six, wrote his mother a melodramatic letter telling her that he was so deeply in debt he had decided to leave England 'and pass whatever time I have left in some miserable corner where I shall no longer be a curse to everyone with whom I have any connection.' This fit of gloom was partly induced by the fact that he was in love with a charming and eligible Miss Dawson but his debts put any thought of marriage out of the question. Sarah came rushing to his rescue. Pocketing her pride, she wrote to the Queen begging that he might be given some small post, and she also appealed to Frederick. Victoria appointed Spencer Marshal of the Court while Frederick, faithful to his brother's trust, produced a sum of money large enough to pay off at least some of Spencer's debts and to make a financial settlement which would enable him to marry Miss Dawson. The girl's parents, however, refused to countenance the match; and two years later, with great pomp and state, Spencer married a Miss Henrietta Cornewalle, whom the Lytteltons stigmatized as flighty. The couple were always to be a worry and a financial burden to their relatives but they remained an integral part of the family; Sarah was at pains to keep on good terms with her daughter-in-law whom nevertheless she heartily disliked.

This was by no means the last time that Frederick came to Spencer's rescue. 'Uncle Fritz's' chilly manner had not endeared him to his ebullient nephews and nieces who described him contemptuously as 'U. was an Uncle'. In Glynnese, the private language spoken by Glynnes and Lytteltons, this curious expression signified 'bare types in which the individual and original has been repressed and rubbed out by the conventional and professional. Example: Mrs Gladstone to Lady Lyttelton, "What sort of a person is — ?" Lady L. "Oh, C. was a clergyman." ' Frederick deserved better of the Lytteltons for he had shown great generosity towards them and not only to the spendthrift Spencer. In particular, he had helped George out of a very awkward situation. When the Gladstone family, owing to the failure of a company in which they were concerned, found themselves faced with the necessity of selling land at Hawarden to the value of £200,000, George Lyttelton rashly undertook to buy half of this land in order to keep the property in the family. The payment of so large a sum as £100,000 of course proved to be far beyond his means, so Frederick stepped into the breach and bought the land himself. Again, when George was deeply involved with the Canterbury Association, a society whose aim was to settle colonists in the South Island of New Zealand, Frederick gave the project his support by buying up a large tract of land. Later he handed this New Zealand property over to George's fourth son, another Spencer, who thus became financially independent, the only Lyttelton not to be hampered by shortage of money.

This Spencer Lyttelton was born in 1847, the sixth child Mary had borne in seven years. In spite of the strain this ever-growing family imposed upon their slender finances and also upon the mother's health, George and Mary showed no sign of pausing in their headlong career of procreation. There were problems too at Hawarden Rectory, where Lavinia had given birth to three little girls in four years. Sarah had not been happy about Lavinia's choice of a husband; for all his good qualities Henry Glynne was not a man whom she could unreservedly like and admire. The marriage had nevertheless been a very successful one, marred only by the lack of a son to inherit Hawarden, Henry's baronet brother Stephen being a bachelor. In 1848 Lavinia gave birth to a boy who died as the church bells were ringing to celebrate his arrival. After this child's birth Lavinia never recovered her full health and strength but in spite of warnings from the doctors she once again became pregnant and died in giving birth to a fourth daughter in October 1850.

Sarah took Lavinia's death with curious calm and detachment, but she was much distressed by the plight of the four motherless little girls, all of them pretty and well-mannered, but very delicate. Her wish to give as much time and attention as possible to these children confirmed her in her belief that the moment had come to resign her post as Governess. The two elder royal children, whom she had always regarded as her special concern, had already more or less left her care. Vicky had long ago outgrown her intellectually and had passed into the hands of Miss Hillyard, an excellent and inspiring teacher. In the spring of 1849 Bertie, now aged eight, was judged too old for petticoat government, and put into the charge of a tutor named Henry Birch. Although Sarah had hoped that Samuel Wilberforce, afterwards Bishop of Oxford, a man she greatly admired, would be the person chosen for this post, she much approved of Birch, and rightly so, since Bertie came to love him dearly and to make good progress during the short time that Birch was in charge. With Vicky and Bertie gone Sarah had no wish to remain at her post. It had proved a very rewarding but strenuous one; she was now in her sixties and felt herself to be in need of rest and relaxation. Towards the end of 1850, a month or so after Lavinia's death, she sent in her resignation.

The parting was a painful one. Sarah's tact and kindness had made her much beloved; on the morning of her departure all the nurses and maids were in tears. The royal children came in one by one to say goodbye. Vicky, intelligent and articulate as ever, 'said many striking and feeling and clever things'. Sarah had always maintained a strict impartiality, but in her heart Bertie came foremost, and she was particularly touched by his reaction to her departure—'The Prince of Wales, who had seen so little of me lately, cried and seem to feel most.' In the evening it was Sarah's turn for tears when she was summoned to say goodbye to Queen Victoria and Prince Albert—'I remember the Prince's face and a few words of praise and thanks from them both, but it is all misty, and I had to stop on the private stair and have my cry before I could go up again.' Hard though it was to say goodbye she did not regret her decision, and after a refreshing sleep in the train on the way home, she realized that at last her work was done, 'and woke with a pleasant *subsided* feeling, and as if the worst was over, and the beginning of rest came into my mind.'

Wisely, Sarah had decided not to settle near Hagley or Hawarden but to set up house with Caroline and Kitty in London. Much of her time, however, was spent with the Glynne children. All her tact and discretion were needed to smooth over the friction which inevitably arose between the various relatives, Catherine Gladstone in particular, 'all kind and loving, but not always *quite* judicious', who were only too anxious to look after the little girls. These children were indeed in need of special care and attention; the eldest proved to be slightly subnormal, the next two died in childhood, and only the youngest, Gertrude, grew up healthy and beautiful, and ultimately married Lord Penrhyn.

Apart from anxiety over the Glynne children the first few years of Sarah's retirement were a quiet and happy time; but in 1857 disaster struck. The tragedy of Hawarden was repeated at Hagley. George and Mary's eleventh child Edward, one day to be Headmaster of Eton, was born in 1855. After his birth Mary was explicitly told that if she were to have any more children it would be at great risk to her own life. Nevertheless, by the summer of 1856 she was again pregnant and in

'Bertie' – the Prince of Wales, aged seven. Painting by Franz Xavier Winterhalter in the Royal Collection.

[195]

February 1857 she gave birth to Alfred, who, ironically enough, was to be a special pet and the flower of the whole family. For a short time all seemed well, but then Mary began to fail. (The trouble seems to have been kidney disease.) In July she took to her bed and a month later she was told that she must die. Her outlook remained refreshingly humorous and matter-of-fact. 'I can't think of anything poorer than Sunday at Hagley without me,' she remarked, the Glynnese meaning of 'poor' being 'denuded of due and decent decoration, example, the hinder part of a French poodle or a pig without a tail.' She told her mother-in-law 'not to fash herself' with the care of the children, adding with more truth than tact, 'You are too old.'

Sarah took this admonition well and acted upon it. After Mary's death on 17 August she was careful never to interfere at Hagley but to be always ready and at hand when needed. Her first task was to try to comfort George, who gave way completely to his grief. Sarah was wise enough not to attempt to check him, realizing that for a person of his manic-depressive temperament this abandonment to sorrow was a necessary safety-valve. Unlike his uncle Althorp in similar circumstances he could find relief and even pleasure in sport and especially in cricket, a taste which he shared with all his eight sons. Sarah's brothers had been keen cricketers, but she herself had no enthusiasm for the game, although she was glad to see George forgetting his sorrow for a few hours—'it is amazing how all our plans and arguments are mixed up with *cricket* nowadays, and all the time I understand no more of the subject than an owl.'

On her mother's death the eldest daughter Meriel, then aged seventeen, took over the management of the house and the children; and when she married in 1860 these duties devolved upon the second daughter Lucy. Sarah frequently stayed at Hagley but she took no part in household matters and offered no advice unless consulted. Instead, she sat in the Tapestry Room, which became her special sanctum and a centre for the whole family where they would gather to enjoy what was then the novelty of five o'clock tea and to exchange jokes and gossip. In the evenings she would read aloud, perhaps Jane Austen or *The Rivals*, or a bowdlerized version of *Adam Bede*. Herself a good linguist she taught French to the younger children, meanwhile insisting on strict punctuality and unobtrusively instilling a little necessary discipline.

George Lyttelton never wholly recovered from the blow of Mary's death, but in 1869 he married Sybella Mildmay, a young and childless widow. The marriage pleased Sarah, who praised the bride for her kindness and quite outstanding tact. Sybella was in fact a very remarkable character. As a girl she had been forced into marriage against her will with a mentally unstable man who went completely insane on their honeymoon. Although she had never made any pretence of loving him, because, as she insisted, she had taken him for better or for worse she refused to allow him to be put into an asylum but instead looked after him herself until his death six years after their wedding. When her family protested against her marrying a middle-aged widower with twelve children she retorted that now she would please herself and that George was the man of her own free choice. She made him an excellent wife and bore him three more daughters, all of whom, and Hester in particular, grew up to become gifted and notable women. The older children, who were for the most part married and away from home by the time of their father's second marriage, came to have a great regard and affection for their stepmother.

Sarah must have shared their opinion of Sybella for it was with her and George rather than in her own home with Caroline and Kitty that she decided to end her days. In March 1869 she renewed old acquaintance and visited Queen Victoria, 'H.M. very fat and rather red, but by no means disagreeable to look at—and quite as charming as ever in manner and kindness.' The Queen, making 'a comical little face', touched upon the dangerous subject of Gladstone and the Irish Church, but for the most part they talked of friends and families or laughed together over ridiculous anecdotes. They were not to meet again. In July Sarah celebrated her eighty-second birthday. She was in good health and spirits but in October, while staying at Hagley, she was taken seriously ill. The doctor told her that she might make one more journey, but only one; if she went back to her home in London she must stay there till she died. Sarah elected to remain at Hagley. She lived for another six months, well enough to enjoy to the full the last of the many Christmases she had spent there, and happy in the company of children and grandchildren. Towards the end she suffered quite severely, and she was often only semi-conscious; but there were lucid moments when she could greet her grandsons with a delighted smile or look out a piece of jewellery to give as a wedding present to her granddaughter Lavinia, who was engaged to Edward Talbot. She died on 13 April 1870 with all her children round her, Billy reading the Commendatory Prayer, George holding one hand, Caroline the other, and Spencer, whom she had dearly loved in spite of his failings, standing at the foot of the bed.

[197]

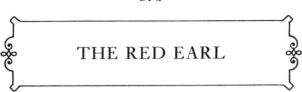

7

THE RED EARL

'The liberal deviseth liberal things, and by liberal things shall he stand.'

Isaiah Chapter 32 verse 8.

'The Red Earl'. Caricature by Harry Furniss, 1910.

[198]

'If ever there was a genuine Liberal he is that man'—so Lord Granville wrote of his cousin John Poyntz, fifth Earl Spencer, who has also been called the last of the Whigs. Granville's description is the more accurate of the two. Although personally John Poyntz Spencer might seem the apotheosis of Whiggery, aristocratic, rich, the owner of magnificent houses and vast estates, a power in Parliament and a little king in his own neighbourhood, politically he looked forward rather than backward, to the coming Liberals rather than to the departing Whigs. His chosen political leader was Gladstone, his closest political friend Campbell-Bannerman, the first two genuinely Liberal Prime Ministers (Rosebery was essentially Whiggish), men of a new breed, sprung from a commercial background, with a new outlook and new standards. In his adhesion to these new ideas lies Spencer's political importance—but what was he like as a person?

The question is not easy to answer. Many people have described him but all of them have looked at the public character; if they have touched at all on the private individual it is only to describe his magnificent physical appearance. 'A wealthy nobleman of manly character, a prominent and popular figure in society,' 'Spencer's lofty character, grace and dignity of manner, transparent sincerity, wide experience of affairs, and imperturbable fortitude in the midst of perils,' 'a noble fellow, such lofty simplicity, such sovereign and steadfast unselfishness,' 'a grand fellow, courageous, hard-working, the incarnation of common-sense, firm yet conciliatory'—the eulogies go on and on with hardly a word of criticism. A fault or two added to this catalogue of virtues would have made its subject appear more human. Sir Charles Dilke, not altogether an unprejudiced witness, mentions Spencer's 'vanity', and Margot Asquith quite mistakenly dismisses him as stupid; but the worst that anyone else can find to say of him is some such innocuous phrase as 'deficient in initiative and intellectual force'. Even when writing of his important relationship with the Victoria University Alfred Hopkinson goes no further by way of description than a mention of 'the Chancellor, Lord Spencer, the most stately and dignified figure who ever took part in public ceremonial within living memory.'

How to get at the man behind the public figure, the ceremonial trappings, the great beard? The obvious comparison is with his uncle, Althorp of the Reform Bill. The resemblance between the two men is striking. Physically of course they were completely different. The fact that John Charles Spencer was a plain, ungainly and very ordinary-looking man makes him seem accessible while John Poyntz Spencer is lost to us behind his splendid exterior. Otherwise uncle and nephew are cast in the same mould. When young both were regarded as below rather than above the intellectual average. Nobody expected great things of either of them; yet both of these apparent mediocrities leapt at one bound to a position of great political importance without serving the usual apprenticeship in lesser offices (John Charles's post at the Treasury can hardly be dignified by the name of political office). Both of them had great influence in Parliament, John Charles in the Commons, John Poyntz in the Lords, although neither of them was a good speaker. Both fall into the category of 'failed Prime Minister' for both had that prize within their reach not once but several times. John Charles simply did not want to be Prime Minister; John Poyntz lost his chance once because of Queen Victoria's aversion to Gladstone, once because of his own ill health. Both of them unwillingly caused the downfall of a government in which they held office. Both of them, in spite of their Whiggish and aristocratic background, inclined to what would now be called the left in politics, John Charles co-operating with Brougham and Whitbread, John Poyntz supporting Gladstone. Apart from politics their lives followed almost precisely the same pattern. Their love of sport and in particular of hunting, even their Mastership of the Pytchley was, of course, part of their common Spencer inheritance. Both made happy marriages, both mourned the unexpected death of a wife, both died childless leaving the title and property to a brother. Finally, both inspired quite unusual liking and respect; whatever might be the violence of political feeling against them—and during John Poyntz's time as Viceroy of Ireland it was violent indeed—no one had a word to say against their personal characters.

John Poyntz Spencer was born at Spencer House on 27 October 1835. The veil which hides him from posterity descends very early. We have only one glimpse of him as a child, the picture of a ten-year-old boy leaning out of the schoolroom window intent on watching hounds streaming across Althorp park in the direction of Cottesmore where they were to kill their fox by candle-light. This passion for hunting was not one which Althorp, to give him the courtesy title which came to him that same year, could share with his father, one of the few Lord Spencers who never became Master of the Pytchley. Perhaps because of the many years he had spent either at sea or abroad the fourth Earl was no great sportsman, his favourite hobby being the collecting of fine porcelain. He did not find it easy to get on happy terms with his children, being all too ready to raise objections and to say 'No', but although he was strict he was never unjust and his relationship with his son, though not close, seems to have been a satisfactory one.

The eulogies of Althorp begin at his first school, the headmaster telling his parents that 'he had earned the greatest respect from all his school-fellows by his remarkable truth and rectitude.' 'It is very pleasant to hear all they say of Althorp,' Sarah Lyttelton wrote of him at the age of eleven; 'he must be a very nice boy, so gentlemanlike and good and popular—not clever, but not silly or idle.' A year later, when he was about to go to his public school which for him as for his uncle was to be Harrow and not Eton, she wrote, 'He seems to me to be a very nice, civil, gentlemanlike boy, and I trust will get on well with the others.' Her wish was fulfilled; at Harrow he made many friends including Frederick Cavendish, whose career was to be so tragically linked with his own. Although he was not a prominent boy in the school he was certainly a popular one; a contemporary remembered him as 'a general favourite and most respected'. The reference to respect, the term used by his previous headmaster, is worth notice; few people knew John Poyntz Spencer well enough to be able to say that they loved him; but everywhere he went, in Parliament, in the Cabinet Room, at Viceregal Lodge, in the wildest and most disaffected regions of Ireland, even in the hunting-field, he never failed to win respect.

Already he was seriously interested in politics, a fact which may explain the active part he took in the school debating society although in later life he was to detest public speaking and to do it very badly. He also helped to found an essay society to which old Harrovians were to be invited. 'It will be a very useful thing in the school and encourage reading, which is not much done now,' he wrote to his father, 'and will also show those devoted to games that old Harrovians do not patronise them alone for their games but can also pay attention to mental acquirements in the school.' The tone of this letter suggests a sober-sided and rather priggish schoolboy; but in letters to their parents children are inclined to write what they know those parents would wish to read. In fact Althorp was one of those whom he described as devoted to games, in his case cricket. Bookish he certainly was not, but when at Harrow he may have appeared unusually serious because his time there was overshadowed by anxiety and grief. His mother died in 1851 after a long illness; and shortly afterwards his elder sister Georgiana also died as the result of an attack of measles. He was now thrown very much into the company of his one remaining sister, Sarah, or 'Tallee', as she was always called, with whom he developed a very close relationship. Lady Stanley of Alderley could find nothing better to say of Tallee than that she was 'plain but sensible'. Lucy Lyttelton, who loved her dearly, wrote of her more kindly—'I have delightful sits and trolls and "sweet converse" with old Tallee, whose goodness and charm to my mind give her grace and beauty that win me more than a lovely face.'

Writing four years later to describe a visit which she had made to Althorp House in 1854 Lucy makes clear that although these two early bereavements were very deeply felt they were not allowed to cast too deep a gloom over everyday life:

> When we were there then Aunt Yaddy was Tallee's friend Miss Seymour, Uncle Fritz sat at the head of the table, the house was full of company and amusement but at grave moments the shadow of those two first great griefs one might still fancy hanging over the house.

The Aunt Yaddy to whom Lucy refers is Adelaide Seymour, whom Lord Spencer married that same year 1854, three years after the death of his first wife. His choice was a very happy one. She bore him two children, a son and a daughter, and she proved an excellent stepmother to Althorp and Tallee. When Althorp became Earl Spencer he made a will in which he left her an annuity, 'as a mark of my great love and esteem for her, and a return inadequate as it is for the obligations I feel for the devoted love to her husband my father and her motherly kindness to my sister and myself.' It was he, and not her own children, who erected the panelling in Great Brington church that is her memorial.

In 1854 Althorp went up to Trinity, Cambridge as his uncle had done before him. On the advice of the headmaster of Harrow but somewhat against his own wishes—'I should prefer if anything being as quiet as possible'—he entered not as an ordinary commoner but as a nobleman. To his annoyance he discovered that the entry of a nobleman into the University was certainly not a quiet one. In chapel he was obliged to sit perched up beside the Master and to walk out immediately after him before all the other members of the congregation. Worse was to come when he attended the University sermon at Great St Mary's:

> When we arrived at the church he [his tutor] ushered me into the vestry where Whewell [Master of Trinity] and all the Heads of Colleges and Doctors were assembled to await the Vice-Chancellor. I then had to be formally introduced and to form part of a mace-preceded procession to a very conspicuous gallery where I was placed on the right of the Vice-Chancellor. We only then had a sermon of enormous length and depth and marched away in similar pomp.

The 'splendid dinner' which followed provided some compensation for all this trying ceremonial. Among his Lyttelton cousins Althorp was famous for what they referred to as 'the Spencer appetite'. Family legend had it that on one occasion at the end of a particularly hearty meal he demolished a whole apricot pie and repeated this feat the same day at late dinner.

Like many another undergraduate before and since Althorp found that 'it is very difficult I fear to settle down very regularly to work in the evenings as there are so often parties which must be attended.' The only thing to which he settled down very regularly was hunting with the Cambridgeshire where he made a name for himself as a hard rider. Although he was receiving an allowance of £600 a year, a munificent sum in his day, to his distress at the end of his second year he found himself in debt. His father, who hid much generosity and understanding beneath a gruff exterior, realized that the root of the trouble was not extravagance but lack of experience in handling money, and paid up his son's liabilities to the tune of £400.

When Althorp went down from Cambridge in 1857 he left with a nobleman's degree, having taken no examination. He had achieved no sort of academic distinction nor had he made a mark at the University in any other way. Hunting and politics were the two subjects which occupied his time and attention. Already he had been discussing with his father the possibility of standing for Parliament, and six weeks after leaving Cambridge he announced his candidature for South Northamptonshire at the forthcoming general election. In April he was duly elected and entered the House of Commons as a supporter of Palmerston.

His time there was to be unexpectedly short. In the nineteenth century there was no Autumn session; and when the House rose he had a clear six months before him. The Grand Tour of Europe with which so many Spencers had completed their education had fallen out of fashion; instead, he set out on a journey round the United States and Canada. He crossed the Atlantic in the Cunard liner *Europa*. Among his fellow-passengers was the famous American showman Barnum, travelling in company with a Miss Williams, a Welsh singer whom he cherished and cosseted not from love but from cupidity, hoping to make large sums from her tour of America. At the Captain's table Althorp was pleased to find himself 'in a very pleasant little society' including William Cunard, son of the owner of the shipping line, and his wife 'a most agreeable, handsome young woman, a great friend of the Seymours, and a confidante, I guess, of the young ladies.' At the home of Lady Clinton, who was aunt both to him and to her, Althorp had already met Charlotte, the loveliest of these three lovely Seymour sisters, whose beauty was the talk of London society.

Arrived in New York Althorp found everyone talking of 'the terrible thunder-cloud ready to explode and separate the North and the South'. America had been a wise choice for him. Like his uncle he cared very little for the works of art which were the special attraction of the European Grand Tour. Politics were his interest; and here he could discuss American political problems and study the American attitude towards the British political situation, and in particular, the great Mutiny then raging in India. 'We must be losing an awful amount not only of money and of life, but of the estimation in which the people of India held us there,' he wrote to his father. 'There is very strong sympathy here felt for our side, particularly in Boston and the South.' Socially as well as politically Althorp preferred the Northerners to the Southerners—'There is more of business, more of toughness in the Northern American, but intrinsically these rough diamonds are better people, more intelligent and more warm-hearted.' This judgement shows the Liberal outlook that was always to characterize him; most Englishmen of his background preferred the aristocratic Southerners.

Not all of Althorp's time was devoted to serious political discussion. He enjoyed the company of American women and he paid them what he obviously intended to be the highest possible compliment, 'the best American ladies could often be taken for English women'—and this in spite of the fact that he had just seen the reigning belle of Saratoga, 'a most beautiful and refined-looking girl', sitting out-of-doors in a public place and drinking sherry cobblers with a young man, behaviour which would have put any English girl quite beyond the pale. Though considerably surprised Althorp was not in the least shocked by these emancipated American girls. His views are admirable even though his prose may be a little rough:

They get to learn the tricks of the world by themselves before they marry, become much better managers of their husbands and themselves than if tied too closely to their chaperon, and they say such a thing as a girl going wrong is never known, and they evidently make most loving and devoted wives. Another thing about it is that young men have excellent opportunity of really arriving at the character of a girl, and of course a girl has an opportunity to judge of a man.

From New York Althorp went to Trenton and Saratoga and on to Quebec, and in October sailed down the Mississippi in a river steamer. Now that he was in the South he had some sensible observations to make about slavery. He argued that if the slaves were to be freed the plantation owners might not find themselves as much out of pocket as they feared since the number of slaves and the cost of their maintenance remained static but the number of free labourers and the amount paid them in wages could vary with the state of the cotton market.

Althorp returned to England in time to spend Christmas at home with his family. Four days later on 29 December 1857 his father died suddenly. The young man of twenty-two who had only sat in the House of Commons for a few months was now a member of the House of Lords and owner of two magnificent houses and of a vast estate of approximately 27,000 acres. What he needed was a wife; and by good fortune the right girl was at hand. In May he proposed to Charlotte Seymour, and although it was said that she could be 'almost glacial' to young men she accepted him readily enough. His family were delighted. 'Althorp'—so his relations continued to call him although he was in fact Lord Spencer—'is to marry Miss Charlotte Seymour,' Lucy Lyttelton wrote. 'She is good, lovely, darkish, and everything delightful.' The two were married on 8 July 1858 at St James's Piccadilly.

The marriage was a marriage of true minds but of contrasting tastes and temperaments. She was loquacious and he was silent; she was outgoing and openly affectionate, he was shy and difficult to get to know; she loved foreign travel, he preferred to stay at home; she had a strong constitution and he in spite of his fine physique was delicate and often unwell; he came from a Whig background, she from a Tory one, although her family had been followers of Peel rather than members of the die-hard wing of the party. Reading descriptions of husband and wife only one phrase stands out as characterizing them both; they are both described as 'truthful and just'. There had to be give and take between them, she, for instance, adapting herself to his political views while he gave way to her preference for holidays abroad. She was one of the most famous beauties of her day and inevitably, she was nicknamed 'Spencer's Fairy Queen'. It seems that she may have been as good as she was beautiful; writing in December 1859 that shrewd judge of character, Sarah Lyttelton, praised her unreservedly. In the last sentence the faint hint of something missing could refer to the absence of a child:

I conclude Caroline gave you all the news up to yesterday ... of how pretty Charlotte looked and flitted about the evening before dressed in mourning, with one brilliant little diamond high upon her fair forehead. She has gone today, by herself, through *horrid* weather, to attend the distribution of a clothing club at the dirty, pokey village of Little Brington, because she was invited by the clergyman. Her manner to everyone of all classes is just perfect, and she must be beloved by all when she is known. There never was a more *lucky*—that is, a more *blessed*—marriage than his as far as a wife goes to make up happiness, which is a great way.

On coming into his inheritance Spencer's first concern was with the renovation

Charlotte Seymour (1835–1903), who married the fifth Earl Spencer on July 8, 1858. Painting at Althorp by G.F. Watts, O.M.

[206]

and improvement of Althorp and its surroundings. Financial necessity had forced his uncle to turn the park into grazing for sheep and cattle; now it was to be laid out afresh and the parts nearest the house made into gardens and pleasure grounds. The house itself was in need of repair and redecoration; and much papering, painting and gilding had to be done. The bailiff's account of the work in hand mentions the decoration of the nurseries which, sadly enough, were never to be inhabited.

Spencer's preoccupation with the work at Althorp is an indication of his growing interest in his home and his home county. Like all his family he was essentially a neighbourly man, deeply rooted in his own countryside. His involvement in all kinds of Northamptonshire affairs is well illustrated by his concern over the restoration of Brixworth Church, the biggest and arguably the most important Saxon church in Britain. Spencer was no connoisseur of ancient churches, but everything in Northamptonshire interested him. Having subscribed a large sum to the restoration fund he was alarmed to hear rumours that the money was to be used in ways which amounted to reconstruction rather than restoration. 'I have the strongest wish,' he wrote to the vicar of Brixworth, 'that whenever restoration of old work in whatever shape it is found, is done that no innovation should be made, or the least damage done to what exists already.' If eminent Victorian architects and ecclesiologists had been of his opinion we should not have had to lament the irreparable damage done to so many ancient churches. (It is only fair to add that in the same letter Spencer suggested seeking advice from Sir Gilbert Scott who could on occasion be the most ruthless of all restorers.)

At home in Northamptonshire his favourite occupation was, of course, hunting. In 1861 when he became Master of the Pytchley, an office which was all but hereditary in the Spencer family, that famous hunt had fallen on evil days. Hounds were first-class and foxes plentiful, but the hunt members had earned a shocking reputation for bad manners and lack of discipline. The Pytchley 'Wild Boys' were notorious; 'Don't go Pytchleying here' was a common form of rebuke to anyone misbehaving in the hunting field. Charles Payne, the famous Pytchley kennel-huntsman, bemoaned himself that 'mine has been a hard-fought battle for eight years with the wildest field in England.'

To control these tough customers and to instil some manners into them would have been a difficult task for anyone, and more particularly for a young man in his twenties even though that young man was an Earl and Master by almost divine right. The Wild Boys, however, met their match in Spencer. His rule as Master of the Pytchley was prophetic of days to come in Ireland. He did not like coercion but

[207]

if coercion had to be 'he would see that it was both efficient and effectual. He controlled his field as firmly as he controlled his pack of hounds; grumblers complained that they were dressed by the right and drilled like a regiment of dragoons before he would allow hounds to enter a covert. On one occasion a Wild Boy old enough to be Spencer's father rode his horse into the middle of a pond and remained there. When asked why he had taken up so strange a position he replied, 'I'm trying to find somewhere where I won't be accused of heading the fox.'

When teaching politeness to such offenders Spencer remained impeccably polite himself. He never swore, not even when knocked off his own horse on his own property by a thrusting stranger. 'Did you come a very long way to do this?' was his only remark to the offender, spoken as he was being carried off on a stretcher. He could however, wither people with his sarcasm. One episode was gleefully remembered for many years. Galloping across Holdenby park he heard the thunder of hooves behind him and without turning his head shouted some particularly scathing rebuke, only to find himself a moment later overtaken by a herd of stampeding cattle.

Spencer enjoyed shooting, and rifle shooting in particular, almost as much as he enjoyed hunting, an enthusiasm which fitted very well with his interest in the Volunteer movement. He presented a cup to the newly formed National Rifle Association to be competed for every year at a meeting held on his own property at Wimbledon, and when he gave Wimbledon Common as a gift to the nation he stipulated that the N.R.A. should always be allowed access. The annual meeting there became something of a social event; and Charlotte Spencer would entertain large house-parties for it, the guest of honour on one occasion being the Sultan of Turkey, Abdul Aziz.

From the time of Robert, first Baron Spencer, when Anne of Denmark visited Althorp, down to the wedding-day in 1981 when his remote descendant Diana Spencer herself became a member of the Royal Family, the link between Royalty and the Spencers had always been a close one. It was therefore natural that John Poyntz Spencer should be appointed Groom of the Stole to the Prince Consort, the same position which his ancestor Sunderland had held under George I. In 1719, the year of Sunderland's appointment, the Groom of the Stole had been the member of the Royal Household nearest to the monarch, with right of access to him at all times. For that reason the post was usually given to a personal friend or favourite; Bentinck, for instance, held it under William III and Bute under George III. With the decline in royal power came a decline in the importance of the Groom of the Stole. For a young man like Spencer in the early stages of a

Shooting at Wimbledon, 1864. Painting at Althorp by Henry Tanworth Wells. The fifth Earl lies on the ground; the Countess sits on a chair beside him. Those in the background include the Earl of Wemyss, the Duke of Westminster and the Earl of Ducie.

political career the post held no attractions; but it still preserved a certain political flavour which made him fear that if he accepted it he might find himself obliged to serve under a government of different views to his own. In Sunderland's day the Groom of the Stole had been required to be constantly in waiting, and even in 1859 Spencer feared that the duties might encroach too much upon his time. 'I should regret extremely,' he wrote to Colonel Biddulph, Master of the Royal Household, 'to be obliged to be away from home any length of time, and not to have leisure to attend to my duties in the country, and I should also be sorry to give up the idea of taking a political part in Parliament.'

Reassured on these two points Spencer accepted the post and served as Groom of the Stole from July 1859 until the death of the Prince Consort in December 1861. The next year, by Queen Victoria's special wish, he was offered and accepted the same post in the household of the Prince of Wales. Here, however, his position was far from satisfactory. He knew that the Queen had pressed for his appointment because she believed that he would be a good influence on the Prince, but he found himself unable to exercise influence of any sort. Nominally the Groom of the Stole was still the senior Household official but in fact he was no more than an ordinary Gentleman-in-Waiting, his original powers having passed into the hands of the Comptroller, who was under no obligation to consult him or to give him any information. In consequence Spencer felt himself to be no more than 'a state occasion attendant', a position very irksome to a young man who liked to lead an active life and who genuinely welcomed responsibility.

Spencer's time with the Prince of Wales was therefore not a very happy one but it had its pleasant moments, one of them being a visit by the Prince to Althorp in February 1863. Charlotte Spencer found him an easy guest, joining happily in dancing and parlour games and paying polite attention to the right ladies, a form of discretion for which princes are not always noted. He distinguished himself out hunting by gallantly charging a formidable brook and clearing it. (Fifty years later two riders who had seen this leap watched another Edward Prince of Wales jump the same brook at precisely the same place.) On another day he found the pace too hot for him and having lost the hunt called at a neighbouring house where to the horror of the butler he would take no refreshment but beer and bread and cheese.

In 1866, when the Prince of Wales once again hunted with the Pytchley a great dinner was given in his honour at Althorp. Knowing his host's aversion to cigars the Prince wickedly pressed one upon him. Unlike Christopher Sykes and other devoted sycophants, Spencer was certainly not prepared to be butchered to make a royal holiday, but he accepted the cigar and smoked it to the end without turning a hair, thus disappointing the Prince's primitive sense of humour.

A month after his first visit to Althorp the Prince of Wales married Princess Alexandra of Denmark. The outburst of popular enthusiasm which greeted Alexandra's arrival went unparalleled until Charles Prince of Wales announced his engagement to Lady Diana Spencer a hundred and twenty years later. On both occasions the nation had been passing through a period of depression. In 1981 Britain was suffering badly from inflation and unemployment. For fifteen months before March 1863 all outward signs of joy and jollity had been swamped by the gloom of Queen Victoria's mourning for the Prince Consort. A wedding was an excellent excuse for everyone to throw off austerity and sadness and to set about the pleasant business of enjoying themselves. Both brides were very young and

Opposite: The Prince of Wales shared the Red Earl's interest in shooting.

[210]

[211]

very pretty, both had charm. The people in the streets welcomed them with uninhibited rapture and turned them both into cult figures.

The wedding of Edward and Alexandra took place on 10 March in St George's Chapel, Windsor. The Spencers were of course among the guests; and some of those present thought that Charlotte, radiant in a dark blue dress that had belonged to Marie Antoinette, outshone even the beautiful bride. These two lovely young women were to become good friends, Alexandra describing Charlotte as 'the nicest woman I have ever seen'.

At Althorp life was gay and social. In the winter if frost stopped hunting there would be parties on the ice and skating by torchlight. Charlotte delighted in entertaining her friends and in being entertained by them. She had a good singing voice, a great social asset in those days when music was home-made, and she was clever at arranging tableaux, a popular form of amusement at house-parties. Both she and her husband loved dogs, in particular dachshunds, terriers and retrievers. She enjoyed all outdoor games but although she was a reasonably good horsewoman she did not hunt. Spencer's absorption in that sport was proving too much for his health. During the hunting season he would be out from eight in the morning till eight at night, usually without food of any sort, and he was not strong enough to stand the strain. In 1863 he developed a patch on his lung, and when ordered by the doctors to winter abroad he resigned the Mastership and spent several months in Egypt.

In the summer of 1865 the Spencers accompanied the Prince and Princess of Wales on a visit to Denmark. Edward and Alexandra were naturally anxious to take their baby son with them to show him to his Danish grandparents. Queen Victoria, who disliked and disapproved of Alexandra's relations, very reluctantly gave the necessary permission for the child to leave England, stipulating that he should only remain in Denmark for six weeks and should then be sent home with the Spencers. Most of the visit was spent at Fredensborg, the summer retreat of the Danish Royal Family. Here the accommodation was uncomfortable, the food plain and monotonous (red-currant jelly was the invariable dessert), and the entertainment unsophisticated, consisting of such simple amusements as croquet, bicycle rides, and pillow-fights. Alexandra was in her element, but Edward was intolerably bored. He was much happier during a brief visit to Sweden which the Spencers also enjoyed greatly. Meanwhile Queen Victoria was writing imperious letters demanding that the baby be sent home as promised. His parents were very loath to part with him, but back he had to go and the Spencers with him while the rest of the party remained behind for another few weeks.

Princess Alexandra passing through the City of London on her way to her marriage to the Prince of Wales, 1863. Detail from a contemporary lithograph.

[213]

Lord John Russell, later first Earl Russell. Painting by G.F. Watts, c.1851.

That same summer, at the personal request of the Prince of Wales, Spencer had been made a Knight of the Garter. When in 1866 he sent in his resignation as Groom of the Stole he may have felt that during his time in that office he had achieved nothing of significance; but at least it was clear that the Prince had learnt to know and appreciate him at his true worth.

Free of his post in the Prince's Household and no longer Master of the Pytchley Spencer was giving more and more of his time and attention to public affairs and politics. In 1865 he had been appointed to the Chairmanship of a Commission set up to investigate the cattle plague then raging throughout the country. He had proved an excellent chairman and gained much useful experience. Although a fellow peer said of him that 'on his feet in the House of Lords he seemed to me to have no command of happy expression' he had already made his mark in that House. The old Whig faction could not feel at home in what was now the Liberal party. When in 1866 Lord John Russell brought in a Reform Bill these dissidents banded together in a group which John Bright christened 'the Adullamites'. Few modern Members of Parliament would recognize the quotation, but the Victorians were better acquainted with the Old Testament, and the House gleefully seized upon the reference to a passage in the first Book of Samuel, 'And David escaped to the cave of Adullam, and everyone that was in distress, and everyone that was in debt, and everyone that was discontented, gathered round him there.'

The Adullamites in the House of Lords went so far as to consider forming a separate centre party; and in January 1867 Lord Elcho wrote to Spencer asking him to become the official leader of this group. His list of what he believed to be Spencer's qualifications for that position shows how deeply the Whigs were rooted in the past and how little they understood the shape of Liberal things to come. It also shows what a high reputation this young man of twenty-nine had already won for himself:

> You have a hereditary title to the headship of the Whig or Constitutional as opposed to the Democratic Liberals. You have station, wealth, and a large Whig house in the centre of London. Personally you are very popular. You have plenty of ability and business experience. At the head of the Cattle Disease Commission you did your work excellently well. You speak well*—in short I am certain that all these men would accept your leadership not only without hesitation but with gratitude.

Elcho had mistaken his man. Spencer might have a hereditary title to the headship of the Whig faction but both his judgement and his personal feelings were drawing him in the opposite direction. Loyalty and common sense combined to convince him that it would be the height of folly to split the Liberal party. He turned down Elcho's proposal declaring that he did not believe that the Radicals were as bad as they were painted—'I have confidence that they, including Gladstone, are Constitutional Liberals, and until they distinctly show by their acts that they are not, I am prepared to support them and think that that support should be given heartily and without wavering.'

The mention of Gladstone is significant. It was Gladstone whom Spencer instinctively recognized as the coming man in the Liberal party and the leader to whom he could give unswerving support and loyalty. Of all the Liberals who had been brought up in the Whig tradition Spencer and Lord Granville were the two who best appreciated Gladstone. 'Pussy' Granville, being Hary-o's son, was cousin to Spencer, and the two were to work closely together during the coming years.

---

* The only other person recorded as praising Spencer as a speaker is Sir John Lefevre who described him as 'confident, fluent and to the point.'

[216]

Between Gladstone and Spencer there existed not only political affinity but personal friendship. In August 1868 Catherine Gladstone wrote to Charlotte warmly inviting them both to stay at Hawarden, a visit which had to be postponed because of the general election that put Gladstone into power as Prime Minister. 'My mission is to pacify Ireland,' he declared while chopping down a tree in Hawarden park. If he were to fulfil that mission he would need an able man to act as Viceroy and to give him unreserved support. He first offered the post to Lord Hartington and to Lord Halifax; both refused it. He then offered it to Spencer, who accepted although with some surprise.

Spencer had an obvious claim to a place in Gladstone's ministry but he could not have expected to be given such an important one. The Viceroy, or Lord-Lieutenant as he was usually called, was the Queen's representative in Ireland and the head of the Irish administration. By the mid-nineteenth century much of his power had passed into the hands of the Chief Secretary, who was a member of the British Cabinet and in close touch with the Prime Minister; but although the Lord-Lieutenant was not quite as powerful as he had been the post was still one of great political importance. It was also an extremely prestigious, and an extremely expensive one. The Lord-Lieutenant was of course the leader of Irish society, treated almost as royalty and entertaining on a more than royal scale. All this cost money. The Viceroy's salary was in the neighbourhood of £20,000, but his expenses were reckoned at double that amount. In 1871 in a letter to Hartington Spencer set out his accounts. The monthly sum could be as much as £3,800. The number of servants employed was thirty-nine, excluding the stables but including a mysterious character described as a rachet marker. Between two and three hundred meals were served every month, luncheons and ball suppers counting for only half a meal. (Presumably afternoon teas did not count at all.)

The post was invariably held by a high-ranking peer, preferably one with political experience and if possible with some knowledge of Irish affairs. Spencer was young and inexperienced; he had never held office and he knew nothing of Ireland. On the credit side, he had made a name for himself in the House of Lords, he had proved an excellent Chairman of an important Commission, and he was known to have a good head for business. A man of commanding presence—during the sixties he had grown the great red beard which became the delight of

Opposite: William Ewart Gladstone. Painting by Sir John Everett Millais, 1879.

[217]

The Christmas Waltz. Music title, 1865.

cartoonists and earned him the nickname of the Red Earl—he would look the part to perfection, while his beautiful wife would be an ideal hostess. And, an essential qualification, he was very rich.

In January 1869 on their way to Ireland, the Spencers paid their postponed visit to Hawarden, where they watched Gladstone fell yet another tree. The next day, on a cold, wet winter morning they arrived in Dublin to be welcomed with great pomp and state and entertained at a grand reception followed by an official luncheon. The day ended in the comparative peace and privacy of a household dinner for twenty-nine people.

This crowded day was typical of Spencer's life for the next five years. Much of his time was taken up with social duties, ball after ball, dinner after dinner. The most magnificent of all these events were the Drawing-Rooms held in St Patrick's Hall in Dublin Castle. About a thousand guests attended, dressed as if for Buckingham Palace, the men in Court suits, the women with feathers in their hair and Court trains. The Viceroy was expected to kiss every lady presented to him, with the result that Spencer's red beard became white with powder and he was obliged to retire several times during the evening to brush it clean again. (The legend that Victorian ladies put nothing on their faces beyond a discreet dab of *papier poudré* is clearly untrue.) Charlotte Spencer was ideally suited to this way of life. She was an admirable hostess and she had that rare beauty that lights up a room and gives a special glow at any party. But it was not her beauty or what her brother described as 'her inherent talent for receiving' which made her the ideal

Vicereine so much as her obvious enjoyment of the part she had to play. Functions which other women would have attended merely from a sense of duty were to her a real pleasure. Later she was to count these years spent in Dublin as the happiest time of her life.

Charlotte was, however, a woman who could see beyond all the pomp and circumstance of Dublin Castle and Viceregal Lodge to the other Ireland of poverty and hatred and injustice. In letters to her sister she wrote of 'unjust oppression', 'tyranny of ascendancy', and 'the bitter spirit of the scene', adding the sad and truthful comment, 'the atmosphere seems tainted with the breath of injustice—everything is crooked and out-of-joint.' This was the Ireland with which her husband had to deal. Gladstone's policy for the redress of Irish grievances was three-pronged. First came the disestablishment of the (Anglican) Church of

The courtyard of Dublin Castle. Mid–nineteenth–century engraving.

[219]

The Viceregal Lodge, Phoenix Park, Dublin. Mid-nineteenth-century engraving.

Ireland, then a Land Act planned to give security of tenure and to encourage a better relationship between landlord and tenant, and thirdly, the reform of Irish university education.

As his uncle had done in 1833 Spencer pinned his hopes to church disestablishment. Charlotte was echoing his views when she wrote, 'I don't for a moment pretend to say that the Church question is the cry of the poor but I believe nevertheless that it is at the root of all the troubles of this country.' The existence of a richly endowed established church serving some 700,000 Protestants out of a population containing four and a half million Catholics was a crying scandal. To remedy it was a long overdue reform, but it was not the answer to the Irish question. In July 1869 the measure disestablishing the Church of Ireland became law. The Irish Roman Catholic hierarchy were moderately pleased; the Protestant bishops were moderately distressed; but the ordinary people remained unmoved. The favourable popular reaction on which both Gladstone and Spencer had counted never materialized.

Gladstone's Land Act of 1870 came nearer to the root of the difficulty. The Act was important as a first step in the right direction, signalizing a change in the spirit of British policy towards Ireland, but in practice it proved something of a disappointment. While Gladstone was pushing these measures through Parliament, hoping that they might prove the solution to the Irish problem, Spencer was dealing with that problem at first hand in Ireland, where he was responsible for the day-to-day maintenance of law and order. He might believe with Gladstone that Irish violence was the product of Irish grievances, but it was his business to suppress that violence whatever might be its origin. Judging by Irish standards the country was passing through a comparatively peaceful period; but in the wild regions of the West, and particularly in Mayo, West Meath and King's County, murder, shooting and agrarian crime had become endemic. Spencer was conciliatory but he was also firm. If conciliation would not work coercion it must be. He would treat the 'Ribbon Men' of the West as he had treated the Wild Boys of the Pytchley. To do this he needed stronger powers than he already possessed, and he demanded permission to suspend Habeas Corpus.

This permission was not granted* but instead Gladstone agreed to bring in a Peace Preservation Act. This stringent measure not only reinforced Spencer's power but it gave him some unexpected free time:

> I am quite at leisure since the Peace Preservation bill has been announced. It is very remarkable how Irish difficulties collapse before a bold front. The ordinary box of business took me often three hours' hard work. Within the last week or ten days it is an occupation of about twenty minutes.

When and if Spencer had time to spare his great delight was to snatch a day's hunting with the Meath, the Ward, or the Kildare hounds. In 1871 when Chichester Fortescue resigned the post of Chief Secretary, Spencer was anxious that Hartington should take his place, and when writing to beg Hartington to accept the appointment he held out one supreme inducement, 'You will get an occasional gallop over the finest grass country in the world.' Hartington duly became Chief Secretary and it is to be hoped enjoyed some good gallops.

In spite of continuing violence Spencer still thought that somehow the Irish people might be brought to acquiesce in the status quo and to support the existing system of government. Because he knew them to be what he called 'an image-loving people' he believed that the presence in Ireland of a member of the Royal Family would encourage loyalty towards the Crown and he supported Gladstone's scheme to provide the Prince of Wales with an 'Irish Balmoral'. Queen Victoria,

---

* In 1871 Spencer again asked permission to suspend Habeas Corpus; and this time it was granted.

The fifth Earl Spencer on 'Misrule', accompanied by the Countess Spencer on 'Goldfinch' and Goddard (first whip), with Pytchley Hounds in Althorp Park near Chowler's House. Painting at Althorp by John Charlton, 1878.

however, refused to consider any idea of giving the Prince a residence in Ireland or allowing him to take any part in the affairs of that country, and this in spite of the fact that an official visit by the Prince and Princess in 1868 had been greeted by an unprecedented outburst of popular enthusiasm, Alexandra in particular captivating the Irish with her beauty and charm. A second visit by the Prince during Spencer's term of office was not so successful, perhaps because on this occasion he left his wife at home. The crowds, however, cheered his companion, the Duke of Connaught, shouting for 'Prince Pat', one of the Duke's names being Patrick.

Meanwhile Spencer was much involved in the third item of Gladstone's Irish policy, the provision of better university education. This apparently innocuous subject was to prove the greatest stumbling-block of all. Trinity College was a Protestant institution; the Queen's Colleges founded by Peel were stigmatized as 'godless'; and the Catholic University which Newman and Cardinal Cullen had started in Dublin proved a failure. The Catholics were clamouring for an efficient university which should be exclusively Catholic; but Gladstone wished to create a genuinely national and non-sectarian one. With this end in view he put forward a plan to bring together in one body Trinity College, the Catholic university in Dublin, and such of the Queen's Colleges as were to be allowed to survive. 'With the massive insensitivity which that most subtle of men could sometimes display,' writes Professor Lyons, 'he thus succeeded at a single stroke in alienating every section of Irish opinion.' Spencer, who regarded the scheme as 'a very ticklish affair', put the same point more briefly and bluntly, 'We shall rouse Trinity to wrath and shall not gratify the Roman Catholics.'

In March 1873 the Irish University Bill was heavily defeated in the House of Commons. Gladstone resigned; but Disraeli refused to take office, and the Liberal ministry staggered along until January 1874 when Gladstone asked for a dissolution. The general election which followed went against the Liberals; and Gladstone resigned. Because the Viceroy's appointment was a political one Spencer also resigned, and on 24 February he left Ireland, leaving behind him a reputation for firmness and courage combined with a sympathy with Irish grievances.

Although he had told Hartington that he thought he would be sorry to leave Ireland Spencer probably did not feel very much regret. As he wrote to Gladstone

Will Goodall breaking up fox, the fifth Earl in the background. Painting at Althorp by John Charlton, 1878.

[223]

in a masterly understatement, 'Certainly Ireland is not satisfactory to govern.' He was going back to England to take up another and very different appointment in which he certainly would find satisfaction; for the second time he was to be Master of the Pytchley.

Spencer's second Mastership, lasting from 1874 to 1878, was a golden age in the history of that hunt. He was an older and wiser man than he had been in 1861 and he carried the authority of an ex-Viceroy. The Wild Boys had also grown older and wiser; and the time had come when it was possible to relax discipline and allow riders to enjoy themselves (hunting is, after all, supposed to be a pleasure). Spencer showed splendid sport, hunting hounds himself two days a week with as much skill as any professional huntsman. A set of rules which he drew up for the guidance of whippers-in show that he controlled the hunt in the same spirit in which he had sought to control Ireland:

In conclusion, I would say, be as quiet as possible in the hunting-field, be strictly just towards the hounds and your horses, keep your temper and your head, and have a reason for everything which you do. These are maxims which I shall try and keep myself.

At hound-work Spencer was by now as expert as his uncle had been and he was of course a far better horseman. One of his favourite hunters was a horse bought in Ireland and originally called Home Rule because its sire was Irish Statesman. Spencer had demurred at the name. 'Sure, your Honour,' came the reply, 'then call him Misrule because that's all we Irish have ever had from any statesman.' The joke pleased Spencer; Misrule it was, and later he chose to be painted riding this curiously named horse.

Spencer of course excepted, the Liberals were usually regarded as an 'unEnglish' set of intellectuals, with no liking for sport, a view particularly prevalent during the election of 1874 which resulted in a win for the Tories. Outraged by this horrid aspersion on his party Granville issued a challenge to the new Ministry 'to pick their best men and pit them against a like number of the defunct Liberal government for a ride across country.' Spencer was to be number one in the Liberal team. The challenge was taken up by Ward Hunt, a bulky Member of Parliament who hunted with the Pytchley and was reputed to weigh twenty-five stone in hunting kit with saddle. Hunt pointed out that the only Liberal who could possibly match him weight for weight was the Lancashire cotton-spinner, John Bright, and even he might have to put up a smaller man

'The death of the Fox'. Watercolour drawing by John Charlton, published in *Twelve Packs of Hounds*, 1891. This drawing is dated 1878–79, and the Master of the Woodland Pytchley, the Red Earl, stands beside the huntsman. The Empress of Austria is in the background.

behind him. 'Bright is no good,' Granville replied; 'he cannot pronounce the name of your hunt.'

During Spencer's second Mastership the Empress Elizabeth of Austria twice rented a house in Northamptonshire in order to hunt with the Pytchley. It was Spencer's business to find someone to pilot her in the hunting-field. Knowing that she was a brilliant and utterly fearless horsewoman he picked 'Bay' Middleton, a rider as brilliant and as fearless as herself. The Empress was one of the most noted beauties of Europe, and her appearance in the hunting field caused a great sensation. Dressed in a blue habit trimmed with gold buttons which showed off to perfection her slim figure and tiny waist, and wearing three pairs of gloves to protect her lovely hands she would follow Bay Middleton anywhere and the faster the going and the more hair-raising the jumps the better pleased was she. Unfortunately her relationship with Bay was not confined to the hunting field. How far the affair went is anyone's guess; gossip had it that they were lovers.

All this while Spencer was aware that hunting was absorbing too much of his time and attention to the detriment of his other interests. 'Please forgive my politics,' he wrote to Hartington in the autumn of 1876, 'I indulge in them to neutralize my hunting which engrosses me sadly.' Once again he was feeling the physical strain to be too great but when he resigned the Mastership in 1878 he told Lord Braye that he had done so 'because it absorbs my time and mind too much, and I can't do anything else with satisfaction, and politics least of all.' So had his uncle Althorp felt when he too had decided to give up hunting.

Spencer, however, had no intention of abandoning hunting altogether as Althorp had done. In September 1878 he stayed with the Emperor and Empress at Godollo in Hungary. He always played down any idea of danger, and now he succeeded in convincing Franz Josef that the disorders in Ireland had been much exaggerated and that the Empress could safely spend some weeks there in order to enjoy the thrills of Irish hunting. A house was accordingly taken for her in County Meath where she arrived in January 1879 to be met and welcomed by Spencer. On her very first day out she caused him a moment of acute horror and dismay when her famous black hunter Domino bolted with her. Fine rider that she was, she gave the horse his head, and soon regaining control, cantered him safely back.

From 1876 to 1878 the Spencers had been living at Harleston Hall while yet more repairs and alterations were being carried out at Althorp. The South Wing

Opposite: The Empress of Austria at Althorp, 1878. Colour plate by De Grimm from *Vanity Fair*.

was entirely recast and the hall altered and much enlarged. Charlotte had a knowledge and appreciation of art which was of help to her now in the necessary rearrangement of pictures. Spencer himself knew as little about art as he did about literature. Margot Asquith declared that she never saw him open a book and quoted him as saying, 'I enjoyed that book, *Jane Eyre*, you know, by George Eliot.' He had a poker face and a pawky sense of humour and maybe he enjoyed pulling the leg of a young woman who thought herself so much more clever than he was. Whether or not he really believed George Eliot to be the author of *Jane Eyre* he had the good taste to read and admire *Middlemarch*. Books, however, were of little interest to him and even when on holiday he admitted to difficulty in finding time for reading. (A reader such as Gladstone does not find time for reading; he breaks off reading in order to find time for other matters.) This was the man who in 1880 became in effect Minister for Education. When the Liberals returned to power after the general election of that year Spencer was given a place in the Cabinet as Lord President of the Council, the Minister responsible for the supervision of education. Strangely enough, he found the work very congenial. His lack of academic qualifications was no drawback because the education for which he was responsible was of a very basic kind, his business being to administer Forster's great Education Act of 1870. The object of this measure was to abolish illiteracy by bringing elementary education within the reach of every child in the country; and the schools set up with this end in view taught little else but 'the three Rs'. The main problem was one of religious differences, a subject with which Spencer was already all too familiar because of his Irish experience. Such schools as already existed had a religious basis and bias. The new Board Schools were planned to supplement but not to supersede these schools, with the result that in many areas a Church school was the only one available. For Nonconformists this was a real grievance. Conversely, Nonconformists were satisfied with the non-sectarian religious teaching given in the Board Schools which Anglicans and Roman Catholics regarded as totally inadequate.

Education was not Spencer's only business as Lord President. He was concerned with agricultural affairs and although he had no official connection with Ireland his advice was constantly sought on Irish problems and he was even sent to Dublin to confer with his successor, Lord Cowper, and to report on the position there. Since Spencer had left office the situation had greatly changed both in Ireland and at Westminster. In April 1875 a young Protestant landlord had stood as Home Rule candidate at a by-election in Meath and won the seat. His name was Charles Stewart Parnell. Within three years this proud, reserved, passionate man had become Leader of the Irish Party and begun a successful campaign of obstruction in the House of Commons. Meanwhile in Ireland the continuing agricultural depression had caused many tenants to fall into arrears with their rent. Failure to pay rent meant eviction, and evictions provoked outrages such as shootings, maiming of animals and even murder. The Land League which Michael Davitt founded in 1879 to help evicted tenants practised a form of intimidation called boycotting after a Captain Boycott who was its first victim. Any landlord or agent who evicted tenants and anyone renting a holding from which the tenant had been evicted was shunned and subjected to complete social ostracism. Gladstone's Land Act of 1881 giving tenants 'the Three Fs', fair rent, fixity of tenure and fair sale, failed to improve the situation. The Land League certainly, and Parnell probably, continued to encourage the wave of violence sweeping over the country. The Government lost patience; and in October 1881 Parnell was arrested and clapped into prison.

Although he was enjoying preferential treatment and suffering no real hardship Parnell was naturally anxious to emerge from 'cold Kilmainham jail' while Gladstone was equally anxious to reach a settlement. By the end of April 1882 both sides had come to an informal agreement known as the Kilmainham Treaty. The Government agreed to amend the Land Act and promised, at least implicitly, to abandon coercion, while Parnell undertook 'to use his influence against intimidation and to co-operate cordially with the Liberal party in forwarding Liberal principles and measures of general reform.' On 2 May he was set free.

By this time a change of personnel in the Irish administration had become necessary. Both Lord Cowper as Viceroy and W.E. Forster as Chief Secretary had proved unequal to the task they had been set, and not surprisingly, since as Spencer put it 'an angel from heaven would not have made the rough smooth or Ireland happy during the last two years.' He himself was now to be sent to attempt the impossible.

At the time of his appointment as Viceroy for the second time the outlook in fact looked brighter than for many years past; and it was generally believed that the Kilmainham Treaty might be the beginning of a new deal for Ireland. Nevertheless, Spencer had nothing to gain and much to lose from a second term of office. As his uncle had accepted the position of Leader of the House of Commons so he now accepted the position of Viceroy simply from a sense of duty—'It is everyone's duty to give his help where it is wanted and I should be a coward to refuse if I am told to do this.'

The new Chief Secretary was to be Lord Frederick Cavendish, who was linked

Front page of *The Illustrated Police News* for May 20, 1882.

to Spencer by ties of blood and friendship. The ramifications of the great Whig cousinry were immense and its hold on political office extraordinary. Spencer, Granville, and the two Cavendish brothers, Hartington and Lord Frederick, were all descended from the first Earl Spencer; and Frederick Cavendish had married another cousin, Lucy Lyttelton, who was niece to the Gladstones through her mother, Mary Glynne.

The only person who was really pleased at the prospect of living in Ireland was Charlotte Spencer. She however remained behind when her husband left for Dublin on the night of 5 May 1882. On 6 May he wrote to tell her of his official entry, 'the best reception I ever got in Ireland'. Late that afternoon Spencer and Frederick Cavendish returned from Dublin Castle to Viceregal Lodge, Cavendish walking through Phoenix Park with the Permanent Under-Secretary, Thomas Burke, and Spencer riding on ahead. He had barely reached his room at the Lodge when he heard an appalling shriek and, looking out of the window, saw a man running towards him and shouting 'Mr Burke and Lord Frederick are murdered.'

Spencer seldom spoke of the horror of that moment. Sometime that evening he wrote his wife a letter very different to the cheerful one bearing the same date, 6 May, in which he had told her of his good reception in Dublin:

> We are in God's hands. Do not be filled with alarm and fear. I was alone and have no apprehension.
>
> God knows how I feel—this fearful tragedy—two such men at such a time. I dare not dwell on the horror for I feel I must be unmanned.
>
> I am very calm.
>
> Do not, loved one, come unless you feel more unhappy in London than here. There is no danger really whatever.
>
> See dear Lucy if you can tell her that I am not made of ice but I dare not face what has occurred. God help and comfort her and all his relatives.

Under his impassive exterior Spencer was an emotional man curiously given to tears. 'I am always liable to be moved by cheering,' he had written to Gladstone on a happier occasion, 'and you had a narrow escape of [seeing] your President of the Council sobbing at your side.' Now, when he forced himself to look at Frederick Cavendish's dead face, he broke down and wept.

While England and Ireland rang with cries of horror and dismay Spencer's

[229]

The arrival of Earl Spencer in Dublin after the Phoenix Park murder, 13 May, 1882. Engraving in
The Graphic.

reaction was a typically prompt and practical one. Cavendish and Burke had been
murdered almost under his own eyes in full public view in the grounds of Viceregal
Lodge. Something was clearly wrong with the Irish police force, the body
responsible for security. On the very next day, 7 May, he wrote to Gladstone
demanding to be sent 'some distinguished and experienced officer to take charge
of the Magisterial Executive and to help the heads of the Police.' Immediately he
set about the business of reorganizing the Royal Irish Constabulary and carried it
through successfully although the opposition to reform was so great that at one
time the entire Dublin police force resigned.

George Otto Trevelyan, the man who was to take Frederick Cavendish's place,
travelled to Dublin on the night of 10 May in the same boat as Charlotte Spencer.
She had insisted on joining her husband, protesting that 'I do not in the least care
how dull or quiet or prison-like the life is there.' Prison-like Viceregal Lodge had
indeed become. If Charlotte wished to take exercise she could only do so under the
eyes of police and sentries in a locked enclosure known as the pound. If she and

[230]

Spencer went out driving the footmen carried arms and the ADC hid a revolver under the rug as an extra precaution. Spencer had to abandon hunting although he argued that when galloping after hounds he would be as safe as in the House of Lords.

He knew very well that all these precautions might prove useless. His was the first name on the black list kept by the 'Invincibles', the secret society responsible for the Phoenix Park murders. Only a month after those murders he was riding through Dublin with a strong cavalry escort when a well-dressed woman ran forward and snatched his horse's bridle in what he described to Queen Victoria as a very small and pretty hand. She was Parnell's sister Anna, and she meant no harm; but the incident showed how easily any guard could be penetrated.

Spencer himself remained unperturbed. He never looked beyond the cares of the day, leaving the morrow to take thought for the things of itself; and, like Winston Churchill, the greater the burden of responsibility on his shoulders, the better did he sleep of nights. His capacity for sheer hard work astonished everyone. The spate of interviews, letters and papers with which he had to deal was nothing to him in comparison with the hated task of speech-making, from which he was now free:

> Three or four days of this kind of work is equal to half-a-day with a speech before me. . . . Every speech I had to make shortened my life. I get quite clear of this here, and consequently I feel much fresher really than I did in London. My brain never feels exhausted, I eat well, sleep well, and enjoy my rides.

Only three weeks after the Phoenix Park murders he was planning a tour through the most lawless and disaffected parts of the country—'It does them good to let them see that there is a Government in person.' Accordingly in September he travelled through Mayo and the neighbouring counties surrounded by a cavalcade of police, soldiers and detectives. He described this dangerous tour as 'delightful', noting that on three occasions he had been able to enjoy rides of from twenty to thirty miles across wild moorland country. In Dublin his chief recreation was cricket. Throughout the summer of 1882, when the staff at the Castle and Viceregal Lodge lived the life of a beleaguered garrison, he did his best to keep them happy by organizing cricket matches and playing in them himself.

The strain of living in these conditions drove Trevelyan to the verge of a nervous breakdown. Spencer was so well aware of the danger in which he himself stood that he felt it necessary to let someone in authority know that the Chief

Secretary was not to be relied upon. 'If I have a fall or disappear as any of us may at any moment,' he told Granville in a letter marked 'Very Secret', 'I think it well that my experience of so rising and prominent an official should be known to someone.'

The public outcry at the Phoenix Park murders had driven the Government to revert to a policy of coercion. Spencer set about the business of suppressing crime and disorder with such determination that soon the Irish were calling him 'the Red Earl' for reasons other than the colour of his beard. Parnell even went so far as to couple his name with 'the congenial work of the gallows'. Spencer was a just man, but just men can make mistakes. In August 1882 a family was murdered at Maamtrasna. Those responsible were caught and tried and three were hanged. Two of them died protesting the innocence of the third, a boy named Myles Joyce who had expected a reprieve that never came. Irish public opinion flared up in fury against Spencer. Sir Charles Dilke, on a visit to Viceregal Lodge, described how he took Spencer out for a much-needed walk, watched, of course, by plain-clothes policemen. Crowds of people were enjoying a Sunday afternoon's outing, and the Viceroy was universally recognized, but only one man raised his hat, and wherever they went they were met by cries of 'Murderer'. Another day, when Dilke was driving in an open carriage with Charlotte Spencer, a cyclist rode through the cavalry escort (another instance of the uselessness of that form of protection) and coming alongside the carriage, remarked in a conversational tone, 'Who killed Myles Joyce?'

The atmosphere of hatred was too much for Trevelyan. Although he was only in his early forties his hair and the lashes of one eye turned snow-white. He was recalled to England to become Chancellor of the Duchy of Lancaster, and his place in Ireland was taken by Henry Campbell-Bannerman who appeared more concerned by the bad state of the drains of the Chief Secretary's house than by the imminent danger of assassination. Campbell-Bannerman was as imperturbable as Spencer himself. The two worked together in good accord and their Irish partnership was the beginning of a long and warm friendship.

If in Ireland Spencer was execrated in England he was becoming as Edward Hamilton put it, 'quite the man of the day'. Of all his Liberal colleagues he was at this period the one closest to Gladstone both personally and politically. Catherine Gladstone too liked him greatly and on his visits to England took every opportunity 'to *pet* as it were dear Lord Spencer'. In 1884 he was given the chance to escape from Irish difficulties and dangers by becoming Viceroy of India but he turned the offer down. In June 1885 the Liberal ministry fell, and Spencer returned to England. In July he was guest of honour at a banquet arranged by

George Goschen and presided over by Hartington. History was again repeating itself; forty-nine years earlier Members of Parliament had given a banquet in honour of Althorp and his share in the passing of the Reform Bill.

Unlike nearly every other English statesman Spencer's spell of office in Ireland had greatly enhanced his reputation. He left behind him a country where violence was less prevalent and life and property more secure than they had been for several years, but he knew in his heart that this was not a lasting gain. Although he was now free of the burden of Irish administration he was more deeply involved than ever in the ferment of Irish politics. Since the establishment of the Union no English statesman had seriously contemplated the possibility of Irish Home Rule; but when on holiday in the summer of 1885 Gladstone underwent what Philip Magnus describes as 'a seismic conversion' and returned home a convinced Home Ruler. For the present, however, he said nothing of his change of heart. To quote Magnus again, 'Gladstone disclosed his mind fully only to God, his family and Lord Granville.' Spencer's name should be added to that list; Gladstone confided freely in him because Spencer too had seen the light and decided in favour of Home Rule.

Many people were to believe that this change of heart was due simply to his personal loyalty to Gladstone. They were mistaken; Spencer had come to his own conclusions some time before Gladstone's conversion. He was a pragmatist who was not afraid to change his mind. In Ireland he had come as near as anyone could to making a success of a policy of coercion, but he realized clearly that his success was only a temporary one. In the long run coercion must provoke more violence, more resistance; yet England could not govern the unruly disaffected Irish without employing coercion. Spencer saw only one solution; the Irish must govern themselves.

At the beginning of December he was summoned to Hawarden for a private conference. Up to now Gladstone had refused to take either the Liberals or the Irish party into his confidence; but on 17 December news of his conversion to Home Rule appeared in the papers, a piece of indiscretion on the part of his son Herbert which was known as 'the Hawarden Kite'. At once the split in the Liberal party became apparent. Nearly all the old Whigs joined Hartington in opposing Home Rule; only Granville and Spencer stood by Gladstone, and of the two Spencer was by far the most influential. Morley described him as 'hardly of less weight than Mr Gladstone himself'. His known integrity and his long experience of Irish affairs made him a key man. That the Viceroy who had earned a great reputation by his apparently successful use of coercion should now change front and declare 'I consider our old methods of government in Ireland quite useless', made a deep impression on wavering minds. On the opponents of Home Rule the impression was of course less than favourable. Dighton Probyn, that faithful servant of Charlotte Spencer's friend, the Princess of Wales, wrote, 'A man of that sort advocating Communism shakes my belief in all things mortal;' and the Prince of Wales himself declared that if Spencer continued to support Home Rule 'I lose for ever all the high opinion I have held of him as a politician and a man of honour.' Even in the hunting-field the atmosphere was perceptibly chilly; and for a time, while tempers ran high, the Spencers found themselves ostracized by London society, many people making a point of refusing invitations to Spencer House.

On 20 January 1886 the Conservatives were defeated in the House of Commons. Gladstone became Prime Minister, and on 8 April introduced a Home Rule Bill. Two months later it was defeated on its Second Reading, ninety-three 'Liberal Unionists' voting against it. A general election followed; the Gladstonian Liberals lost; and Spencer, who had returned to the Cabinet in his old position of Lord President, found himself again out of office.

His return to private life did not mean that he lacked occupation. He was already Lord-Lieutenant of Northamptonshire, and in 1889 he became chairman of the newly-formed County Council. Lunatic asylums were among the Council's responsibilities; and one day Spencer was walking in the grounds of the local asylum when he was accosted by two keepers:

'Now, now, you come back quietly with us.'
'My good man, I'm Lord Spencer.'
'That's what they all say here.'

In 1890 he became Master of the Pytchley for the third time. Things did not go as smoothly as they had previously done; he was too busy to give his full time and attention to the hunt, and the experiment of appointing a Field Master under him was not a success. But he showed admirable sport, and when he resigned in 1894 his name became a legend in the Pytchley country where he is remembered as one of the greatest Masters that hunt has ever known.

Much of Spencer's time was devoted to spreading the gospel of Home Rule. Swallowing his dislike of public speaking he addressed meetings up and down the country, sometimes displaying more zeal than tact. His indiscretions provoked Sir William Harcourt into quoting the same text that had been applied to Father Ignatius, and to describe him as 'one of those children of light who have all the innocence of the dove but none of the craft of the serpent.' At these meetings Spencer sometimes found himself sitting on the same platform as those Irish members who had abused him so fiercely. On one occasion he shook hands with Parnell, and he showed generosity when that proud man crashed to ruin. In 1890 Captain O'Shea brought a suit for divorce against his wife Katharine, citing Parnell as co-respondent. The resulting scandal shattered the Irish party and put an end to all hopes of Home Rule within the foreseeable future. Had Parnell quietly withdrawn instead of standing his ground the result might have been less catastrophic. In an effort to force him to do so Gladstone, backed by the leading Liberals, wrote him a letter which amounted to an ultimatum demanding that he retire from politics. 'In that whole gathering of ex-ministers,' writes Professor Lyons, 'the only man who doubted the rightness of putting the screw on Parnell was the man who had perhaps suffered most from him in bygone days, Lord Spencer.'

In December 1891 five leading Liberals, Gladstone, Rosebery, Harcourt, John Morley, and of course Spencer, met for an informal conference at Althorp. Morley describes the scene in the candle-lit library where the Caxtons and so many other treasures were kept: 'A picture to remember, Spencer with his noble carriage and fine red beard, Mr Gladstone seated on a low stool, discoursing as usual, playful, keen, versatile, Rosebery saying little but now and again launching a pleasant *mot*, Harcourt cheery, expansive, witty.' Within a few months the Liberals were back in power, and Spencer again in the Cabinet, but this time as First Lord of the Admiralty. No position could have better pleased him. Both his father and his uncle Robert had served in the Navy and risen to the rank of Admiral; his grandfather had held the office that was now his own. His first task, however, was an unpleasant one and had nothing to do with the Navy. He was deputed to persuade Granville to relinquish his claim to the Foreign Secretaryship and to content himself with the Colonial Office. Granville's powers were failing; but he himself could not recognize this and he was described by Spencer as feeling 'very sore'. With Rosebery as Foreign Secretary Charlotte Spencer had her own part to play. Since he was a widower someone had to be found to perform the official functions of the Foreign Secretary's wife. 'There is only one lady who fulfils the requisite conditions beyond all doubt or comparison,' Rosebery wrote to Queen Victoria, 'he means Lady Spencer.' Charlotte therefore undertook such duties as presenting the Ambassadors' wives to the Queen and acting as hostess at Foreign Office parties.

Although he knew the effort was a hopeless one in February 1893 Gladstone brought in another Home Rule Bill. This time it passed the House of Commons only to be thrown out by the Lords. Spencer's speech in support of the measure was a failure; as Morley put it, quoting Tennyson, 'He has not the glory of words,' adding, however, 'his character is one of the best possessions of our Party.' In December an Opposition motion called for an immediate expansion of the Navy, a policy with which Spencer was in full agreement. He had taken over the Admiralty at a critical time when Britain was in danger of falling behind in the race for naval supremacy both as to numbers of ships and as to their design and equipment. The Board of Admiralty demanded an increase in the Naval Estimates. Now, for the first time, Spencer came into serious collision with Gladstone. In vain did he point out that he had cut the Board's figures by half, before giving them to the Cabinet (in fact his proposed increase now only amounted to three million pounds); Gladstone refused to consider any increase whatsoever. Such an idea went against both his love of economy and his pacifist principles. The old man of eighty-three could not be moved; as he himself said, 'You might as well try to blow up the Rock of Gibraltar.' Spencer, however, proved equally adamant; he was prepared to lose his Prime Minister rather than lose his battleships. Gladstone was astonished. He had always regarded Spencer as a malleable character like Pussy Granville; now he discovered his mistake. The Cabinet was solid in support of Spencer; and Gladstone retired to Biarritz in a huff. He could either accept the estimates or resign, and he decided to resign. Althorp had twice caused a Cabinet upheaval, once when Goderich resigned and once when William IV chased the Whigs out of office; now his nephew had brought about the resignation of the Prime Minister whom he had served so long and so loyally.

Gladstone was large-minded enough to bear no malice. He decided to recommend Spencer to Queen Victoria as his successor; but the Queen pointedly omitted the courtesy of asking his advice, and instead picked on Rosebery. Again like his uncle, Spencer had missed his chance. Instead he remained at the Admiralty to implement the programme he had defended so stoutly. HMS *Magnificent*, launched in 1895, was the prototype of a class of battleship far in advance of any existing ship; HMS *Havock* was the first destroyer. Less spectacular but equally important was the change from gunpowder to cordite and the invention of the quick-firing gun. When in July 1895 the Liberals went out of office Spencer left the Navy modernized and far better equipped than it had been for many years previously.

Both Spencer and Charlotte were sorry to leave the Admiralty, Spencer because, as he told Queen Victoria, 'I have immense satisfaction in my work here',

Charlotte because she much enjoyed living in Admiralty House. Now she turned her attention to yet another scheme for the rearrangement and alteration of Althorp. Though he was a rich man Spencer was finding himself short of funds. His estates nominally produced an income of between £46,000 and £47,000 but the continuing agricultural depression had much reduced their value. Money could only be found by selling some of the family treasures. The choice lay between the pictures and the great Althorp library. Reluctantly Spencer decided that the library must go. He was clearly right in his choice; books in private houses can neither be properly secured against thieves nor easily made available to scholars. Althorp, however, lost its unique glory; no other private house contained a library approaching this one in scale or magnificence. The collection was bought by Mrs John Ryland for £250,000—one of the Caxtons would now fetch several times that figure—and formed the nucleus of a public library which she gave to Manchester in memory of her husband. In 1892, the year of this momentous sale, Spencer had become Chancellor of the Victoria University, a federal university which included Manchester. Though the Rylands Library belonged to the City* the University was much involved in its creation and management, and it was the Vice-Chancellor who took Spencer to see his treasures in their new home. The two men went alone at Spencer's special request because he feared that he might find the occasion a very painful one. He was, however, genuinely pleased to see the books so well cared for and he found consolation in the thought that they had remained in England but easily available to scholars from all over the world.

The collection was so large that every downstairs room at Althorp had been filled with books and their absence left the house looking very bare. Charlotte seized the opportunity to set about alteration and redecorating, and she even began to collect books for herself in an endeavour to fill some of the empty shelves.

Strange though it may seem the man who had left Cambridge with only the equivalent of a pass degree and who once declared Modern History to be 'hardly a subject requiring a Professor to teach it', now became seriously concerned with university affairs. In 1902 it was proposed that the Victoria University, a body composed of three colleges, one at Leeds, one at Liverpool, and Owen's College at Manchester, should be divided into three separate universities. As Chancellor Spencer was much involved in the complicated negotiations which this entailed and although he strongly disapproved of the proposed scheme once it was decided upon he gave it his full support. He became Chancellor of the newly-formed

* In 1972 it was merged with the University Library to form the John Rylands University Library.

Manchester University, and on his visits to the North on university business he would stay with the Vice-Chancellor, especially endearing himself to the younger members of the family.

At the other end of the educational scale as President of the National Education League Spencer was concerned with the improvement of the primary schools. He travelled all over the country advocating the addition of elected members to the School Boards, the creation of County Education authorities, and the provision of 'a public school under popular management within the reach of all the children of the country'. So often did he speak on these subjects that in one speech he characteristically likened himself to 'a horse that has run in too many races and has in consequence grown somewhat stale'. Although not a good speaker he could on occasion produce a memorable phrase; in one of his speeches on education he declared, 'In the past we have been living in an age of toleration, but we have now arrived at an age of equality.'

In 1899 Campbell-Bannerman became Liberal leader in the Commons and the effectual leader of the party as a whole. Three years later, on the death of Lord Kimberley, Spencer himself became Leader in the Lords since Rosebery remained sulking in his tent like Achilles. When the party split on the Boer War issue Spencer strongly backed Campbell-Bannerman's firm though unpopular 'pro-Boer' stand. Already it was becoming clear that one of these two old friends must become the next Liberal Prime Minister.

All seemed set fair in private life as in politics. Now that Spencer was out of office there was time and opportunity to gratify Charlotte's liking for foreign travel. Like most members of Society with a capital S they took a cure each year at some German spa; and they also visited France, Spain, Italy and Egypt. In 1895 they travelled round the world, stopping off in India, Ceylon, Hong Kong, Japan, Canada, and the United States. While they were away they received news of the death of Charlotte's sister, Lilah Lady Clifden. Her grandson, Luke White, had always lived with her; and on their return the Spencers took charge of this boy.

In the summer of 1902 the Spencers as usual took a cure at Bad Nauheim. In spite of her sixty-six years Charlotte seemed radiant as ever in health and beauty, but on returning to England she felt slightly unwell. Cancer was diagnosed and a major operation performed. At first she appeared to make a good recovery but in June 1903 she suffered a severe stroke. For four months she lay without speaking or moving, dying at last on 31 October.

Her death was a great grief to her many friends, including Queen Alexandra, who had sent almost daily to enquire. To her husband it was a near mortal blow. The strain of those last silent months had broken him down; his own health gave way, and a year after her death he developed serious heart trouble. Nevertheless his political future had never looked brighter. In October 1904 the Parliamentary journalist, Henry Lucy, in an article discussing the composition of the next Liberal Ministry, suggested Spencer for Prime Minister. A year later, when Balfour's Government was clearly tottering to its fall, a more famous journalist, W.T. Stead, gave as his opinion that the two most likely candidates for the position of Liberal Prime Minister were Rosebery and Spencer, Campbell-Bannerman coming a poor third. Of the two Stead much preferred Spencer—'He is by heredity, by character, and by achievement marked out for high position.' Most Members of Parliament would have chosen Campbell-Bannerman; but Stead expected him of his own accord to stand down in favour of Spencer. Campbell-Bannerman told a friend that he and Spencer had already come to precisely the opposite arrangement; because it was advisable that the Prime Minister should be in the House of Commons Spencer would stand down in favour of Campbell-Bannerman. There is, however, no other mention of this agreement between the two friends and if it was ever made it must have been merely a tentative plan.

In February 1905 a document was published which became known as 'Lord Spencer's manifesto to the Liberal Party'. In fact, it was nothing of the sort. Spencer had promised to speak at a meeting in support of Corvie Grant, the Member for Warwick. He was unable to keep this engagement and instead sent a letter setting out his personal views on such questions as Free Trade, Home Rule, Education, and the situation in South Africa. (As might have been expected his opinions on all these subjects were those of an orthodox Gladstonian Liberal.) Because of the importance attaching to Spencer's name the 'manifesto' was regarded as an official declaration of Liberal policy. This elderly man of seventy, with the mark of death clear upon him, was hailed as the future Prime Minister.

It was not to be. In September 1905 he suffered a stroke when out shooting on his Norfolk property. His recovery was only partial although he himself was slow to recognize this. As soon as he was fit to travel he went out to take a cure at Bad Nauheim and on his return dined with Morley at Boodles. 'I could not hide from myself,' Morley recorded, 'that he had some notion of being invited to take first place if our party won the election.' Ten days later Spencer had another stroke; never again would he be able to fill even a minor office. When Balfour resigned in December 1905 it was Campbell-Bannerman who became Prime Minister. Spencer lingered on for four-and-a-half years, dying on 13 August 1910. Perhaps it was as well that he had failed to reach the heights; he was not quite of the stuff out of which successful Prime Ministers are made. Let him speak his own epitaph—'I have done my utmost to do my duty and no man can do more than that.'

EPILOGUE

Dieu Defend le Droit.

Spencer motto.

Edward John, eighth Earl Spencer. Painting by Rodrigo Moynihan, presented to Lord Spencer, when Viscount Althorp, on attaining his majority, in 1945, by the tenants of the Althorp farms. Painting at Althorp.

The marriage in St Paul's Cathedral of Lady Diana Spencer
to H.R.H. the Prince of Wales.

With the death of the Red Earl the Spencer pattern changes. For generations the emphasis had been on politics and on hunting. Now these two interests fade into the background. Members of the family continued to hunt, but the Red Earl was the last Lord Spencer to be Master of the Pytchley; and today the kennels at Althorp stand empty. In his early years the sixth Earl was a Member of Parliament; but his successors have played no part in political life. Instead, during the twentieth century the two dominant themes have been an ever deepening concern with the upkeep and preservation of Althorp and its treasures, and an increasingly close connection with the Royal Family culminating on that wedding-day in July 1981 when Diana Spencer herself became a member of that family.

Helped and encouraged by his half-brother, the Red Earl, Charles Robert Spencer, known familiarly as Bobby, entered the House of Commons in 1880 as Liberal member for North Northamptonshire. Aged only twenty-two, his youthful high spirits made him well liked in the House. 'He is so young, so light-hearted, so glad he is alive and a Member of Parliament that we on the wrong side of fifty renew our youth in him,' wrote Sir Henry Lucy. 'For himself it is a special delight to sit up in the gallery beside Earl Spencer with his elbow resting on the rail. There is no possible place in which he could display to such advantage his incomparable shirt-front, his irreproachable cuffs, and his miraculous collar.'

Bobby Spencer's collars were always to be miraculous, higher, stiffer, and more glossy than any worn by ordinary mortals. Correct and immaculate clothes were matters of serious importance to him; all the anecdotes told about him are concerned with dress. No less a person than Gladstone decribed his maiden speech as 'highly effective'; but the speech which passed into parliamentary legend was one in which this dapper aristocrat informed the House that he was not an agricultural labourer.

Like other members of 'the smart set' Bobby Spencer was often to be found at the Whig stronghold of Holland House where the middle-aged Lady Holland liked to surround herself with young men. No one could tell whether he was there as one of her favourites or as an admirer of her adopted daughter Marie, whose parentage remains to this day an unsolved mystery. He was, however, only one of many, and in July 1887 he married Margaret Baring, daughter of the first Lord Revelstoke and sister to Maurice Baring, the well-known author and man of letters. In her own quiet and unspectacular way Margaret was a remarkable person. Not very good-looking, and painfully shy with strangers, she blossomed

Charles Robert (Bobby), sixth Earl
Spencer (1857–1922). Painting by
Sir William Orpen, R.A., exhibited
at the Royal Academy in 1916.
At Althorp.

and shone in the privacy of the family circle or in the company of those who shared
her own interests. Like all the Barings she was a good linguist and well read both in
French and English—the Red Earl once asked her to compile a list of books for his
own reading—but her greatest love was music. A talented violinist, she had
studied at the Royal College of Music and played second violin in a very competent
quartet. After her marriage she regularly conducted a choir of 500 voices drawn
from all over Northamptonshire. The Spencers' home was Dallington Hall, a not
over-large house between Northampton and Althorp. She would fill it full to
bursting with a party of musical friends large enough to form an orchestra; and
they would spend happy days making music for themselves or playing at charity
concerts.

 This shy woman, who disliked parties and was totally free from snobbery, might
seem an odd wife for the one-time socialite Bobby Spencer, who, if Frederick
Ponsonby spoke truth, 'should not have been but distinctly was a snob'. The
marriage, however, was a very happy one. He shared her love of music and enjoyed
playing her accompaniments while she in her turn took the deepest interest in his

The sixth Earl at a meet of the
Pytchley Hunt in Althorp Park in
1914.

parliamentary career. Only twice in her life was she seen to burst into tears, once
when the old family nannie died and again when she heard the news of his defeat in
the 1895 election. On one occasion she even overcame her shyness sufficiently to
make a speech. When an election meeting was getting out of hand the agent,
hoping that the rowdy element might be chivalrous enough to listen to a lady,
asked her to say a few words. He wrote a sentence or two on a piece of paper which
she pinned to her muff and read out with great effect; but the effort involved was
too much for her and three weeks of sleepless nights followed.

To her husband Margaret Spencer was a joy and a support; to her children she
was a loved and loving mother, filling their lives with interest and laughter. She
encouraged them to share her love of books and music, reading to them both in
French and English, usually from old favourites of her own, but sometimes from
The Jungle Book, the latest novelty of the day. Of an evening, when they had gone
to bed, she would carry her Stradivarius violin up to the night-nursery and lull
them to sleep with the strains of Schumann's 'Träumerei'. When on 4 July 1906
she died of heart failure after giving birth to a third daughter all the warmth and

The sixth Earl as Lord Chamberlain at the Coronation of King George V in June 1911.

happiness of family life died with her. Her sister Susan, who had married the royal physician, Sir James Reid, did what she could for her desolate nephews and nieces but she saw too little of them to be a real help, although when their father inherited the title in 1910 and moved into Althorp there were great Christmas gatherings of Spencers and Reids, with private theatricals, usually in French, snowball fights and skating, or, in better weather, hunting and bicycle rides. In day-to-day life inevitably it fell to the eldest daughter, Delia, to try to take the place of a mother to her brothers and sisters. She was to grow up into an outstanding and much-loved character—'a cheerful saint', she has been called—but at sixteen she was too

[244]

Bobby at home, with 'Jock'.
Photograph taken at Althorp by Sir
James Reid, Christmas 1911.

young to prove a complete success in this difficult position, lacking, as she did, any real help or encouragement from her father. Shattered by the loss of his wife the once light-hearted Bobby Spencer froze into a remote and chilly character, who did his duty by his children but failed to develop any warm or loving relationship with them. For the rest of his life he wore tokens of mourning and wrote on black-edged paper. He never spoke of his wife; little Margaret, who had been named after her dead mother, knew nothing about her and never heard her name mentioned.

Although he regained his seat in 1900 and for a while served as Junior Whip Spencer made little impact on political life, being known to fame chiefly as the

'An Expert in Ceremony'. Cartoon by Spy in *Vanity Fair*.

Opposite, below: Bobby's private army of Brownies. Photographed at Althorp by Sir James Reid, May 1917.

best-dressed man in the House of Commons. The only offices he held were ones which though in origin political were in practice concerned with duties about the Court. In 1886 he had been made Groom-in-Waiting, in 1895 Vice-Chamberlain, and finally in 1905 Lord Chamberlain of the Household. Since this last post was always held by a peer he was now created Viscount Althorp. His father had filled the same position; but what had been for Frederick Spencer a pleasant retiring post after a lifetime spent in the Navy was for the son the peak of a career which in the course of the years had come to centre not on Parliament and politics but on the Court and the Royal Family.

[246]

Above: Family group at Althorp, taken by Sir James Reid, Christmas 1911. On the right is Bobby, on the left Jack. Delia is second from the left, at the back.

Viscount Althorp (Jack), hunting at Althorp, 1911.

The position of Lord Chamberlain suited Spencer admirably. Like his royal master, Edward VII, he was an expert on dress and etiquette, on uniforms and medals, and he shared Edward's mania for punctuality. He frequently accompanied the King when travelling abroad and in consequence amassed a remarkable collection of foreign Orders, one journey being known as 'the Hennessey trip' because everyone on it received three stars. Staying with Queen Alexandra's Danish relations he found the food just as dull and the entertainment just as tedious as his half-brother had done some forty years previously. He was happier on a State visit to Berlin in 1906 when his brother-in-law, Sir James Reid, who was also a member of the royal suite, wrote home, 'Bobby is all right, very fussy, but quite in his element and delights us all.'

After Edward VII's death Spencer remained on as Lord Chamberlain to George V but in 1911 he resigned because of ill health and retired to Althorp. In the summer of 1913 he entertained King George and Queen Mary, come to attend

Jack's Coming of Age: with his father, June 1913.

army manoeuvres, which that year centred on Northampton. When war broke out in August 1914 he was of course too old for active service but he wore uniform as honorary Colonel of a battalion of the Northamptonshire Regiment and he interested himself in the doings of the troops who camped in the park and used it as a training-ground. His three sons were all in the fighting services. Albert Edward John, named for his godfather, Edward VII, served in the Life Guards and was wounded in the early fighting; George and Cecil were both in the Navy. Cecil, a professional naval officer who won the Distinguished Service Cross, was a handsome young man of unusual charm and ability; and his early death as the result of a riding accident in Malta cut short a career of great promise. When the war ended Lord Spencer settled down once more to the comparatively uneventful life of a country magnate. His health, however, was not good; and he died suddenly on 26 September 1922.

His successor was a much more considerable personality although Bobby Spencer was not quite the nonentity that his preoccupation with dress and protocol might lead people to suppose. The seventh Earl is a difficult character to assess. To people he did not know or did not like 'Jack' Spencer could be forbidding, gruff, and at times positively rude, but to friends or sometimes to mere acquaintances whom he found congenial he showed himself a kind, considerate and warm-hearted person. He has been described as 'an ingrowing character'; perhaps the shyness which he inherited from his mother combined with his upbringing by an unsympathetic father to turn him in upon himself and to blunt his perception of other people. A man totally lacking in any sense of the appropriate he would say or do precisely what he himself thought true and right without the faintest regard for the reaction his words or deeds might produce. The 'coffins' story, still current in Northamptonshire, is a good example of this strange obtuseness. The Spencer vault under Great Brington church was overcrowded, and many of the coffins were in a state of disintegration. Spencer had the place cleared and the bodies, or what remained of them, burnt. The action was a sensible one; but he never thought to consider its effect on his more conventional neighbours who still shudder with horror at the thought of his casual method of disposing of the bones of his ancestors.

This able but difficult man had the good luck which so often attended the Spencers; he married a wife as good as she was beautiful. Cynthia Hamilton, daughter of the third Duke of Abercorn, was one of those rare women of whom people speak only in superlatives of praise. Not merely was she a great beauty; she was an exceptionally loving and sympathetic person, possessed of what St Paul

The entrance hall at Althorp, described by Pevsner as 'the noblest Georgian room in Northamptonshire'. A photograph taken in 1921.

Albert Edward John ('Jack'), seventh Earl Spencer (1892–1975). Painting by Augustus John, O.M. Exhibited at the Royal Academy 1930. At Althorp.

describes as 'the spirit of wisdom and understanding'. If her husband was in-growing she was essentially out-going, and so filled up what was lacking in him. And she was also highly intelligent. Like most girls of her class and generation she had received very little formal education, but she set out to educate herself, and so well did she succeed that she could easily hold her own in the company of the scholars and *savants* whom her husband frequently entertained at Althorp. She had a son and daughter of her own, and she acted almost as stepmother, but a very loving and beloved one, to her husband's young sister Margaret. She knew and was known to all the workers and tenants on the Althorp estate, a most welcome guest at any house or cottage for miles around.

Cynthia Spencer's beauty and charm did not fade with the years as a story dating from the Second World War makes quite clear:

One evening she had to officiate at a Women's Land Army function at which, of course, she wore uniform. As she was walking back afterwards she was accosted by a body of roistering Americans; she is fresh and very pretty, with nothing to

Cynthia Hamilton, Countess
Spencer (1897–1973). Painting by
Sir William Nicholson, 1932.
At Althorp.

reveal the truth that she is a grandmother. They asked what the initials W.L.A. meant on her shoulder. With her customary sweetness of manner she replied that they stood for Women's Land Army. 'Oh, no, they don't,' the G.I.s chorussed; 'they mean We Love Americans,' whereupon they danced ring-a-ring-of-roses round her in the middle of Piccadilly.

The relationship between Jack and Cynthia Spencer is in some ways reminiscent of the relationship between George VI and Elizabeth the Queen Mother, to whom Cynthia Spencer acted as Lady of the Bedchamber, thus maintaining the link between the Spencers and the Royal Family. Jack Spencer himself held no position at Court nor did he take any part in politics. As a young man at Trinity, Cambridge he had joined a dining-club deceptively known as the True Blue. The whig aristocrats who belonged to this exclusive society were too conservative to recognize the change in the significance of party colours and continued to call themselves after the 'buff and blue' of Charles James Fox. The club owned some very fine plate which Jack Spencer, always concerned with the preservation of anything of artistic or historical interest, carried off at the beginning of the Second World War and put into safe-keeping until 1945. True blue he became also in the more usual sense of the term, for he forsook the Whig and Liberal tradition of his family and declared himself a Tory of the most reactionary variety. He was once heard to remark, keeping a perfectly straight face, that he thought the Great Reform Bill, which his great-uncle had so valiantly supported, had gone very much too far. His activity on behalf of Toryism was, however, confined to the presidency of the Kettering Conservative Association.

Jack Spencer took little or no interest in the other traditional concern of his family. As a young man he had enjoyed hunting but in later life he gave it up entirely. He did, however, keep up some connection with the Pytchley, performing such functions as the presentation of a testimonial to the famous huntsman, Frank Freeman, and keeping the coverts on his property in reasonable order although more from a sense of duty to the neighbourhood than from any real interest in the sport.

The Spencers had always been known as good landlords and good neighbours; their roots went very deep into their native soil. Jack Spencer loved and served Northamptonshire well, devoting much of his time and energy to local affairs. For many years he was Lord Lieutenant of his native county. On the County Council he was the longest serving member, and he was also Chairman of the Northampton General Hospital Management Committee. In this capacity he did exceptionally valuable work, presiding over the change from voluntary to National Health status, and the building of new wards and out-patients' accommodation. He found time too for many smaller and less important local committees where his ability and conscientious devotion to duty won him great liking and respect.

At the very centre of Jack Spencer's local patriotism was his love for Althorp. To all Spencers the great house has always been home, beloved as no other place could be, but in him this sentiment became the ruling passion of his life. He was not a man born with exceptional artistic taste, a natural connoisseur; rather, as Queen Mary acquired her knowledge of antiques through her interest in the royal collections so did he learn his expertise through his love and care for Althorp and the treasures it contained. He knew the history of every picture, each stick of furniture or piece of china, and he cherished them all with the informed devotion which Althorp of the Reform Bill had bestowed upon prize bulls and sheep. Had the great library remained *in situ* doubtless he would have studied it with equal care for he was already something of a bibliophile. As a member of the Roxburghe Club, a society responsible for the publication of choice books of historical or literary interest, he edited a beautifully produced volume of the correspondence between David Garrick and Georgiana Poyntz, wife of the first Earl Spencer. He found much satisfaction in overseeing the rearrangement and cataloguing of the family archives, putting the muniment room into apple-pie order and opening it to writers and research-workers from all over the world. In his lonely old age he liked to spend much time there chatting to these scholars and enjoying their company. To one American historian he told how he had once come in to have a word with his distant cousin Winston Churchill, then doing research for his biography of the great Duke of Marlborough. He found Churchill smoking the inevitable cigar—'I ripped it right out of his mouth and stamped it out on the floor.'

Jack Spencer's generosity did not stop short at the muniment room. He gladly lent valuable pictures to exhibitions and he went so far as to open Althorp to the public though it was pain and grief to him to see strangers tramping through his home. Nothing, however, pleased him more than to show the house and its contents to anyone who could appreciate them properly. Schoolboys and actresses were as welcome as art historians and experts so long as they were prepared to show an intelligent interest. Most people looked back on these tours as happy and privileged occasions, remembering their host as the kindest, most informative, and most courteous of guides; but he could be severe on anyone who made what he regarded as a foolish mistake. He was once kind enough to take the grandson of one of his friends all round the house. Contemplating a picture depicting heaps of dead game this clever but shy fifteen-year-old ventured on an identification— 'Landseer?' 'No,' came the reply, uttered in fierce, barking tones, 'SNYDERS!' Annihilated, the boy made no further attempt to display any knowledge of art.

The knowledge and expertise of 'the Curator Earl', as Spencer was nicknamed, became generally recognized; and he was asked to serve on many important bodies concerned with art, antiques, and the management of museums. He was a trustee of the Wallace Collection, he represented both the Victoria and Albert and the Imperial War Museum on the Museums' Commission, and he served on the Advisory Council of the Victoria and Albert, finally becoming its chairman. When he retired from this position the museum authorities commemorated his years of service by organizing a special exhibition of the treasures of Althorp, a mark of recognition which greatly pleased him.

Jack Spencer was a valued member of all these bodies, but he could also be a disconcerting one. When he became Chairman of the Advisory Council he opened the first meeting he attended in that capacity by remarking that the Director of the Museum had asked him to say a few words about their late Chairman, Lord

Edward John, Viscount Althorp, and Frances Roche, daughter of the fourth Lord Fermoy, before their marriage in Westminster Abbey in June 1954.

Harlech, recently dead—'Well, whenever he and I came to this meeting he always annoyed me by sitting down in *my* chair.'

His taste in art was eclectic and not altogether conventional; typically enough, he chose Augustus John to paint his own portrait rather than a more academic and generally accepted artist. As might have been expected, painter and sitter did not agree well together, and the resulting portrait is not so happy as the one that hangs beside it, Sir William Nicholson's exquisite likeness of Cynthia Spencer. That beautiful and beloved woman died in 1972 after a long and distressing illness, leaving her husband desolate. He did not, however, have to endure any long period of loneliness for he died three years later on 9 June 1975, aged eighty-three.

Jack Spencer's last years might have been more happy had he been able to establish a more warm and close relationship with his children and grandchildren.

[256]

The porch at Althorp, re-designed by Henry Holland in 1791.

His only son Edward John, or Johnnie, carried on the family tradition of personal service to the Monarch by becoming equerry to George VI and later to Queen Elizabeth. In 1953, when about to accompany the Queen on a royal tour of Australasia, he announced his engagement to Frances Roche, daughter of Lord and Lady Fermoy, a very pretty and attractive seventeen-year-old still at finishing-school in Florence. They were married a year later, and made their home on the Sandringham estate at Park House where Frances herself had been born on 20 January 1936, the day when King George V died in nearby Sandringham House.

John Spencer had inherited his family's interest in agriculture. After his marriage he resigned his post as equerry in order to follow a course at Cirencester Agricultural College, and then started farming seriously both in Norfolk and at

Althorp. A person with an instinctive sympathy with young people, he devoted much time to the promotion of boys' clubs, becoming President of the Northamptonshire Association and Chairman of the National Association of Boys' Clubs. Like so many Spencers he was a keen cricketer, and also a good shot; but his favourite hobby was photography. He was a schoolboy when he took his first photograph, a snapshot of Queen Mary planting a tree in the park at Althorp. During the royal tour in the Antipodes he shot several films, and on his return made over £2,000 for charity by showing them up and down the country. His career as a photographer culminated on that day in February 1981 when his daughter Diana and the Prince of Wales officially announced their engagement. Camera in hand, he mixed with the crowd outside Buckingham Palace, telling the astonished television interviewers that he was there to take a picture of the scene when and if his daughter came out on the balcony—'I've photographed all the other important occasions in her life, and I'm not missing out on this one.'

The four Spencer children Sarah, Jane, Diana, and Charles, were fortunate in enjoying a particularly close and loving relationship with both their father and their mother; but the relationship between those parents themselves was not so happy, and in 1967, their marriage finally collapsed. The break-up of the family combined with the distress provoked by two divorce cases and three suits for custody inevitably had a traumatic effect upon the children but perhaps they did not suffer so badly as some other children have done in similar circumstances because both their father and their mother were at pains to prove to them that though the pattern of their lives might alter their parents' love for them could never change. Sarah and Jane were already at boarding-school when their parents parted, and the six-year-old Diana was immediately sent off to a small school at Thetford, later following her sisters to West Heath in Kent. The divorce through, Frances Althorp married Peter Shand-Kydd and went to live on the island of Seil, near Oban. The children dearly loved their mother; and the holidays spent there were happy times full of such enjoyable occupations as boating, fishing and lobster-potting. Park House, however, remained home. There the nearest children of their own age were the young Princes, Andrew and Edward, at Sandringham House, only half-a-mile distant, but although near neighbours they did not become the close friends that the gossip-writers would have us believe. The royal children were seldom at Sandringham, and the two families met only as children do who live in the same neighbourhood and whose parents and grandparents are friends. There was no climbing over the park fence, only the occasional tea-party or a swim in the swimming pool which 'Johnnie' Spencer had imported specially from America because it incorporated more safety precautions than any British-designed pool. In the absence of their mother he felt himself doubly responsible for the children's safety and happiness; and his plans for their entertainment could be delightfully imaginative. To reward Diana for bringing home a good report from school he added a special attraction to her seventh birthday party by hiring a camel called Bert from Dudley Zoo and having a platform built so that the young guests could easily climb on to the back of this beast. Needless to say, the party—and the camel—went with a remarkable swing.

Perhaps because of the break-up of the parents' marriage their two grand-mothers were particularly important people in the children's lives. Lord Fermoy had died in 1954; and in 1960 his widow was appointed Lady of the Bedchamber to Elizabeth the Queen Mother, thus strengthening the existing connection with the Royal Family. Before her marriage Ruth Lady Fermoy had been a concert pianist; and she passed on her love of music to her granddaughters, with whom she was always in very close contact. The children saw less of their Spencer grandmother. Frances Althorp had not shared the family feeling for Althorp nor had she taken them there very frequently. On the whole, they feared rather than loved their grandfather. Jack Spencer could always express his feelings better in writing than in speech. After his wife's death one of the older girls, perceptive enough to realize something of his loneliness, began to write to him regularly from school. He replied with charming, deeply affectionate letters; and only then did she recognize the love which lay hidden beneath his gruff and undemonstrative manner. But if grandfather was alarming, grandmother was the reverse, loving, sympathetic, and full of wonderful ideas. Althorp itself was a welcoming house, where in spite of the inevitable prohibitions, 'Don't touch this, don't break that', children could feel happy and at home. Their special kingdom was the long range of attics crammed full of unwanted lumber where they could discover such fascinating and forgotten objects as chamber-pots or unearth piles of old diaries and albums. Here on rainy days they could amuse themselves happily for hours together. In fine weather there was no shortage of outdoor occupations: the eldest daughter Sarah was a keen horsewoman but none of the other children enjoyed riding, least of all Diana who was to marry into the most notable of all horsey families.

When in 1975 John Spencer inherited the title Althorp became the family home; but after his marriage the following year to Raine, Countess of Dartmouth, his children by their own choice spent less and less time there. By now the two elder girls were grown up while Diana was a bouncing, irrepressible sixteen-year-old who as yet gave little promise of the beauty which was to enchant the world.

Althorp was more accessible to West Heath than her mother's distant home in Scotland, and she would come there when she was given a weekend off from school. One such brief holiday was the occasion for her now famous meeting with the Prince of Wales, one of the guns in her father's shooting party. That encounter in a muddy Northamptonshire field led in due time to the splendours of Buckingham Palace and the pomp and circumstance of the wedding in St Paul's. Among the crowds who watched that magnificent procession and the stately ceremonial of the marriage service there must have been many who remembered the long line of monarchs behind the bridegroom and his mother. Did anyone give a thought to the forebears of the very young and very lovely bride, the politicians and statesmen, the scholars and art-collectors, the farmers and sportsmen, the beautiful and gifted women, Georgiana and Harriet, Sacharissa and Spencer's Fairy Queen, the loyal servants of the Crown who fought for King Charles or cherished Queen Victoria's children, an ancestry fit for a queen?

On the balcony at Buckingham Palace, 29 July, 1981.

SELECT BIBLIOGRAPHY

An exhaustive bibliography would be out of place in a book of this nature. I have therefore listed only books which are basic authorities for each chapter, omitting books used for background reading, and books dealing with only one issue. Thus in the list for chapter six I have not included Professor Lyons' invaluable *Ireland since the Famine* or his biography of Parnell. An exception to these rules occurs in the list for chapter three where I have included *Lord Melbourne's Susan* because it deals with an episode which, to my knowledge, is not recorded elsewhere.

Throughout the book I have made constant use of *The History of the Althorp and Pytchley Hunt*, by Guy Paget (Collins, 1937).

PROLOGUE
Here the two most important books are *Five Northamptonshire Families*, by Mary E. Finch (Northamptonshire Record Society, 1958), and *A Short History of Althorp and the Spencer Family*, by W.E.K. Spencer (1949) The guide books to Northamptonshire by Nikolaus Pevsner, Tony Ireson, and J.A. Gotch have also proved useful.

CHAPTER ONE
Two essential books are *Sacharissa* by Julia Cartwright (Seeley, 1893) and an anonymous *Life* of Waller appearing in an eighteenth-century edition of his poems, *Poems Written upon Several Occasions and Several Persons by Edmund Waller Esq, the Eighth Edition, to which is Prefixed the Author's Life* (London, 1711). *Letters from Dorothy Osborne to Sir William Temple* edited E.A. Parry (Griffiths, Cobden and Weld, 1888) gives a contemporary view-point.

CHAPTER TWO
Robert Spencer, Earl of Sunderland by J.P. Kenyon (Longmans Green 1958) is the chief authority. Two other important books are *A Character of a Trimmer* (Cambridge 1948), a biography of Halifax by H.C. Foxcroft, and *Marlborough's Duchess* by L. Kronenberg (Weidenfeld and Nicolson, 1958).

CHAPTER THREE
There are so many books dealing with 'the Devonshire House Set' that selection is difficult. I am chiefly indebted to *Georgiana; Extracts from the Correspondence of Georgiana*

Duchess of Devonshire edited by the Earl of Bessborough (Murray, 1955), *Lady Bessborough and her Family Circle*, edited by the Earl of Bessborough and Arthur Aspinall (Murray 1940), *The Face without a Frown* by Iris Leveson Gower (Muller 1944), *Hary-O, Letters of Lady Harriet Cavendish* edited by Sir George Leveson Gower and Iris Palmer (Murray 1940), and *Dearest Bess* by D.M. Stuart (Methuen 1955). *Lord Melbourne's Susan* by Dorothy Howell Thomas (Gresham Books 1978) provides some new material while *The Grand Whiggery* by Marjorie Villiers (Murray 1939) is useful for general reference.

CHAPTER FOUR
Here my chief sources have been *A Memoir of John Charles Viscount Althorp, Third Earl Spencer* by Sir Denis le Marchant (Bentley 1876) and *Whig Renaissance; Lord Althorp and Reform 1782–1845* by Ellis Archer Wasson, which is as yet unpublished.

CHAPTER FIVE
The Life of Father Ignatius of St Paul by Father Pius (Devine) (Duffy, Dublin, 1866) is the only book dealing with the Honourable and Reverend George Spencer. There are several short pamphlets, but they are hagiography rather than history.

CHAPTER SIX
This chapter is based on *The Correspondence of Sarah Lady Lyttelton* edited by the Hon Mrs Hugh Wyndham (Murray 1912) and *The Lytteltons* by Betty Askwith (Chatto and Windus 1975).

CHAPTER SEVEN
No biography of 'the Red Earl' exists. *The Red Earl; the Papers of the Fifth Earl Spencer* edited by Peter Gordon (Northamptonshire Record Society, 1981) is invaluable, but unfortunately only the first volume, 1835–1885, is as yet published. Among the many biographies of contemporary statesmen and politicians the most useful are the various *Lives* of Gladstone, and *C.B.: a Life of Sir Henry Campbell-Bannerman* by John Wilson (Constable 1973). *Charlotte, Countess Spencer* by F. Seymour (Marks, Northampton, 1907) is very helpful.

EPILOGUE
The only book I have used here is *Princess* by Robert Lacey (Hutchinson, 1982); otherwise the Epilogue is based entirely on personal information and newspaper cuttings.

SOURCES OF
ILLUSTRATIONS

The references are to the numbers of the pages on which the illustrations appear

Reproduced by Gracious Permission of Her Majesty the Queen: pp.71, 89

Aedes Althorpianae, by T.F. Dibdin: pp.1, 14, 15, 27, 37

Althorp, The Rt.Hon. the Earl Spencer: frontispiece, facing p.49, facing p.65, facing p.80, facing p.128, p.206, p.209, p.222, p.223, facing p.240, p.242 (Photographs by Beedle & Cooper); 70, 252, 253 (Photographs by Harry Spencer, A.R.I.B.A.); 115, 119 (Photographs from *Sir Joshua Reynolds*, by Sir Walter Armstrong, 1900)

The Rt.Hon. the Earl of Bessborough: p.101 (Photograph by the Royal Academy of Arts)

BBC Hulton Picture Library: pp.34, 95, 131, 176, 179, 180, 187, 188, 195, 211, 218, 219, 220, facing p.224, facing p.225, pp.228, 230, 243

British Library: pp.76, 151, 154, 191

British Museum, Department of Prints and Drawings: facing p.129

The Rt.Hon. the Viscount Cobham, Hagley Hall: pp.173, 174 (Photographs by the Courtauld Institute of Art)

Country Life: pp.22, 73, 251, 257

The Devonshire Collection, Chatsworth. Reproduced by permission of the Chatsworth Settlement Trustees: facing pp.32 and 48; pages 78, 82, 85, 90, 91, 92 (Photographs by the Courtauld Institute of Art)

The J. Paul Getty Museum: p.47

The Henry E. Huntington Museum and Art Gallery: facing p.113

The Life of Father Ignatius of St. Paul, by Father Paul, 1866: p.148

The Paul Mellon Centre for Studies in British Art: p.99

National Portrait Gallery: pp.18, 19, 38, 40, 41, 48, 54, 57, 88, 97, 106, 136, 164, 198, 216

National Trust: facing p.33, p.69

New York Public Library: p.74

Northampton Studies Collection, Central Library, Northampton: p.156

Oscott College: p.165
Press Association: facing p.241, p.261
Private Collections; pp.43, facing pp.64, 86, 99, 120, 135, 213
Sir James Reid's Family Albums: pp.244, 245, 247, 248, 249 (Photographs by
  Derrick Witty)
Rothamsted Experimental Station Library: pp.140, 143 (Photographs by Derrick
  Witty)
John Rylands University Library of Manchester: facing p.81
Harry Spencer, A.R.I.B.A.: pp.13, 20, 25, 53, 77, 246
Lady Strickland-Constable: p.124
Universal Pictorial Press and Agency, p.256
Yale Center for British Art, Paul Mellon Collection: facing p.112

The author would like to express her gratitude for the kindness and co-operation
of those owners who have allowed the pictures in their collections to appear in this
book.

INDEX

Numbers in italics refer to illustrations

Achorne, Stanesley, library of, 81
Acklom, Esther *see* Althorp,
   Viscountess
Acklom, Mrs, 126, 129, 140
Albert, Prince Consort, 181, 182,
   184, 185, 186, 189, 194, 209, 210;
   Champion's drawing of, *180*; John
   Spencer appointed Groom of the
   Stole to, 208–9
Alexandra of Denmark, Princess of
   Wales, 210, 212, *214*, 222, 234,
   238, 248
Alfred, Prince, 188, 189
Alice, Princess, 188, 189
Alington, Hester, 171
Althorp, Charles Edward Maurice,
   Viscount, 258
Althorp, Esther, Viscountess, 125,
   126, 127, 128
Althorp, Frances, Viscountess, *256*,
   257, 258, 259
Althorp, Viscounts *see* Spencer,
   Earls
Althorp, 11, 12, 22, 32, 36, 39, 42,
   50, 52, 63, 64, 76, 77–8, 79–80,
   118, 142, 152, 157, 172, 200, 207,
   208, 212, 225–6, 235, 237, 241,
   244, 248, 254–5, 259, 260; Tudor
   house built by Sir John Spencer,
   12; hawking tower in park, 15, *15*;
   staircase, 36, *37*, art collection, 51,
   52, 76, 142; engraving of (c.1702),
   53; Library, 66, 72, 76, 80–81,
   81(facing), 237; stables, 68, *73*;
   'Chace Book', 79; Chapel
   Brampton home farm, 127, 144;
   Prince of Wales's visits to, 210;
   Empress of Austria at, *225*
   (facing); Library sold, 237; family
   group at (1911), *247*; Viscount
   Althorp, 'Jack', hunting at, *248*;
   entrance hall, *251*; porch, *257*;
   opened to the public, 255
Anderson, Henry, 21
Andrew, Prince, 258
Anne, Queen, 51, 65, 66
Anne of Denmark, Queen, 16, 208
Arlington, Henry Bennet, first Earl
   of, 52–3

Arran, Anne, Countess of, 65
Arthur, Prince, 188–9
Asquith, Margot, 199, 226
Athanasian Creed, 158, 160
Attwood, Thomas, 135

Bacon, Francis, 20–21
Baring, Hon. Margaret *see* Spencer,
   Margaret, Lady
Baring, Maurice, 241
Bateman, Anne Spencer,
   Viscountess, 68
Bedford, Anne Egerton, Duchess of,
   71
Bedford, Diana Spencer, Duchess
   of, 70–72
Bedford, John Russell, Duke of,
   71–2
Bessborough, Frederick, Earl of
   (Viscount Duncannon) 89–90,
   103, 104, 105, 110
Bessborough, Henrietta ("Harriet"),
   Countess of (Viscountess
   Duncannon), 80, 84, 88, 93–4, *95*,
   97, 103, 105, 106, 107, 108–12,
   118; marriage to Frederick
   Duncannon, 89–90; Hoppner's
   painting of, *101*; illness, 100; love-
   affair with Granville Leveson-
   Gower, 103–4; and marriage of
   Hary-o to Granville, 108–9; and
   Caroline's affair with Byron, 109–
   10; becomes guardian of Susan
   Churchill, 110–11; death of, 111;
   Rowlandson's watercolour
   drawing of, *112* (facing)
Biddulph, Colonel, 209
Bingham, Lady Lavinia *see* Spencer,
   Countess
Birch, Henry, Royal tutor, 193–4
Blandford, George Spencer
   Churchill, Marquess of, 110
Blenheim Palace, 72
Blomfield, Charles (later Bishop of
   London), 153, 157, 159, 160
Bloody Assize (1685), 58
Boundes (Robert Smythe's home),
   39
Bradwell Ox, *140*

Bright, John, 214, 224–5
Bristol, Frederick Hervey, Earl of
   (and Bishop of Derry), 90–91
Brixworth Church (All Saints), *206*,
   207
Brougham, Henry Brougham, first
   Baron, 123, 132, 139, 141, 145, 200
Buckingham, George Villiers, first
   Duke of, 19
Buckingham Palace, 260, *261*
Burke, Edmund, 87
Burke, Thomas, murder of, 229–30
Butler, Josephine, 145
Byron, Lord, Caroline Lamb's affair
   with, 109–10

Campbell-Bannerman, Sir Henry,
   199, 232, 238, 239
Canning, George, 132
Carey, Lady Elizabeth, 13
Carisbrooke Castle, Isle of Wight,
   34, 35
Carlisle, Frances Spencer, Countess
   of, 67
Carlisle, Lucy, Countess, 33
Caroline of Ansbach, Queen, 70
Caroline of Brunswick, Queen, 104–
   5, 130–31; Trial in House of
   Lords of (1820), *131*
Carr, Dr, 121
Carteret, Lady Georgina *see*
   Spencer, Lady Georgina
Cassano-Sera, Duke of, 81
Castlemaine, Barbara Villiers,
   Countess of, 45, 52, 56
Catlin, Mary, 12
Cavendish, Lady Arabella *see*
   Sunderland, Countess of
Cavendish, Lord Frederick Charles,
   201; appointed Chief Secretary of
   Ireland, 227, 229; marriage to
   Lucy Lyttelton, 229; murder of,
   229–30
Cavendish, Lady Frederick *see*
   Lyttelton, Lucy
Cavendish, Lady Georgiana ('G') *see*
   Morpeth, Lady
Cavendish, Lady Harriet (Hary-o)
   see Leveson-Gower

Cavendish, Lord George, 86
  see also Devonshire, Duke of
Chadwick, Professor, 166
Chapel Brampton (Althorp home
  farm), 127, 144
Charles I, King, 21, 28–9, 30–32,
  33, 33–5, *36*, 40
Charles II, King, 35, 39–40, *43*, 44,
  52, 55, 56–7, 58
Charles, Prince of Wales, 210;
  marriage to Lady Diana,
  241(facing), 260
Chatham, Lord, 75
Chatsworth House, 94, 96, 104, 109
Chesterfield, Lord, 70
Chillingworth, William, theologian,
  30
The Christmas Waltz, music title for,
  218
Churchill, Lady Anne see
  Sunderland, Countess of
Churchill, Susan ('Lord
  Melbourne's ward'), 110–11
Churchill, Winston, 255
Civil War, 28–36
Clancarty, Earl of, 58, 64–5
Clancarty, Elizabeth, Countess of,
  58, 64–5
Claremont (Royal home), 189, 191,
  191
Clifden, Lilah Lady, 238
Clifford, Augustus (Bess's son), 98,
  102, 104
Clinton, Lady, 140, 203
Corn Laws, 130, 145, 146, 191
Courtney, Eliza, 102, 104
Coutts, Thomas, banker, 98, 99
Cowper, Lord, Viceroy of Ireland,
  226, 227
Cromwell, Oliver, 29–30, 36–7, 44
Cruikshank, George, *129* (facing)
Cunard, William, 203

Dallington Hall, 242
Danby, Thomas Osborne, first Earl
  of (and first Duke of Leeds),
  52–3, 63
Dartmouth, Raine, Countess of,
  marriage to John, eighth Earl
  Spencer, 259
Davitt, Michael, 227
Declarations of Indulgence, 59, 60
Denison, Evelyn, 124
Derby, Alice, Countess of, 12
Derby, Fernando, Earl of, 12
Devonshire, Elizabeth, Duchess of
  see Foster, Lady Elizabeth
Devonshire, Georgiana, Duchess of,
  80, 84–108, 111–12, 118;

Reynolds's paintings of, *80*
  (facing), *91*, *92*; Downman's
  watercolour drawing of, *82*;
  marriage, 84–7; her passion for
  gambling, 87; and political
  activities, 87, 93–4, *95*;
  Devonshire House set, 87–8;
  Elizabeth Foster's friendship with,
  90–93, 99; birth of daughter
  Georgiana, 92–3; and of daughter
  Harriet, 96; Viscount Howick's
  friendship with, 97–8, 100; debts
  of, 94, 98, 99, 112; birth of
  son William, 99; and of Eliza
  Courtney, 100; ill-health of, 104,
  105–6, 107–8; and death, 108;
  Rowlandson's watercolour
  drawing of, *112* (facing)
Devonshire, William, fifth Duke of,
  90, *91*, 94, 96, 98, 105, 106–7;
  marriage to Georgiana, 84–7;
  Batoni's painting of, *85*; and
  friendship with 'Bess', 90–93, 94,
  96, 99–100; children of, 92–3, 96,
  98, 99, 102; death of Georgiana,
  108; and marriage to 'Bess',
  108–9
Devonshire, eighth Duke of see
  Hartington, Marquess of
Devonshire House (Devonshire
  House set), 87–8, *91*, 94, 97–8,
  103, 104, 107, 108, 109, 111, 114,
  118; gambling table at
  (Rowlandson), *74*
Diana, Princess of Wales, 23, 70, 79,
  95, 181, 208, 210, 258, 259–60;
  marriage to Prince Charles, *241*,
  241 (facing), 260
Digby, Lady Anne see Sunderland,
  Countess of
Dilke, Sir Charles, 199, 232
Disraeli, Benjamin, Earl of
  Beaconsfield, 223
Dominic, Father, 167, 171
Dorset, Anne Countess of, 12
Dorset, Thomas Sackville, Earl of,
  12
Douglas-Home, Lady Margaret, 245
Dublin Castle, 218, 229, 231;
  courtyard, *219*
Duncannon, Viscount (son of
  Harriet Bessborough), 122–3, 126
  see also Bessborough, Earl and
  Countess
Durham, Lord, 'Radical Jack', 139
Durham Ox, *143*

Edward, Prince of Wales (later
  Edward VII), 184, 186–8, 189,

190, 193–4, 221–2, 234, 248, 250;
  Winterhalter's painting of (aged
  7), *195*; John Spencer appointed
  Groom of the Stole to, 209–10;
  visits to Althorp, 210; marriage to
  Alexandra of Denmark, 210, 212,
  214; in shooting dress, *213*; visits
  to Ireland, 222
Edward, Prince, 258
Egerton, Lady Anne see Bedford,
  Duchess of
Egmont, Justus van, *57*
Elcho, Lord, 215
Elizabeth I, Queen, 18–19
Elizabeth II, Queen, 257
Elizabeth of Austria, Empress, 225;
  at Althorp, 225
Elizabeth, Princess (Charles I's
  daughter), 33–6
Elizabeth, Queen Mother, 253, 257
Ellesmere, Thomas, Lord, 12
English College, Rome, 161–2
Essex, Robert Devereux, second Earl
  of, 19
Essex, Robert Devereux, third Earl
  of, 28
Essex, Arthur Capel, Earl of, 57
Eton College, 149–52, 153, 176, 177,
  194; School Room at, *151*
Evelyn, John, 51, 53, 66
Exclusion Bill (1680), 45–6, 55–6, 63

Falkland, Lucius Carey, Lord, 27–8,
  30, 31
Fane, Lady Maria, 107
Fermoy, Lord, 257, 258
Fermoy, Ruth Lady, 257, 258
Fitzherbert, Mrs, 94, 96; secret
  marriage to Prince of Wales, 96–7,
  104; Reynolds's painting of, *97*
Foster, Lady Elizabeth ('Bess': later
  Duchess of Devonshire), 90–93,
  94, 98, 99–100, 102, 103, 105,
  108; Reynolds's painting of, *90*;
  birth of daughter Caroline, 96;
  and of son Augustus Clifford, 98;
  marriage to Duke of Devonshire
  (1809), 108–9
Foster, John, 104
Foster, W.E., 227
Fox, Charles James, 87, 93–4, 96,
  106, 110, 117, 118, 252;
  Reynolds's painting of, *86*;
  marriage to Mrs Armistead, 105;
  appointed Foreign Secretary, 107;
  death, 108
Franz Joseph, Emperor, 171, 225
Frederick, Duke of York (George
  III's son), 123

Frederick, Prince of Wales (son of George II), 70
Freeman, Frank, 254

Garrick, David, 79, 255
George I, King, 66–7, 208
George II, King, 70
George III, King, 88, 93, 123, 130, 208
George IV, King, 130–31; as young Prince of Wales, 88, *89*; and secret marriage to Mrs Fitzherbert, 94, 96–7; and marriage to Caroline of Brunswick, 104–5
George V, King, 248, 257; Coronation of, *244*
George VI, King, 253, 257
George, Dr, Master of Eton, 76
Gibbon, Edward, 103
Gladstone, Mrs Catherine (*née* Glynne), 184, 192, 194, 217, 232
Gladstone, Herbert, 233
Gladstone, W.E., 146, 193, 197, 199, 200, 215, 226, 229, 230, 235, 241; marriage to Catherine Glynne, 184; John Spencer's friendship with, 215, 217, 218, 232; Irish Policy, 217, 219–23, 227, 233; and support for Home Rule, 233, 234, 235–6; Spencer's conflict over Naval Estimates with, 236
Gloucester, Henry, Duke of, 33–5
Glynne, Catherine *see* Gladstone, Mrs
Glynne, Henry, Rector of Hawarden, 184, 193
Glynne, Lavinia (*née* Lyttelton), 174, 184, 193, 194
Glynne, Mary *see* Lyttelton
Glynne, Sir Stephen, 178, 193
Goderich, Frederick Robinson, Viscount, 132, 236
Godley, Mr, tutor, 149–50, 151, 153
Godolphin, Sidney, Earl of, 55
Goschen, George (Viscount Goschen), 233
Graham, Sir James, 183
Grammont, Corisande de, 104, 107
Granville, Lord ('Pussy': Hary-o's son), 199, 215, 224–5, 229, 232, 233, 235, 236; *see also* Leveson-Gower
Great Brington, St Mary's Church, 31, 32, 46, 48, *156*, 157, 161, 162, 202; monument to first Baron Spencer, *20*, 21; and Spencer memorial tombs, *22*; George Spencer becomes Rector of, 157–8, 160; Spencer vault under, 250

Grenville, Lord, 107
Grey, Charles Grey, second Earl, 97–8, 99, 100, 132, 133, *135*, 136–7, 139
Grey of Dilston, John, 145

Hagley, Worcestershire (Lytteltons's home), 163, 175, 176, *176*, 178, 184, 185, 194, 196, 197
Halifax, Dorothy, Viscountess ('Poppet'), 26, 31, 40, 42
Halifax, George Savile, first Marquess of, 40, *41*, 42, 44, 45–6, 55, 56
Halifax, Gertrude, Marchioness of (2nd wife of George Savile), 42
Hamilton, Lady Cynthia *see* Spencer, Countess
Hamilton, Emma, Lady, 84, 104
Hamilton, Sir William, 104
Harcourt, Sir William, 234–5
Harleston Hall, 225
Harley, Robert, first Earl of Oxford and Mortimer, 66
Harrow, 201, 202
Hartington, Spencer Compton, Marquess of, (later 8th Duke of Devonshire), 221, 223, 225, 229, 233
Hartington, William George Spencer, Marquess of, (later sixth Duke of Devonshire), 99, 102, 105, 121
Hawarden (Gladstones's home), 184, 193, 217, 218, 233
Hawarden Rectory, 184, 193
Hayter, Sir George, *128* (facing), *136*
Helena, Princess, 188
Henrietta Maria, Queen, 21, 33, 34
Hobhouse, John, 137
Holdenby (Holmby) House, 31, 32, 33
Holland, Henry, architect, 80
Holland, Lady, 146, 241
Holland House, 241
Holywell House, near St Albans, 72
Hood, Admiral, 94
Hopkinson, Alfred, 199
Hoppner, John, *77*, *101*
Hunsdon, Elizabeth, Lady, 12–13
Hunsdon, George Carey, Lord, 12
Hunt, Ward, 224
Huskisson, William, 130, 132
Hyde, Lawrence, 55

Ignatius of St Paul, Father *see* Spencer, Hon. and Rev. George

Illustrated Police News, cover of, *228*
Institute of Charity, 167
Ireland, 225, 226–32; John Spencer's Viceroyship of, 217–23, 227–32, 233; disestablishment of Church of, 220–21; Land Act, 220–21, 227; Peace Preservation Act, 221; suspension of Habeas Corpus, 221 & n; reform of university education, 220, 222–3; Kilmainham Treaty, 227; Phoenix Park murders, 229–30, 231, 232; Home Rule for, 233–6
Irish Coercion Bill, 137–8, 139
Irish Party, 227, 233
Irving, Edward, 161
Isle of Wight: Carisbrook Castle, 34, 35; Spencers's holiday house on, 153, 162; Osborne, 189

James I, King, 16, 19, 20–21
James II, King (James, Duke of York), 33, 45, 52, 55, 56, 57–62, 63; Lely's painting of, *54*
John Rylands University Library, 237 &n
Johnson, Dr Samuel, 79
Jones, William, orientalist, 80
Jonson, Ben, 15, 16

Keble, John, 138, 166
Kent, Duchess of (Queen Victoria's mother), 163
Kenyon, J.P., 50
Kilmainham Treaty, 227
Kimberley, Lord, 238
King, Charles, Huntsman of the Pytchley Hunt, *120*
Kitson, Katherine, 12
Knapton, George, *70*
Knightley, Sir Richard, 12
Knightley, Susan, 12

Lamb, Augustus, 109
Lamb, Lady Caroline (Harriet Bessborough's daughter), 96, 100, 103, *106*, 107, 108, 109; Byron's affair with, 109–10
Lamb, William *see* Melbourne, Lord
Land League, Ireland, 227
Lansdowne, Lord, 79
Lawrence, Sir Thomas, *135*
Leicester, Lady, 23, 26, 31–2, 33, 35, 36
Leicester, Robert Sidney, second Earl, 23, 24, 26–7, 28, 29, 31–3, 35, 36, 38, 44
Leicester, Philip, third Earl *see* Lisle, Lord

Leveson-Gower, Granville, 103–4, (later Lord Granville), 108–9
Leveson-Gower, Harriet ('Hary-o': later Lady Granville), 96, 98, 99, 104, 107, 108–9, 118–21, 177, 214
Liberal Party/Government, 199, 214–15, 217–23, 224, 226–32, 233, 234, 235, 238, 239
Lisle, Philip, Viscount, 28, 32, 36–7, 41
Liverpool, Robert Jenkinson, second Earl, 132
'Louchee' see Williams, Charlotte
Louis XVI, King of France, 98
Louis Philippe, King, reception to, 188, 189
Louise, Princess, 188
Lucy, Sir Henry, 239, 241
Lyttelton, Albert, 171
Lyttelton, Alfred, 196
Lyttelton, Caroline, 174, 182, 184–5, 189, 194, 197, 205
Lyttelton, Edward, 194
Lyttelton, George, fourth Baron, 145, 174, 177, 178, 184, 193, 194, 196–7
Lyttelton, Mrs Henrietta (née Cornewalle), 192
Lyttelton, Hester see Alington
Lyttelton, Lavinia see Glynne, Mrs
Lyttelton, Lavinia, 197
Lyttelton, Lucy, 196, 201–2, 205, 229
Lyttelton, Mary, Lady, 178, 184, 193, 194, 196, 229
Lyttelton, Meriel, 196
Lyttelton, Sarah, Lady, 114, 118, 122, 125, 134, 144, 149, 152, 161, 163, 169–70, 173, 174–97, 201, 205; marriage to William, 153, 174; and death of husband, 163, 177; appointed Lady of the Bedchamber, 178; and Royal Governess, 184, 185–91; resigns post as Governess, 193–4; death, 197
Lyttelton, second Baron (half-brother of William), 175
Lyttelton, Sybella, Lady, 196–7
Lyttelton, Spencer (Sarah's son), 174, 176, 177, 192, 193, 197
Lyttelton, Spencer (Sarah's grandson), 193
Lyttelton, William Henry, third Baron, 153, 164, 174, 174, 175–7
Lyttelton, William ('Billy'), Rector of Hagley, 174, 177–8, 197

Macaulay, Lord, 50, 191
Manning, Cardinal, 161

Marie Antoinette, Queen, 98
Marlborough, Charles Spencer, third Duke of see Sunderland, fifth Earl of
Marlborough, Henrietta, Duchess of (Lady Godolphin), 68, 72
Marlborough, John Churchill, first Duke of, 66, 68
Marlborough, Sarah Jennings, Duchess of, 66, 67–8, 70, 72, 75; Kneller's painting of, 69
Mary of Modena, Queen, 59–60
Mary II of Orange, Queen, 33, 55, 62, 63, 64
Mary, Queen (George V's wife), 248, 254, 258
Melbourne, Lady, 87, 100, 104, 107, 109
Melbourne, Lord, 100, 107
Melbourne, William Lamb, Lord, 107, 109, 110, 111, 140, 141, 183
Middleton, 'Bay', 225
Milbanke, Arabella, 110
Mildmay, Sybella see Lyttelton, Lady
Milton, Lord (later third Earl FitzWilliam), 122–3, 124, 125, 126, 127, 129, 146
Monmouth, James Scott, Duke of, 45, 55, 58
Monteith, Alexander, 172
Morley, John, 235, 236, 239
Morpeth, Georgiana, Lady ('G': Duchess of Devonshire's daughter), 92, 92–3, 98, 103, 104, 105, 118, 121
Morpeth, Lord, 105
Morris, Roger, architect, 68

Nash, Thomas, 13
National Education League, 238
National Rifle Association, 208
Nelson, Admiral and Lady, 80, 83–4, 104
Newman, John Henry, Cardinal, 161, 166, 167, 222
Norris, Lord, 50
North, Lord, 93
Northampton, Lord, 75–6
Northamptonshire Farming and Grazing Society, 143, 145–6
Northumberland, Algernon Percy, Earl of, 27, 28, 33

O'Connell, Daniel, 139
Ogg, David, 59
Ormonde, Lord, 32
Orpen, Sir William, 242

Osborne, Dorothy, Lady Temple, 36, 38, 38, 39, 45
Osborne, Isle of Wight, 189
Oscott College, Sutton Coldfield, 165, 165–6, 168
Ossulton, Lord, 107
Oxford, Lady, 100, 110
Oxford Movement, 138, 166, 177, 189

Paget, Guy, 77
Palmer, William, 166
Palmerston, Viscount, 100, 117, 170, 183–4, 203
Park House, Sandringham, 257, 258
Parnell, Anna, 231
Parnell, Charles Stewart, 226–7, 235
Passionist Order, George Spencer becomes member of (as Father Ignatius), 167–72
Payne, Charles, 207, 209
Peel, Lady Delia, 244–5
Peel, Sir Robert, 191, 222
Pembroke, Countess of, 23
Penn, William, 51
Penryn, Gertrude Glynne, Lady, 194
Penshurst Place (Sidney home), 23, 29, 32, 33, 34, 35, 36, 38
Peterloo Massacre, 129 (facing), 129–30
Phillips, Ambrose, 161, 164, 166, 167
Phoenix Park murders, 229–30, 231, 232
Pierce, Thomas, tutor, 36, 50, 51
Pitt, William, the Younger, 83, 84, 93, 94, 107, 117, 118
Pius IX, Pope, 167
Pole-Carew, Caroline, 174
Pole-Carew, Kitty, 184–5, 194
Ponsonby, Caroline see Lamb, Lady Caroline
Popish Plot (1678), 55
Portsmouth, Louise de Keroualle, Duchess of, 45, 47, 56–7
Poyntz, Georgiana see Spencer, Countess
Probyn, Dighton, 234
Pugin, Augustus Welby, 164, 164–5
Pusey, E.B., 166
Pytchley Hunt, 77, 117, 120, 124, 125, 127, 200, 207, 210, 214, 224, 225, 234, 241, 243, 254
Pytchley Hunt Club, 77
Pytchley 'Wild Boys', 207–8, 224

Queensbury, Duke of, 78
Quin, Lord George, 144, 156

Quin, Lady Georgiana ('Gin' or 'Nig'), 114, 144, 156
Quin, Lady Lavinia, 144–5

Randolph, Dr Francis, 105
Reid, Sir James, 244, 248
Reid, Susan, 244
Reform Bill (1832), 128, 134–7, 136, 175, 254
Restoration, 39–40, 51
Revelstoke, first Lord, 241
Revicski, Count, library of, 80–81
Richmond, Charles Gordon-Lennox, Duke of, 142
Roche, Hon. Frances see Althorp, Frances, Viscountess
Rockingham Hall, 175
Romilly, Samuel, 123, 128
Rosebery, Archibald Philip, fifth Earl, 235, 236, 238, 239
Royal Agricultural Society, 142, 143
Royal Irish Constabulary, 230
Roxburghe Club, 254–5
Rufford (Savile's country house), 42, 45, 46
Rumbold, Sir William, 121
Rupert, Prince, 29
Russell, Lord John, 127, 134–5, 139, 141, 146, 170, 183, 214
Russell, John, 88
Rye House Plot, 57
Ryland, Mrs John, Althorp Library bought by, 237

Sacheverell, Dr, 66
St Christopher, coloured block print, (1423), 81, 81 (facing)
St Joseph's Retreat, Highgate, 172
St Jules, Caroline, 96, 99, 102, 104
Samwell, Anthony, 21
Sancroft, Archbishop, 60
Sandringham House, 257, 258
Savile, Lady Betty, 42
Savile, Sir George see Halifax, Marquess of
Savile, Henry, 40–41, 44
Scott, Sir Gilbert, 207
Seymour, Adelaide Horatia Elizabeth, see Spencer, Viscountess
Seymour, Charlotte see Spencer, Viscountess
Shaftesbury, Anthony Ashley Cooper, first Earl of, 45, 46, 55
Shaftesbury, Anthony Ashley Cooper, seventh Earl of, 138, 158, 190–91
Shakespeare, William, 18

Shand-Kydd, Peter, 258
Sheridan, Mrs Richard, 108
Sheridan, Richard Brinsley, 88, 88, 98, 108, 110
Sidney, Algernon, 28, 32, 36–7, 40, 41, 44, 50, 57, 57, 65
Sidney, Elizabeth, 36
Sidney, Dorothy see Sunderland, Countess of
Sidney, Frances, 36
Sidney, Henry, 26, 41, 42, 44, 45, 46, 51, 60, 61
Sidney, Mary, 36
Sidney, Sir Philip, 23
Sidney, Philip see Lisle, Lord
Sly, Mrs, Royal nurse, 186
Smith, Sidney, 191
Smyth, Robert, 37–9, 50
Southampton, Elizabeth Vernon, Countess of, 18, 19
Southampton, Henry Wriothesley, third Earl of, 18, 18–19, 21
Spencer, Adelaide Seymour, Viscountess ('Aunt Yaddy'), 202
Spencer, Albert Edward John, seventh Earl ('Jack': Viscount Althorp), 79, 250–56; hunting at Althorp, 248; coming of age, 249; marriage to Cynthia Hamilton, 250, 252; Augustus John's painting of, 252, 256; his loving care of Althorp and its treasures, 254–5; death, 256
Spencer, Anne see Bateman, Viscountess
Spencer, Lady Anne see Arran, Countess of
Spencer, Lady Arabella, 65
Spencer, Cecil (son of 6th Earl), 250
Spencer, Charles Robert, sixth Earl ('Bobby': Viscount Althorp), 241–50; elected MP for N. Northamptonshire, 241; marriage to Margaret Baring, 241–4; Sir William Orpen's painting of, 242; at meet of Pytchley Hunt, 243; at Coronation of George V, 244; as Lord Chamberlain, 244, 246, 248; with 'Jock', 245; Spy cartoon of, 246; created Viscount Althorp, 246; private army of Brownies of, 247; death, 250
Spencer, Charlotte Seymour, Viscountess, 203, 208, 210, 212, 217, 226, 235, 236–7, 238; marriage to John Spencer, 205; Watts's painting of, 204; friendship with Princess Alexandra, 212; as Vicereine of

Ireland, 218–19, 220, 229, 230–1, 232; death of, 238–9
Spencer Cynthia, Hamilton, Countess, 259; marriage to 'Jack' Spencer, 250, 252–3; appointed Lady of the Bedchamber, 253; Nicholson's painting of, 253, 256; death, 256
Spencer, Lady Delia see Peel, Lady Delia
Spencer, Lady Diana see Bedford, Duchess of; Diana, Princess of Wales
Spencer, Lady Dorothy see Halifax, Viscountess
Spencer, Edward John, eighth Earl ('Johnnie': Viscount Althorp), 257–9; Moynihan's painting of, 240 (facing); Equerry to George VI and Elizabeth II, 257; marriage to Frances Roche, 256, 257; and collapse of marriage, 258; marriage to Countess of Dartmouth, 259
Spencer, Lady Elizabeth see Clancarty, Countess of
Spencer, Elizabeth Georgina Poyntz, (wife of 4th Earl), 201
Spencer, Lady Frances see Carlisle, Countess of
Spencer, Frederick, fourth Earl Spencer, 114, 144, 147, 149, 150, 155, 168, 171, 175, 192–3, 200, 202, 203, 205, 246
Spencer, George John, second Earl, 80–84, 110, 116, 117, 118, 122, 123, 159, 160, 161, 162, 175, 177; Library built up by, 76, 80–81; engraving of, 77; becomes second Earl (1783), 80; marriage to Lavinia Bingham, 80; as First Lord of Admiralty, 80, 83; and political activities, 81, 83, 107, 141, 163
Spencer, Hon. and Rev. George (Father Ignatius of Saint Paul), 114, 148, 149–72, 175, 177; youth and education, 149–55; Grand Tour of Europe, 155–6; ordained deacon, 157; and becomes Rector of Great Brington, 158, 160; Evangelicalism of, 158–9, 160; converted to Roman Catholicism, 161; and attends English College, Rome, 161–2; as priest-in-charge at W. Bromwich, 162–3; moves to Oscott College, 165; visits to Ireland, 166–7; enters Passionist Order, 168–9; death of, 172

Spencer, George (son of 6th Earl), 250

Spencer, Georgiana Poyntz, Countess of, 78–80, 84, 85, 88, 97, 99–100, 102, 103, 107, 110, 121–2, 255; marriage to John Spencer, 77–8; Gainsborough's painting of, *78*; and Reynolds's painting of, *80* (facing); her passion for gambling, 79–80

Spencer, Lady Georgiana *see* Devonshire, Duchess of

Spencer, Lady Georgiana (sister of 5th Earl), 201

Spencer, Lady (*née* Georgina Carteret), 72

Spencer, Lady Harriet *see* Bessborough, Countess

Spencer, Harry (Dorothy Sidney's son), 32–3

Spencer, Henry (d. 1476), 11

Spencer, Henry, third Baron *see* Sunderland, first Earl of

Spencer, Lady Jane, 258

Spencer, John, of Hodnell, 11

Spencer, Sir John (d. 1522), 11–12

Spencer, Sir John (d. 1586), 12

Spencer, Sir John (d. 1599), 12, *13*

Spencer, John, (son of 1st Baron), 18

Spencer, Hon. John (son of 3rd Earl of Sunderland), 68, *70*, 71, 72

Spencer, John, first Earl, 72, 75, 80, 85, 93; Knapton's painting of, *70*; created Earl Spencer, 75; inheritance from Sarah Churchill, 72, 75; library and art collection of, 76; hunting, 76–7, 79; marriage to Georgiana Poyntz, 77–8

Spencer, John Charles, third Earl (Viscount Althorp), 114–47, 157, 163, 169, 184, 199–200, 236; youth and education, 114–17; Reynolds's paintings of, *113* (facing), *115*; political activities, 117, 122–4, 126, 128–41, 146; and hunting, 117–18, 119, 124, 127, 200; marriage to Esther Acklom, 125; death of Esther, 126–7, 128; farming and stock-breeding, 127, 142–4, 145; Reform Bill, 128, 134–7, 175, 233; Hayter's painting of, *128* (facing); Leader of the House of Commons, 133, 137; and Chancellor of the Exchequer, 133–4, 137; death of father, 141; death of, 147, 168, 192

Spencer, John Poyntz, fifth Earl ('The Red Earl'), 199–239, 241,
242; Furniss's caricature of, *198*; political activities, 199–200, 203, 214–24, 226–36, 238, 239; and hunting, 200, 203, 207–8, 212, 221, 224–5, 234; childhood and education, 200–203; elected MP for S. Northamptonshire, 203; trip to North America, 203–4; death of his father, 205; marriage to Charlotte Seymour, 205; appointed Groom of the Stole, 208–10; made Knight of the Garter, 214; Gladstone's friendship, 215, 217, 218, 232; as Viceroy of Ireland, 217–23, 227–32, 233; appointed Lord President of the Council, 226, 234; Phoenix Park murders, 229–30, *230*, 231; support for Irish Home Rule by, 233–5, 236; appointed First Lord of the Admiralty, 235, 236; Althorp Library sold by, 237; death of wife Charlotte, 238–9; death of, 239

Spencer, Lavinia, Countess, 80, 83–4, 114, 116, 118, 122, 125, 129, 152, 155, 158, 159, 161, 174–5; Reynolds's paintings of, *113* (facing), *119*

Spencer, Margaret Willoughby, Lady, 15, 21

Spencer, Margaret, Lady, 241–4

Spencer, Lady Margaret *see* Douglas-Home

Spencer, Penelope, Baroness, 18

Spencer, Lady Penelope, 29, 42

Spencer, Robert, first Baron, 11, 13–17, 19–21, 208

Spencer, Robert Lord (son of 2nd Earl of Sunderland), 53, 55, 56, 60, 61

Spencer, Robert *see* Sunderland, Robert, second Earl of

Spencer, Robert (b. 1791: son of 2nd Earl Spencer), 114, 122, 147, 156, 168, 175, 192, 235

Spencer, Lady Sarah *see* Lyttelton, Lady

Spencer, Lady Sarah ('Tallee': sister of 5th Earl), 201

Spencer, Lady Sarah, 258

Spencer, William, of Defford, 11

Spencer, Sir William (d. 1532), 12

Spencer, William, second Baron, 18, 21

Spencer House, 76, *76*, 114, 118, 129, 142, 200, 234

Spenser, Edmund, 12

Spithead Mutiny, 83

Stanley of Alderley, Lady, 201

Stead, W.T., 239

Strangford, Isabella, Lady, 36

Sunderland, Anne Churchill, Countess of (2nd wife of 3rd Earl), 65, *65* (facing), 66, 67

Sunderland, Anne Digby, Countess of, 41–2, 51–2, 53, 55, 61, 62

Sunderland, Charles Spencer, third Earl of, 62, 64, 65–8; death of father, 65; marriages of, 65, 67; library of, 66; quarrel with Sarah Churchill, 67–8; appointed Groom of the Stole, 208–9

Sunderland, Charles Spencer, fifth Earl of, 68, 110; becomes third Duke of Marlborough, 72

Sunderland, Dorothy Sidney, Countess of, 23–48, 50; Van Dyck's paintings of, *25*, *32* (facing); marries Henry Spencer, 26; and death of Henry, 31–2; Princess Elizabeth's friendship with, 35–6; marries Robert Smyth, 37–9, 50; letters of, 42, 44–6; relations with son Robert, 50

Sunderland, Henry Spencer, first Earl of, 21, 26–31, 32, 40, 50

Sunderland, Judith Tichborne, Countess of, 67

Sunderland, Robert Spencer, second Earl of, 26, 36, 39, 41, 42, 45, 46, 50–65; marriage to Anne Digby, 41–2, 51–2, 61; Maratta's painting of *49* (facing); as Secretary of State, 55–7; as adviser to James II, 58–61; conversion to Catholicism, 58, 60, 61, 63; death of son Robert, 61; exiled in Holland, 62; as adviser to William III, 62–4; appointed Lord Chamberlain, 64; death of, 65

Sunderland, Robert Spencer, fourth Earl of, 65 (facing), 68

Talbot, Edward, 197

Tankerville, Charles, fifth Earl, 107

Tavistock, Marquess of, 122–3

Temple, Lady *see* Osborne, Dorothy

Temple, Sir William, 23, 39, 40, 55

Tichborne, Judith *see* Sunderland, Countess of

Tractarians, 158, 166

Trevelyan, George Otto, 230, 231–2

Trimmer, Miss, governess, 98–9, 103, 114

Trinity College, Cambridge, 154–5, 202–3, 253; The Quadrangle, at, *154*

Vane, Sir Harry, 40
Viceregal Lodge, Phoenix Park, Dublin, *220*, 229, 230–31, 232
Victoria, Queen, 158, 163, 169, 181–2, *187*, 189, 197, 200, 209–10, 212, 221–2, 235, 236; Sarah appointed Lady of the Bedchamber to, 178; at Windsor, *179*; Sarah appointed Governess to children of, 184, 185–6; and Sarah's resignation, 194
Victoria, Princess Royal ('Vicky'), 184, 186, *187*, 189, 190, 193, 194
Victoria University, 199, 237
Villiers, Elizabeth, 63

Wales, Prince of *see* Charles; Edward; George IV
Waller, Mrs Ann (*née* Banks), 23
Waller, Edmund, 23–4, 26, 29–30, 44, 45, 48, *48*
Walpole, Sir Robert, 70–71

Walsh, Bishop, 162
Webster, Sir Godfrey, 109
Wellington, Duke of, 132, 133, 137, 141
Winterhalter, *188*, 189, *195*
Whigs, 63–4, 66, 81, 87, 88, 117, 118, 122, 128, 130, 132–41, 199, 214–15, 229, 233; Young Whigs, 123–4, 128, 132, 133
White, Luke, 238
Wilberforce, Samuel, 193–4
William III of Orange, King, 45, 55, 60, 61–4, *64* (facing), 65, 208
William IV, King, 137, 141, 236
Williams, Charlotte, ('Louchee'), 90, 92, 98, 99, 104
Willoughby, Sir Francis, 15
Willoughby, Margaret *see* Spencer, Baroness
Wimbledon Common, 208, *211*
Windsor Castle, 181, 183; Queen Victoria on terrace, *179*; reception to King Louis Philippe, *188*, 189;

wedding of Edward and Alexandra, 212
Wiseman, Nicholas, 162
Wiseton Hall, *124*, 125, 126, 127, 137, 142, 147
Woburn Abbey, 72
Worde, Wynkyn de, printer, 81
Wormleighton (Spencer home), 11, 12, 29
Wriothesley, Henry *see* Southampton, third Earl of
Wriothesley, Lady Penelope *see* Spencer, Baroness
Wurtenburg, Duke of, investiture of, 16–17
Wynne, Sir Watkins Williams, 152–3

York, Anne Hyde, Duchess of, 41
York, James, Duke of *see* James II
Young, Arthur, 142
Young Whigs, 123–4, 128, 132

WILLIAM SPENCER (Lessee of Defford, Worcs. under Abbey of Evesham, 1330)

JOHN SPENCER of Defford *m.* Alice Deverell.

NICHOLAS SPENCER of Defford *m.* Joan Polard

THOMAS SPENCER of Defford (possibly the Thomas Spencer of Staverton, Northants – 'Feudal Aids' 1428)

HENRY SPENCER (d. 1476).   *m.* Isabel, dau. of Henry Lincoln.
(Educated at Evesham Abbey.
Lessee of Badby, Northants,
under Evesham Abbey).

(1479) John of Hodnell, Warws. *m.* dau. of Warsted.   Thomas   William   Nicholas

(1485) William of Radbourn & Snitterfield, Warws. *m.* Elizabeth, dau. of Peter Empson of Towcester.

SIR JOHN SPENCER (d. 1522). *m.* Isabel, dau. of Walter Graunts of Snitterfield & Wormleighton.
of Snitterfield & Wormleighton.   (by Elizabeth Rudinge of the Wych, Worcs.)

SIR WILLIAM SPENCER of Althorp, (d. 1532). *m.* Susan Knightley.   Jane Knightley

SIR JOHN SPENCER (d. 1586). *m.* Katherine Kitson.   Isabel, Lady Cotton   Dorothy Spencer

SIR JOHN SPENCER (d. 1599). *m.* 1566, Mary Catlyn.   3 sons.   Mary, Lady Aston

SIR ROBERT SPENCER (1570-1627), created Baron Spencer of Wormleighton, (1603) *m.* 1587, Margaret Willoughby, (d. 1597)

WILLIAM, 2nd BARON SPENCER, K.B. (1591-1636) *m.* 1614, Lady Penelope Wriothesley, (1598-1667)   3 sons.

HENRY, 3rd BARON SPENCER (1620-1643) created Earl of Sunderland (1643)   *m.* 1639, Lady Dorothy Sidney (1617-1684)   5 sons.

ROBERT, 2nd EARL OF SUNDERLAND, K.G. (1641-1702) *m.* 1665, Lady Anne Digby, (1646-1715)   Hon. Henry Spencer

CHARLES, 3rd EARL OF SUNDERLAND, K.G. (1675-1722)   Robert, Lord Spencer
m. (1) 1695, Lady Arabella Cavendish (1673-1698)   *m.* (2) 1699, Lady Anne Churchill (d. 1716)

Frances, Countess of Carlisle   ROBERT, 4th EARL OF SUNDERLAND, (1701-1729)

m. (3) 1717, Judith Tichborne d. 1749.

2 sons.   Lady Margaret Spencer

GEORGE JOHN (1758-1834) 2nd EARL SPENCER, K.G. *m.* 1781, Lady Lavinia Bingham (1762-1831)

JOHN CHARLES, 3rd EARL SPENCER (1782-1845) *m.* 1814, Esther Acklom (1788-1818)   FREDERICK, 4th EARL SPENCER, K.G. (1798-1857)
        m. (1) 1830, Elizabeth Georgina Poyntz (1799-1851)

JOHN POYNTZ, 5th EARL SPENCER, K.G. (1835-1910)   Lady Georgiana Spencer   Lady Sarah Spencer
m. 1858, Charlotte Seymour (1835-1903)

ALBERT EDWARD JOHN, 7th EARL SPENCER (1892-1975) *m.* 1919, Lady Cynthia Hamilton (b. 1897)

EDWARD JOHN, 8th EARL SPENCER (b. 1924) *m.* (1) 1954. Hon. Frances Roche (b. 1936)   Lady Anne Wake-Walker

Charles Edward Maurice
Viscount Althorp (b. 1964)
m. (2) 1976, Raine, Countess of Dartmouth (b. 1929)